CUBA

WHAT EVERYONE NEEDS TO KNOW

ALSO BY JULIA E. SWEIG

Inside the Cuban Revolution: Fidel Castro and
the Urban Underground

Friendly Fire: Losing Friends and Making
Enemies in the Anti-American Century

CUBA
WHAT EVERYONE NEEDS TO KNOW

JULIA E. SWEIG
Second Edition

OXFORD

UNIVERSITY PRESS

Oxford University Press, Inc., publishes works that further
Oxford University's objective of excellence
in research, scholarship, and education.

Oxford New York
Auckland Cape Town Dar es Salaam Hong Kong Karachi
Kuala Lumpur Madrid Melbourne Mexico City Nairobi
New Delhi Shanghai Taipei Toronto

With offices in
Argentina Austria Brazil Chile Czech Republic France Greece
Guatemala Hungary Italy Japan Poland Portugal Singapore
South Korea Switzerland Thailand Turkey Ukraine Vietnam

Copyright © 2009, 2012 by Julia E. Sweig

Published by Oxford University Press, Inc.
198 Madison Avenue, New York, New York 10016

www.oup.com

Oxford is a registered trademark of Oxford University Press

The Library of Congress has cataloged the earlier edition as follows:
Sweig, Julia
Cuba : what everyone needs to know / Julia E. Sweig.
p. cm.
Includes bibliographical references and index.
ISBN 978-0-19-538379-9; 978-0-19-538380-5 (pbk.)
1. Cuba—Politics and government—1959–1990.
2. Cuba—History—Revolution, 1959.
3. Cuba—Politics and government—1990–
4. Cuba—Foreign relations—United States.
5. United States—Foreign relations—Cuba.
I. Title
F1788.S955 2009
972.9106'4—dc22   2009014819
Second edition ISBN: 978-0-19-989-670-7

1 3 5 7 9 8 6 4 2

Printed in the United States of America
on acid-free paper

For Reed, for everything

CONTENTS

The Cuban Revolution
and the Cold War, 1959–91

The Cuban Revolution
after the Cold War, 1991–2006

After Fidel, under Raul

ACKNOWLEDGMENTS

For this second edition, great thanks to my friend Jeffrey Goldberg, who graciously invited me to join him in Havana for his impromptu interviews with Fidel Castro in 2010. Michael Bustamante again lent his elegant editor's touch and all around wisdom to the new material in the second edition. He is a first-class scholar, fine writer, creative thinker, and careful historian.

At the Council on Foreign Relations my thanks go to Dave Herrero and Samantha Fuchs for their superb research assistance and to Richard Haass, James Lindsay, Amy Baker, and Irina Faskianos. I have been very fortunate to have the generous support of the Ford Foundation while researching this book: in particular, I am deeply grateful to Mario Bronfman for his backing and for his friendship.

My thanks always to Saul Landau, devoted teacher and friend since my first trip to Cuba in 1984. I have made many friends and professional colleagues in Cuba since that first visit: thanks for your seriousness, scholarship, and friendship.

Dave McBride, my editor at Oxford University Press (OUP), had the idea for this book as part of OUP's What Everyone Needs to Know series. I am very pleased he invited me to participate and thank him for his guidance along the way.

February 2013

INTRODUCTION

In Washington, D.C., August masquerades as a sleepy summer month. Beltway insiders habitually head out of town, trying to escape the mid-Atlantic swelter. Yet surprise conflicts, refugee crises, and budget showdowns always seem to up-end family plans to unplug. At least that is the running joke.

For as long as I can remember, rumors of Fidel Castro's death have tended to surface in August as well. But in the summer of 2010, as if to preempt the news cycle, the aging Cuban revolutionary leader seized the stage of a national conference in Havana to make a six-minute speech warning of a potential nuclear crisis involving Iran. It was Fidel's first public appearance since falling gravely ill in 2006. Save for a steady stream of published *reflexiones* or the occasional video clip, Fidel's legendary ubiquity in Cuban private and public discourse had notably faded. On this occasion, Fidel once again grabbed the soapbox, attempting to alert Cubans and global public opinion to a looming catastrophe in the Middle East. The next week, *Atlantic* magazine journalist Jeffrey Goldberg published a cover story called "The Coming War with Iran." I remember thinking that if Fidel saw the piece, he might take it as confirmation of his anxieties and validation of his seriousness as a student (if no longer protagonist) of international relations.

Later that month, I was not too surprised to receive a phone call from Ambassador Jorge Bolaños, Cuba's lead diplomat in Washington. Though on vacation, I was planning to go to Cuba a few weeks later and assumed his call was about my trip. Instead, Bolaños got right to the point. "Julia," he asked, "can you put me in touch with Jeffrey Goldberg?" Washington is a small town, so while perhaps comically presumptuous, it was not really a stretch for the ambassador to think that one writer who happens to be Jewish might be able to track down another prominent writer who recently had been named one of the "Forward 50" Jews in the United States by the *Jewish Daily Forward*. As it turns out, Jeff and I have been friends for years.

"Fidel can see you this weekend," Bolaños briskly told an also-vacationing Goldberg. Evidently, Castro wanted to compare notes about the brewing standoff over Iran's nuclear program. Given Fidel's notorious media savvy, I suspect he also viewed Jeff as a vehicle to send several messages—to Washington, Tel Aviv, Tehran, and to the left-leaning American and Latin American publics for whom his words still hold substantial cachet.

Three days later, Jeff and I sat in disbelief in the Miami airport waiting to board a sold-out flight to Havana. Because of the loosening of U.S. government restrictions on travel to Cuba, over the past several years Cuban-American families have filled more than 30 flights a week to the island, weighed down with everything from toiletries to flat screen TVs to multiple layers of clothing (thus avoiding steep taxes on excess luggage). More and more Cuban-Americans, as well as those who identify as diaspora Cubans, are traveling to their homeland, whether to visit, vacation, or, under the guise of remittances, invest in their families' emerging small businesses. But most Americans who are not of Cuban descent are still banned from the 30-minute puddle jump, unless licensed by the Treasury Department.

During his tenure in power, the usually loquacious Fidel relished interviews with visiting reporters and editors. Over the years, he had met with hundreds, maybe even thousands, of Americans—members of Congress, cabinet secretaries, Nobel Prize winners, religious leaders, intellectuals, Wall

Street CEOs, even rock stars and fashion models. Yet ever since contracting a severe intestinal infection four summers earlier, the aging *comandante* had not spoken to one major American journalist. Although we understood Fidel wanted to talk about the Middle East, we had no idea what to expect.

Our first meeting took place in an office Fidel keeps at the Palacio de Convenciones, an imposing conference center. Fidel's wife Dalia, son Tony, and personal doctor joined us for the nearly three-hour discussion, together with a translator and a small security detail. An avid and careful reader, Fidel showed Jeff the blue journal of notes he had taken on the *Atlantic* piece, and the two spoke at length about the Obama administration's limited policy choices with respect to the Iranian nuclear program. Fidel also discussed a number of unexpected themes: his experience of anti-Semitism as a boy, his respect for the suffering Jews experienced historically (especially during the Holocaust), and his distaste for Ahmadinejad's knee-jerk anti-Israel hostility.

This was the first time I had seen Fidel Castro in nine years, let alone since his illness and retirement. Notorious for his stamina as a talker, Fidel in the past seldom left me with the impression that he was a good listener. But during our substantive conversation, and later, over lunch in an adjacent dining room, he seemed relaxed, peppering Jeff and me with questions about our kids and their education. He also spoke repeatedly about living out of office in an entirely different way than he had for most of his life.

As if to prove the point, Fidel invited us to join him for an outing at the national aquarium the following day. Originally we had plans to see Adela Dwornin, the president of the Comunidad Hebrea (i.e., the Jewish Community) in Cuba. Fidel asked us to bring her along. Che Guevara's daughter, Alina (a marine biologist), was there too, along with Guillermo Garcia, a leading conservationist whose father was a guerrilla fighter from Fidel's days in the Sierra Maestra.

Seated together in the bluish light of the underground observation room, we watched mesmerized as three dolphins gracefully played and danced under water, accompanied by three young handlers, no oxygen. Between acts, the divers gestured for us to approach the glass—Fidel first. They taught him how to communicate with the animals, and for about 10 minutes he stood alone with his nose and hands pressed against the glass tank, bobbing up and down, following the divers' cues. We took our turn too.

During a lull in the ethereal Cirque de Soleil–type performance, Fidel leaned over and asked about my plans for the rest of the week. I told him I had a number of meetings scheduled and then popped a question I had been waiting to ask for ten years. For my first book, *Inside the Cuban Revolution,* I interviewed dozens of Cuban participants in the 1950s underground insurgency. But while in office, Fidel had several times rebuffed, or more likely ignored, my efforts to interview him. With a little more time on his hands, Fidel now agreed to speak with me about that fateful chapter in Cuban history. At his suburban Havana home the next day for a final good-bye chat with Jeff on his way to the airport, we decided I would return two days later.

I developed ten questions, assuming I would be lucky if we got through two or three. We sat in a room evocative of the American "Florida rooms" of the mid-20th century: wicker furniture painted lavender, rocking chairs, a television and VCR, stained glass, plants. Adjacent to Fidel, a table held the props of most people in their late 80s: several pairs of glasses, TV remotes, a glass of water, a stack of papers and books (including my own).

But before addressing my historical inquiries, Fidel had something else to share. "I'm going to give a speech tomorrow at the University of Havana to mark the beginning of the new school year, and I have been working on the text." The speech would mark his first open-air appearance since just before falling ill in 2006. He recited some of the first lines in a dry tone—nothing of the legendary orator. For the most part, his remarks focused on developments in the Middle East, perhaps a subject far removed from the daily routines of his prospective audience of Cuban students. Having grown up in the wake of the materially and ideologically trying "Special Period" following the Soviet collapse, Cuban youth today are not nearly as politicized as when Fidel's own generation entered student life. It clearly bothers the now former head of state that the next generation appears less interested in ideas and more interested in stuff. Fidel thus sought to energize their collective political and international consciousness. Yet he also seemed intent on proving that after facing mortality and a long, difficult recovery, he could still regale the crowd with a real stem-winder.

I spent six hours with Fidel that day. After rehearsing his speech, he answered each of my questions and encouraged me to keep them coming even when I was sure fatigue or boredom would have set in. At the time of our conversation, he was preparing to release a new volume of memoirs and thus proved to be particularly attuned to the period of time covered in my first book. At one point I made reference to a shipment of weapons from Costa Rica to the Sierra Maestra in 1958. Annoyed that I had used a different and quite possibly better source to describe this event, Fidel asked his wife to get the editor of his memoirs on the phone. I shuddered at the prospect of Fidel's editor having to answer to the dictates of such a noto-riously punctilious man. Friendly competition between histo-rians over the provenance of a source is one thing; kibitzing with a living world historical figure about whose sources are more accurate was quite another.

By late afternoon, Fidel offered to answer any historical ques-tion I could muster. I asked if his definition of "historical ques-tions" included discussing the transformations taking place in Cuba since he stepped down from power—recent history, but fair game, I hoped. His answer—a firm and definitive no—confirmed what I had observed and what his passionate detractors still find hard to accept: Fidel was not governing, neither from behind the scenes nor in any other way. The current leadership certainly consults him about the strategic direction of the country. But since 2008, it appears Fidel has agreed to stay out of Raul's way and quietly back his decisions. Both Fidel's columns about contemporary international affairs and his memoirs are conspicuous for what they lack: commentary on Raul's rather substantial agenda for revamping *sin prisa, pero sin pausa* (not in a hurry, but without delay) the political, economic, and social modus operandi that had prevailed for most of the previous half century.

The now digitally savvy Cuban state media has grappled with how to portray this new division of labor. When Fidel was in power, every utterance, public appearance, or meeting with a foreign dignitary claimed front-page coverage. In contrast, during the acute stage of his illness, very little information about his condition surfaced. As his recovery became more secure, Cubans adjusted to the once omnipresent head of state in retirement mode, donning an Adidas track suit instead of the olive drab of an active military commander. At least in 2010, Fidel, still sought the occasional public appearance and today maintains a political base among party old-timers and revolutionary die-hards. *Granma*'s coverage of our visit gave an idea of the media's struggle to convey the new rules of the game. Two photos above the fold: one with Fidel in a plaid shirt, slacks, and sneakers playing host at the aquarium; the other, a picture of President Raul Castro in a suit and tie, seated in a stiff protocol meeting during a state visit. The message in these images seems quite clear: Raul is running the country, including foreign affairs, and Fidel is definitively retired, with enough time on his hands to spend a couple of days talking Middle East politics, playing with dolphins, or revisiting his own history.

Back during lunch on the first day of meetings with Fidel— the day before the dolphin show—I had tried to get us away from the Middle East and change the geographic focus of the conversation to our own neck of the woods. These days, Latin America is neither Washington's complacent imperial backyard nor Fidel's proving ground for revolutionary insurgencies.

Still, many of Fidel's political children—whether because they spent substantial time in revolutionary Cuba, were at one point inspired by its example, or participated in revolutionary movements that Cuba cultivated and helped arm—now lead everything from labor and social movements to foreign ministries and governments throughout the region. Even though market economies and multiparty democracies prevail over anything resembling the Cuban Revolution's model of one-party state socialism, Latin America's ideological diversity, gradual leftward turn, and ever-growing diplomatic independence from the United States represent a long-term foreign policy victory for Fidel of literally continental proportions.

But when I failed to draw from him a Latin American geopolitical tour d'horizon, Jeff tried another, more direct approach. "So, are you still exporting the Cuban model?" Fidel did not miss a beat, but his response, once Jeff reported it the following week, made headlines around the world: "The Cuban model? It doesn't even work for us anymore."

Ten words out of ten hours of talks that week brought Fidel the kind of spotlight I suspect he was after by inviting Goldberg to interview him, but on the wrong subject—not the Middle East, but Cuba itself. Around the world and in the United States, the media blizzard conveyed shock, and a bit of disbelief, that the architect of the Cuban Revolution was ready to admit "the Cuban model" had run its course. But in a sense the foreign media were the last in on the news. By 2010, the failure of the Cuban economy and government to generate productive jobs and an open society—coupled with the thousand other outmoded, expensive, and corruption-inducing elements of this "model"—had become the primary topic all Cubans talked about, starting with the sitting president Raul Castro himself. "¿Cómo va la cosa?" (How is *the thing* going?), Cubans jokingly ask each other these days, referring to ongoing internal debates about reform. International reporting, however, at times still focuses on whether a recovered Fidel is really in charge and whether his known allergy to capitalism will ever yield to the pragmatic changes his brother has long regarded as essential in order for the Revolution to leave any meaningful legacy.

Publishing this line compelled the retired commander-in-chief of the Revolution to comment on politics at home for the first time in four years. A few days after Goldberg's blog post, Fidel made an indoor appearance at the University of Havana to release the latest volume of his memoirs. Taking a short detour from his historical remarks, he admitted the quote was accurate but insisted Jeff's published interpretation was incorrect. Both Jeff and I took the quote to be a recognition that Fidel had absorbed and endorsed Raul's case for a substantial (if gradual and still rhetorically "socialist") overhaul of the terms of Cuba's social contract. In fact, Fidel now claimed rather cryptically, he had meant "exactly the opposite." "My idea, as the whole world knows, is that the capitalist system no longer works for the United States or the world.... How could such a system work for a socialist country like Cuba?"

Of course, in reporting the remark Jeff had implied nothing of the kind. But the purpose of Castro's demarche was to reassure his revolutionary base that Cuba could withstand changes his brother would soon introduce without importing the orthodox capitalism Fidel had decried for decades and against which he had defined the Cuban Revolution itself. In other words, Fidel sought to assure his political followers that change would not mean abandoning Cuba's ability to make decisions for itself or reneging on the state's commitment to social welfare and education via some kind of shock therapy. Thus, in a roundabout way, and without commenting directly on his own achievements or failures in domestic economic matters (likely the subject of more intractable debate than his accomplishments in foreign affairs), Fidel had given his implicit endorsement to Raul's leadership and the changes now occurring under his watch.

Indeed, within a matter of weeks, Raul went on to launch a series of measures first hinted at when he formally assumed the presidency in 2008—namely, massive layoffs from state jobs and more space for small-scale (for now) private enterprise. Cubans have greeted the early stages of implementation with both guarded optimism and, in other corners, skepticism or anxiety. Now an octogenarian himself, Raul Castro uses moderate, politically cautious, and euphemistic language—"updating of the Cuban socialist model"—to describe what may well turn out to be Cuba's most radical, if moderately paced political, social, and economic renovation since the 1960s.

Before the media kerfuffle prompted by Jeff's reporting, my week with Fidel had ended on the historic neoclassical steps— the *escalinata*—of the University of Havana. The speech to open the school year was scheduled for 7:30 AM, before the heat set in. By the time I arrived, ten thousand people had already gathered in the surrounding streets—a large group to be sure, and especially for so early in the morning, but still distinct from the hundreds of thousands that had congregated to hear Fidel's speeches in the 1960s.

At approximately 7:25 AM, Fidel's motorcade arrived. The audience of university students and professors went wild. After preliminary remarks and a musical tribute to the retired leader (a Silvio Rodríguez song with the lyrics "Yo soy un hombre feliz" ["I am a contented man"]), Fidel took the podium, scanning the cheering crowd and waving to his admirers. He began the speech with the lines he had practiced in front of me a day earlier, describing how on the same spot 65 years ago to the day, he had first acquired a political "conscience of [his] duties." Yet in a clear reference to his health trials of the previous years, Cuba's erstwhile head of state confessed he "never thought [he] would return to these steps." Every single person in the crowd who was close enough for me to see started weeping. For all of their clarity about how Cuba needs to change, Cuban loyalists still revere Fidel for the indelible mark he has made on their country and feel a personal connection to the man who so dominated their lives until recently.

Of course, not all Cubans share the same visceral admiration for the Revolution's chief architect and protagonist. The Castro brothers have obviously never lacked critics, above all in Miami. But like many things in Cuban society, the lasting place of Fidel in the national imagination can also be seen in shades of gray.

Fidel has not spoken to a mass, public audience since the speech I witnessed on the *escalinata*. There are many reasons this could be. But most important is that Cuba has transitioned from the charismatic authority of the kind associated with Fidel's mass mobilizations to a dramatically different kind of leadership. Raul Castro does not hold political rallies. When he does speak in public, his comments seldom exceed 30 minutes, and his detailed evaluations of policy implementation sound more like a CEO reporting to shareholders or a statistics-inclined technocrat than a politician attempting to mobilize nationalist fervor. Compared to the exhausting, adrenaline rush of Fidel's leadership style, many Cubans find this change refreshing. Yet for the 11 million citizens on the island, and the nearly 2 million Cubans in the diaspora, style must ultimately go hand in hand with substance. Raul seems to be acutely conscious of the imperative of delivering on his government's commitments. Going forward, it will have to walk a fine line between upholding the already frayed but vital social safety net on which Cubans depend, while expanding space for private economic activity, slimming an overinflated state, and at the same time mitigating the effects of inequalities that, as it is, have already grown substantially since the emergence of the dual currency economy in the 1990s. So, too, will the government have to make good on widespread talk of political and economic decentralization, to say nothing of pressures for wider political participation and debate. Raul's presidency is delivering results, but it may be another decade until Cuba looks substantially different from the way it does today.

This new edition of *Cuba: What Everyone Needs to Know*, completed three years after the first edition, dives deeper into these ongoing and projected transformations in Cuban society.

September 2012

CUBA

WHAT EVERYONE NEEDS TO KNOW

CUBA BEFORE 1959

What were the main features of Cuban life during Spanish colonial rule?

For nearly 400 years, the island of Cuba was among Spain's foremost and most loyal colonial possessions in the Americas. After "discovering" Cuba on Columbus's first voyage, the Spanish established their earliest settlement on the island at Baracoa, toward the east, in 1511. San Cristobal de la Habana, the future capital, was founded four years later. Governor Diego Velazquez, a conquistador (not to be confused with the 17th-century painter of the same name), quickly succeeded in defeating small pockets of native Taíno resistance. By midcentury, Cuba's indigenous population had declined to less than a few thousand due to disease, mass suicides, and forced incorporation into the ranks of emerging colonial settlements.

Over the next two centuries, Cuba served two primary purposes as a colony. First, with the Florida Straits a natural gateway to Spanish colonial possessions (and their vast mineral riches) in the rest of the hemisphere, Cuba became a key stopping-off point for commerce between the new world and the

Michael Bustamante's contribution to this first section of the book was especially invaluable.

old. Indeed, it was from Cuba that Hernán Cortés launched his expedition that began the conquest of Mexico. Havana thus boomed as a city with a strong merchant and financial tradition. Second, Cuba developed a number of important industries of its own, namely, tobacco, coffee, and sugar. As a result, although the Spanish had settled neighboring Hispaniola first, Cuba emerged as the preeminent Spanish colonial possession in the Americas.

Without a significant indigenous population, African slavery became the primary means to supply labor to Cuba's agricultural industries. The first reports of African slaves on the island date back as early as 1513, and by 1774, a census reported that 25% of Cuba's total population of 173,000 were African slaves (another 18% were free blacks, or slaves that had been permitted to earn their freedom). By the mid-1800s, the combined totals of free and enslaved blacks accounted for well over 50% of the island's population. Slave revolts occurred sporadically throughout the colonial period, and pressure for abolition gradually built as Great Britain first abolished the slave trade (1807), then abolished the institution of slavery altogether (1830s). Yet slavery in Cuba would only be partially eliminated in 1868.

The growth of Cuba's agricultural industries over time drew the island progressively closer to its neighbor to the north, not the Spanish crown. During the 10-month British occupation of Havana in 1762–63, Havana was also temporarily free from Spain's excessive and extensive taxation policies. This economic shift planted the seeds for a wider political change as well, as more Cubans than ever before gained a concrete image of what life free of the Spanish crown might be like. With independence from Great Britain in 1783, ties between the United States and Cuba only increased, as the new country was no longer bound to previous colonial trade agreements with other British colonies throughout the Caribbean. And while Spain attempted sporadically to route Cuban trade through the mother country or within the Spanish empire, sugar exports and other forms of direct commerce with the United States continued to expand (particularly during the era of Europe's Napoleonic Wars) as loyalist Spanish colonial authorities gained more autonomy from the Spanish crown.

Between roughly 1810 and 1825, Spain's colonial empire fell apart, the victim of a substantially declining power base, domestic unrest within Spain, imperial overstretch, and a spate of powerful independence movements led by such dynamic leaders as Simon Bolivar, José de San Martín, and Miguel Hidalgo. Cuba, however, remained "ever faithful," becoming one of Spain's only remaining colonial possessions in the Americas. The reasons for this "loyalty" varied. Grievances against the Spanish state were certainly not lacking, especially among the *criollo* (or Cuban-born) class of merchants, businessmen, and landowners who lacked the privileges of their loyalist *peninsular* (Spaniard elites in Cuba) rivals. Criollos bore the brunt of heavy taxation policies implemented to prop up a weakening Spanish crown, leading many to support independence (as described in greater detail on page 4, "How did Cuba's independence movement gain momentum, and what was its relationship to abolition?"). Moreover, in the wake of the Napoleonic Wars' disruption of Spanish monarchical rule, the proclamation of the Spanish Constitution of 1812, and Spain's transition to a form of constitutional monarchy after an 1820–23 Civil War, criollos' own utter lack of say in the governing of local Cuban affairs seemed all the more hypocritical.

Nonetheless, at the outbreak of independence struggles elsewhere in Latin America, Spain did make key concessions to criollos in Cuba. Royal decrees permitted criollos to openly trade with vessels from other countries in Cuban ports and granted full legal rights to the land they occupied. In addition, many criollos recognized that their own economic clout rested on the institution of slavery. As a result, elites looked with great trepidation to the example of Haiti, where just a few years earlier, Toussaint L'Ouverture had initiated a rebellion that eventually led to the proclamation of a "negro republic."

Fears of unleashing a restless slave population and contending with massive social upheaval tempered the desirability of independence, at least for a time.

Meanwhile, the United States eyed Cuba carefully, looking toward not only commercial opportunities but also territorial expansion. In 1823, Secretary of State and future president John Quincy Adams called both Cuba and Puerto Rico "natural appendages of the North American continent." He reasoned, "There are laws of political as well as physical gravitation; and if an apple, severed by the tempest from its native tree, can not choose but to fall to the ground, Cuba, forcibly disjoined from its unnatural connection with Spain and incapable of self-support, can gravitate only toward the North American Union, which, by the same law of nature can not cast her off from its bosom." At several occasions during the mid-1800s, as Spain underwent a series of domestic dynastic conflicts (the Carlist Wars), the United States offered to purchase Cuba outright, but Madrid refused. As a society in which slavery was still widely practiced, Cuba became a potentially attractive acquisition for those southern states then in the midst of fending off abolitionist drives from the North.

How did Cuba's independence movement gain momentum, and what was its relationship to abolition?

That Cubans did not free themselves from Spain in the early 1800s does not mean they lost their desire for independence. Individual activists and organized movements pushed for the end of Spanish colonial rule over Cuba throughout the 19th century, often inspired by the American, French, and various Latin American revolutions. As early as the first decade of the 1800s, secret societies plotted, revolts were planned and suppressed, and Spanish authorities discovered hidden schemes. Among those early activists well known for pushing the cause of independence are Father Felix Varela, José Antonio Saco (famous for his open appeals for reforming Spanish

administration), and José María Heredia (Cuba's first revolutionary poet).

In some cases, the cause of abolition merged in varying
degrees with the independence drive, as in the work of Saco and
several abolitionist conspiracies. The leadership of free blacks
like José Manuel Aponte (who led a conspiracy in 1812) was
often important. The 1840s "Ladder Conspiracy," an alleged plot
named after a preferred method of torture for slaves, included
the participation of some of Cuba's most well-known criollo
independence supporters, sympathetic to abolition as well.

Another important faction emerged, however, between those
seeking independence and those loyal to Spain: annexation-
ists. Whether driven by commercial ties or fears of black uprisings, some elites who opposed Spain's mismanagement of the
island's affairs opted for incorporating Cuba into the United
States as a way to gain greater freedom while preserving their
privileges and the workings of a slave economy. Annexation-
ists found vocal supporters in the United States and at times
were responsible for armed plots of their own. Perhaps the
most well known are the handful of filibustering expeditions
led by a former general in the Spanish Army, Narciso López,
often with U.S. citizens as mercenaries. Following his capture
and execution, López's supporters throughout the U.S. South
established a secret society that would plot to participate in
several additional conspiracies.

By the 1860s, clamors for independence and abolition had
grown to a fever pitch, especially in the aftermath of the U.S.
Civil War. In 1868, after conspiring with fellow partisans of the
independence cause, Carlos Manuel de Céspedes, a wealthy
landowner from eastern Cuba, issued the Grito de Yara, liberating his slaves and announcing that they were free to join him
in a war against colonial Spain. Ironically, his action had been
indirectly inspired by events in Spain, where reformers had
succeeded in overthrowing the corrupt Spanish government at
the time. As unrest spread across the country, Generals Antonio
Maceo and Máximo Gómez (a Dominican native) assumed

leadership of the rag-tag rebel army. After 10 years of inconclusive conflict, rebels and the Spanish agreed to end the war with the 1878 Pact of Zanjón, an agreement that granted amnesty to those who had participated in the conflict and freedom to those slaves who had fought in the rebel army. Several of Cuba's independence leaders refused to recognize the pact, however, and launched a short-lived attempt at reigniting the rebellion between 1879 and 1880.

In subsequent years, Cuba entered a period of relative calm but significant change. Slavery was formally abolished (at all levels and without exception) in 1886. Cuba's sugar industry also entered a period of crisis in the 1880s as prices fell and growers were forced to mechanize and consolidate production to stay afloat—threatening the livelihoods of midsized planters and the new free slaves whom they employed. Domestic political upheaval in Spain led to the creation of the Liberal (or Autonomist) Party, which promised to carry out reform, grant Cuba greater autonomy, and permit the limited participation of criollos in Spanish legislative affairs.

Who was José Martí?

At this time, the writings and activism of José Martí became central to the struggle for independence, whose epicenter had moved from Cuba to exile, along with many separatist leaders themselves. Born in Havana in 1853, Martí was too young to have played a large role in the Ten Years War, but was exiled to Spain at the age of 17 for his opposition to colonial rule. He eventually settled in New York, where he lived from 1881 to 1895. Essayist, poet, political thinker, organizer—a true cosmopolitan—Martí moved in a wide variety of social circles, alternately organizing support for independence causes and pursuing his art. His writings—both creative and nonfiction—played a fundamental role in creating a broader consciousness on and off the island for the cause of Cuban independence and the humanistic values that guided the struggle.

In addition to passionately supporting Cuban independence, Martí was also wary of U.S. designs—annexationist or otherwise. "I know the monster, because I have lived in its lair," he wrote, "and my weapon is only the slingshot of David." In legendary writings like the 1892 essay "Our America," Martí helped establish the David versus U.S. Goliath mentality that has remained central to Cuba's nationalist ethos ever since. A vocal critic of U.S. imperialism and expansionism, Martí stressed that the Americas should seek to be more unified and that Cuba could and should play a leading role in this effort. Among his greatest concerns were unequal power relations between races and classes, and the dearth of citizenship rights across the region. He argued for education as the basic motor for development throughout Latin America—a concept that would be a foundation of the Cuban Revolution's social policies under Fidel Castro. At the same time, Martí held in high esteem such liberal values as freedom of the press and freedom of speech that were denied him and others in Cuba under Spanish rule. Artistically, Martí is credited as a key founder of Latin American modernism.

In 1892, from New York, Martí founded and assumed leadership of the Cuban Revolutionary Party (PRC), an effort to unify conflicting factions of the independence movement under one umbrella organization. Fundamentally, Martí sought to unite Cubans around a vision of common principles and nationalism, calling in general terms for a Cuba without racial divisions or social cleavages. Over the course of three years, Martí negotiated a fragile consensus among separatist leaders, built the PRC's support in exile, and secured funds and arms for a new revolutionary effort. Meanwhile, on the island, nearly two decades of Spanish promises of reform had shown little results. Renewed economic crisis in 1894 fed the flames of separatism once again. At Martí's personal request, Generals Máximo Gómez and Antonio Maceo agreed to return to Cuba and assume military leadership of a new uprising.

How did Cuba's final war for independence begin?

On February 24, 1895, Cuba's war for independence began with the *Grito de Baire*, a call by insurgents near Santiago de Cuba to begin their fighting. In subsequent months, Maceo, Gómez, and Martí landed on the island to join and lead growing ranks of rebels. Things went poorly at first. By May, Martí was dead, killed in his first and only appearance in battle. But by September, after registering several impressive victories over Spanish forces, rebel leaders met, elected a provisional revolutionary government, and chose to begin an invasion toward the western portion of the island under Maceo's leadership. The campaign was largely a success, with troops crossing into the province of Havana and making their way to the westernmost tip of the island. Spain's captain-general of Cuba resigned his post and was replaced by General Valeriano Weyler, who instituted a brutal counterinsurgency policy of reconcentration, forcing all residents on the island to move to fortified Spanish areas within 8 days or face attack. By the end of 1896, it seemed the Spanish were on the verge of victory: Maceo had been killed, much of the western provinces had been pacified, and the rebel generals were distracted by constant battles with and within the Council of Government, the revolution's civilian authority, over civilian-military prerogatives in the conduct of the war (a tension that would emerge 50 years later among future insurgencies). Still, by the beginning of 1898, rebel control over rural areas had been reestablished, and Spanish morale had been generally weakening.

Why did the United States intervene and how did the Cuban War of Independence come to be known as the Spanish-American War?

The United States watched the war unfold with more than just casual interest. From the beginning, several sectors of political and public opinion clamored for U.S. involvement. In part, this

excitement was generated by Cubans themselves. Rebel representatives based in New York City, led by future Cuban president Tomás Estrada Palma, brought accusations of Spanish
brutality, especially under Weyler, to the attention of the city's
premier institutions of "yellow journalism," namely, the papers
of William Randolph Hearst. With such popular and favorable
press coverage, supporters of Cuban independence were able
to use the United States as a primary base to raise money, mate-
rials, and support for the war. For many Americans, including
among leading African American intellectuals and media, the
continued Spanish presence seemed to fly in the face of the
anticolonial, postemancipation destiny of the Americas.

Yet U.S. opinion was still divided over Cuba's future. By the
time the war broke out, less than 20% of Cuba's sugar mills
were Cuban owned, and at least 95% of all of Cuba's sugar
exports were destined for the United States. United States
owners and investors in the Cuban industry thus watched
with horror as their properties (and the business interests of
the United States) came under threat not only from the cruelty
of the Spanish but also from rebel troops whose insurgency
unleashed an uncompromising slash-and-burn strategy in the
Cuban countryside. For some of these U.S. investors and some
Washington politicians, autonomy but not complete independence for Cuba emerged as an enticing option. The administration of Grover Cleveland refused to grant Cuban rebels
the status of belligerents. Indeed, early in the war, Cleveland's
secretary of state explicitly urged Spain to offer autonomy in
order to avoid ultimate U.S. intervention. After all, more threatening than the prospect of continued violence was Cuban independence. Spain at first refused, convinced at the time of its
ability to win the war. Yet it soon saw autonomy as the only
hope of holding on to Cuba and in late 1897 established a local
autonomous government based in Havana.

For the U.S. press, independence supporters, and the
jingoist impulses that guided much of U.S. public opinion
during this era of international manifest destiny, autonomy

was unacceptable. "You furnish the pictures, and I'll furnish the war," Hearst famously said to one of his cartoonists covering the conflict. Meanwhile, those involved in the Cuban independence movement, like Cuban revolutionaries in the next century, faced a challenging balancing act. They needed U.S. support and recognition as a way of countering Spanish half-a-loaf autonomy impulses while suspecting that too closely courting the United States could well threaten the independence and integrity of their movement (a fear shared by many leaders, including Gómez).

The final push for war came in February 1898, when the U.S. battleship *Maine*, sent to Havana Harbor to protect U.S. interests in the wake of popular riots against Spain, mysteriously exploded. Accusations flew of Spanish culpability. Then President William McKinley attempted to divert the hawkish prodding of his Republican Party colleagues and avoid war by offering to purchase Cuba outright from Spain or serve as a mediator in the conflict. Spain declined both options. The march to intervention thus became unstoppable. Cuban independence fighters were ill-informed of American plans and left out once the war began. The pro-independence Cuban junta in New York had helped to secure passage of the Teller Amendment in the U.S. Congress, a provision under which Washington disclaimed any intent to seek long-term control of the island. It would prove little assurance.

The war was over rather quickly. From the time the United States declared war in late April 1898 to the signing of an armistice in August, hardly three months had passed. During this short period, U.S. forces destroyed the Spanish navy and routed Spanish forces in its other colonial possessions: Puerto Rico and the Philippines. The United States and Spain signed a final peace treaty in December 1898 in Paris. Just as Cuban independence forces had been blocked from occupying key cities once the Spanish were defeated, they were not permitted to participate in the Paris negotiations. The American flag, not the Cuban flag, was raised over Havana. General Gómez, who once trusted American intentions, had been betrayed. He now spoke openly of an "unjustified military occupation."

What kind of independence did Cuba gain and what was the Platt Amendment?

In early 1899, the United States formally began a military occupation of Cuba. Again, McKinley insulted the victorious partisans of Cuban independence by insisting that as many office holders as possible on the island (mayors, etc.—all of whom had answered to Spain) retain their positions to preserve some degree of order, a recurrent theme of American 20th-century expansion. The Cuban economy was in shambles and conditions on the island dire. Gómez and the other leaders of the independence struggle were in little position to resist the American presence, other than through public pronouncements and publications. Many Cubans, however, still trusted in the Teller Amendment and recognized the need for U.S. assistance in rebuilding the economy. Indeed, during the occupation, influxes of American capital and investment further tied Cuba's sugar and other industries to those of the U.S. economy. Although McKinley kept open the door to possible annexation, pressure by anti-imperialists at home and the abiding power of Cuban nationalism prevented an outright takeover. Indeed, when the United States permitted municipal elections on the island, annexationist candidates lost across the board.

In 1900, General Leonard Wood, in charge of the U.S. occupation, called for a constitutional convention, a sign that the United States sought to end its military occupation. Participants in the convention included many well-known independence activists, with the notable exception of Gómez. In 1901, the convention approved a new constitution based largely on the American model. Soon afterward, the U.S. Congress passed the Platt Amendment, an attempt to place limits on Cuba's sovereignty. In addition to constraining Cuba's ability to conduct its own foreign affairs and international financial matters, the amendment granted the United States the right to intervene in Cuba for the "preservation of Cuban independence" and the adequate "protection of life, property, and individual liberty." Cubans erupted into the streets in protest, and for several months the Constitutional Convention rejected the amendment or attempted to add several clarifications to its text. Finally, faced with little other way to secure an end to the American occupation, representatives at the Constitutional Convention approved the provision in a vote of 16 to 11. In the subsequent push for presidential elections, General Wood urged the military government to support the candidacy of Tomás Estrada Palma (former head of the Cuban Revolutionary Party's junta in New York, Martí's right-hand man, and a U.S. citizen who spent decades outside of Cuba) over that of Bartolomé Masó, who, unlike Estrada Palma, had opposed the Platt Amendment. On May 20, 1902, Estrada Palma formally took office and the Cuban flag was finally allowed to fly over Havana.

What were the early years of Cuban independence like and how did the Platt Amendment impact Cuba's political culture?

The Platt Amendment framed much of the disorder that would consume Cuba in subsequent years. After nearly a century of activism in favor of Cuban independence, Cuba's republic quickly descended into a chaotic spin of political infighting, corruption, political violence, and civil unrest. By the 1905 election season, Cuban politicians were starkly divided between liberals and moderates, with little besides personal allegiances separating the two parties. Moderates (supporters of Estrada Palma) committed blatant fraud to keep liberals out, and liberals in turn rose in revolt. In 1906, partisans on both sides called for U.S. intervention; full-scale military occupation subsequently followed. American forces departed by

1909, with José Miguel Gómez of the Liberal Party winning the presidency. Gómez helped to further Cuban economic growth and stabilize the political system. But there were costs: Growth carried the price of extensive foreign ownership, and political stability came with the institutionalization of an extensive system of sinecures and graft. In 1912, U.S. forces once again briefly entered Cuban territory to protect U.S. property against the "revolt" of members of the rogue Independent Party of Color, quickly suppressed by Cuban forces (see page 29, "How did race relations figure into Cuba's political development during the prerevolutionary period?"). United States Marines would again enter Cuban territory in 1917 amid political chaos between liberals and conservatives. They remained until 1923, helping to ensure stability and for a time boost conservative leader Mario García Menocal's increasingly centralized and corrupt rule. Meanwhile, between 1920 and 1921, Cuba's sugar industry had hit the highs and lows of an enormous boom and bust cycle, remembered as the Dance of the Millions.

Throughout the 1920s, public frustration and fervor grew pervasive among an ever-wider swath of Cubans. Intellectuals, labor activists, veterans of the Wars of Independence, and student movements all grew jaded by the failure of Cuba's leaders to fulfill the idealism and potential of the independence movement itself. Dependence on the United States was clear and an embarrassment, the Platt Amendment was a humiliating impediment to Cuban sovereignty, and Cuban politics had been characterized by corruption, low-level political violence, and zero-sum rivalries. Several activists founded the first Cuban Communist Party during this period, and many labor leaders applied the principles of anarchism to their activism. For those intellectuals and students not ready to embrace either of these radical ideologies, anti-imperialist (Augusto Sandino in Nicaragua) and nationalist (the Mexican Revolution) movements throughout Latin America still provided a source of inspiration.

Many Cubans looked to the candidacy of Gerardo Machado for president in 1925 with a renewed sense of hope. Though affiliated with the Liberals, Machado ran with a progressive, nationalist platform: end the Platt Amendment, no presidential reelection, university autonomy, a new and more just commercial treaty with the United States, and greater control over corruption. Once in office, Machado won popular approval because of an enormous public works program for improving Havana.

Yet corruption continued, and soon, Machado revealed his authoritarian impulses, restricting the freedom of political parties, repressing labor movements, and securing a series of illegal extensions of his term. Cuba subsequently descended into cycles of sporadic violence as opposition groups mounted across Cuban society, labor activism increased, and the government attempted to maintain its stranglehold on power. The opposition was deeply divided. Some middle-class opponents of Machado actively hoped for a full-scale U.S. intervention. Others, such as the generally liberal-democratic student movement, remained not so much anti-American as anti-intervention. For a time, the Communists too were able to establish an alliance with Machado supporters due to their joint opposition to U.S. intervention. Radical labor activists, meanwhile, fruitlessly pursued social revolution. Violence and vandalism erupted in the countryside, with U.S.-owned plantations an obvious target—ironically, both for those who opposed the threat of U.S. interference and those who sought to provoke it. In 1933, U.S. Ambassador Sumner Welles arrived in Havana to mediate, primarily between the middle-class opposition and the government. In part because the United States had begun to move away from its interventionist policies under the new administration of Franklin D. Roosevelt, but also because Machado had been a loyal protector of U.S. business interests, Washington resisted greater military intervention. By August, Welles had helped broker a transfer of power. Machado resigned and fled to the Bahamas.

Why does the United States have a naval base at Guantánamo Bay, Cuba?

In addition to various restrictions on Cuban sovereignty, the Platt Amendment stipulated that Cuba would "sell or lease" to the United States lands necessary for coaling or naval stations, in order to "enable the United States to maintain the independence of Cuba." Thus, shortly after the amendment took effect, Cuba's first president, Tomás Estrada Palma, signed a treaty granting the United States a lease in perpetuity to a naval base at Guantánamo Bay, on the eastern tip of Cuba. Under the terms of the agreement, which was renegotiated in 1934 after the Platt Amendment's repeal, in order for the lease to end, both parties are required to consent to its termination. Originally designed as a coaling station for the U.S. Navy, the base is now the oldest U.S. naval installation anywhere overseas and the only American base in a country with which the United States does not have diplomatic relations. During the insurrection in the 1950s, money and weapons occasionally filtered out of the base, destined for the revolutionaries. The base remained a source of employment for locals from the area well beyond the 1960s, a handful of whom still receive a monthly pension from the U.S. government.

Since the triumph of the revolution, the Cuban government has argued that the United States' retention of the base is illegal under the terms of the Vienna Convention of the Law of Treaties, which, though drafted after the 1903 and 1934 lease agreements, stipulates that treaties coerced under the threat of force—the Platt Amendment's right of intervention and FDR's deployment of warships 30 years later during the Machado upheaval—are illegitimate. Moreover, the treaty and its renewal agreement stipulate that the base is to be used for "coaling and naval purposes only." The United States has used the base for much more, including for Haitian and Cuban refugees picked up at sea and more recently for detention facilities, torture, and military trials. Since 1959, the Cuban government has refused to cash the $4,000 annual rent check issued by the

U.S. Treasury and repeatedly demanded for the base to revert to exclusive Cuban sovereignty.

What was the political climate out of which Fulgencio Batista first emerged?

Shortly after the departure of Machado, Fulgencio Batista, a relatively obscure official in the Cuban Army of humble origins, led what is remembered somewhat misleadingly as the "Sergeants' Revolt," a passive and surprisingly swift government takeover in September 1933. Batista's actions led to the establishment of a provisional revolutionary government under the leadership of Ramón Grau San Martín, a progressive professor of medicine who had supported the anti-Machado student movement and did not come from the traditional political elite. Though brief (100 days), Grau's first presidency was of seminal importance to later events in Cuban history, as his government implemented a number of dramatic nationalist reforms. His cabinet unilaterally abolished the Platt Amendment, established a minimum wage, granted women the right to vote, established a ministry of labor, and, perhaps most important, passed a law requiring that 50% of employees in agriculture, business, and industry be Cuban citizens (Spaniards and Americans often occupied key posts in business, while Jamaicans and Haitian immigrants were willing to earn cheaper wages than Cubans in agriculture). Yet in the aftermath of the violent and disruptive Machado period, political chaos reigned supreme: The government lacked support, intransigent plantation owners refused to abide by the government's policies regarding labor rights and wages, and Batista further consolidated his authority over the Cuban armed forces. Antonio Guiteras—veteran of the student movement, well-known radical, associate of Julio Antonio Mella (co-founder of Cuba's first Communist Party), and minister of the interior under the Grau government—played an important role. In addition to shoring up the government's support in eastern Cuba (where he had extensive contacts), he also pushed the Grau administration's limits by backing the efforts of radical labor activists, sometimes affiliated or in alliance with the Communists, then known as the Partido Socialista Popular, or PSP. Deeply disturbed and acting independently of the Grau administration, Batista and the military brass moved to preserve order and protect the security of American-owned properties by clamping down on unrest, violently at times. In the end, Grau faced opposition from all sides—from traditional elites for being too radical, and from radicals like Guiteras for not being radical enough. The government soon collapsed and Batista was allowed to assume de facto control.

How did Cuban politics and U.S.-Cuban relations evolve between 1934 and 1952?

Throughout this period, the United States watched affairs in Cuba with great unease. Yet, under the terms of the Good Neighbor Policy, Washington gave up the rationale to resist the abrogation of the Platt Amendment, conceding its repeal in 1934. Moreover, some opponents of the Machado regime had specifically targeted U.S.-owned property in the hopes of provoking American interference. In Washington's view, Batista was preferable to constant intervention in order to preserve law and order.

But Batista needed civilian legitimacy. With the support of the United States, Carlos Mendieta, a prominent politician who had broken with the Machado government, assumed the office of the presidency. Over the next several years, a succession of governments seemed to return to the old-style political haggling dominant in Cuba prior to 1933. But behind the scenes, Batista maintained order, mediating disputes between political elites and serving as the strong man to guarantee stability against continued unrest. Increasingly, Batista cultivated positive relations with the United States as well, securing favorable trading terms among other benefits. Yet despite his strongman tactics and opposition to the Grau 100-day government, Batista still viewed himself as a reformer bred from the turmoil of 1933. Thus, even as disaffected supporters of the Grau government (including Guiteras) turned further to the left, Batista, ever a chameleon, became more of a Populist. In the late 1930s, he attempted to assume the mantle of reformism, reinstituting Grau's nationalist labor laws, allowing more open labor organizing, and even working in coalition with the Communist PSP (a marriage borne of convenience and popular front politics, not ideological simpatico). In that spirit of reform, and confident of his political staying power, Batista called for a new Cuban constitution and new elections in 1940. The result was one of Latin America's most progressive constitutions at the time, representing a true, if cumbersome, attempt to construct social democracy, in which the state was charged with ensuring social welfare and an expansive range of rights. Batista emerged victorious in the 1940 elections and, despite his continuing and increasingly strong political accommodation with the Communists (among those leftists who had so strongly resisted the United States during the Machado years), forged deeper economic and security ties with an ideologically pragmatic Washington as the United States entered World War II. Cuba's economy boomed as a result of war-related demand and the United States used Cuban territory, including the Guantánamo base, for a host of war-related activities (airfields, supply stations, etc). A number of Cuban military personnel also trained in the United States and contributed to the war effort on the front lines. With the upcoming 1944 elections, Batista planned to turn over power, stepping aside to watch the social democracy he had helped construct out of the turmoil of 1933 continue on.

Ramón Grau San Martín returned to the presidency under the banner of the Cuban Revolutionary Party (recycling the name of Martí's independence-era political organization), popularly known as the Auténticos. As a respected nationalist leader, Grau raised popular expectations for bold reforms. In the aftermath of World War II, Cuba's sugar economy boomed.

Yet Grau's second presidency was a grave disappointment, as public sector corruption returned in a way not seen since the 1920s. Opposition soon grew in the form of the Ortodoxo Party, founded in 1947 under the leadership of charismatic former student activist and frenetic nationalist Eduardo Chibás. A young lawyer, Fidel Castro, would soon become an active participant in Ortodoxo affairs. Meanwhile, despite the repeal of the Platt Amendment, the United States remained highly influential in Cuban domestic affairs, given the extent of its own economic interests in the country and the all-important leverage of its sugar quota. By middecade, U.S. capital controlled over 40% of the Cuban sugar industry, 23% of all nonsugar industry, 90% of all telephone and electric services, and 50% of Cuba's railway services (which were heavily utilized by the sugar industry). Havana, long a tourist destination for Americans, experienced a boom in the sex and gambling industries, both of which were promoted by the American mob as well as Cuban locals.

In 1948, the Auténticos were once again elected to power, with Carlos Prío Socarrás taking the presidency. A well-known former student leader, Prío had been in charge of several ministries under Grau, but forced Grau out on corruption charges once he assumed power. Still, corruption worsened and political infighting deepened. The University of Havana had become the center of outright political gangsterism. Chibás's weekly radio tirades against the improprieties and corruption of the Auténticos reached a new fever pitch and gained more acolytes for the Ortodoxo cause. During the summer of 1951, however, Chibás shot and killed himself on the air, in an apparent radio publicity stunt gone wrong. The result was even more political upheaval.

With the elections of 1952 approaching, the strength of the Ortodoxos worried both Cuban conservatives and the ever-influential United States. Batista entered the field as well, having remained an imposing figure in Cuban politics from a seat in the Senate, which he assumed in 1948. Behind the scenes, Batista and other conspirators in the military were convinced that the nation was descending into political and economic chaos once again. In early March 1952, with Batista's own chance at victory slim in the elections three months down the line, the military launched a coup. Constitutional rule in Cuba thus ended. For all the faults of this period—the extensive corruption and political infighting, the gangsterism and street violence, not to mention the general inefficiency of government as a result of these practices—the years between 1940 and 1952 had nonetheless been a time of relatively open political competition and considerable, though not unlimited, freedom of expression. Incapable of resisting what at the time appeared to be a more or less unified and U.S.-backed military under Batista, Prío's government collapsed and he fled to Miami. Passivity and shock characterized the initial response of the Cuban body politic to the coup.

What were the origins of the Cuban Revolution? How did it succeed?

Among a new generation of revolutionaries, the 1952 coup crystallized the view that brittle democratic institutions, polarization, and corruption had made the path of electoral politics a dead end. Among these was Fidel Castro. A trained lawyer and follower of Chibás, Castro planned to run for congress on the Ortodoxo ticket. But Fidel had also already acquired a taste for experimentation. His first revolutionary venture took place in 1947, when he became involved in an effort to overthrow the Trujillo dictatorship in the Dominican Republic led by the Caribbean Legion (a Pan-American coalition of leftists who sought to overthrow Latin American dictators). At the last minute, he reconsidered his plan to participate, leaving the expeditionary ship and returning to Cuba. The following year in Bogotá, Colombia, Fidel strengthened his revolutionary resume, joining a riot started in response to the assassination of Colombian presidential candidate Jorge Eliécer Gaitán, whose platform had been based on land reform, workers' rights, and the rights of the country's peasants. During the uproar, he helped take over a police station, seized its weapons, and attempted (with little success) to rally government soldiers around the cause of the protestors and the fallen leader. Experiences like these helped fuel not only Castro but an entire generation of activists disillusioned with Cuba's status quo. Their inspirations and influences varied. Moved by the examples of the French, American, and Mexican revolutions, as well as Cuba's own independence struggle, many saw themselves as part of the Latin American antidictatorial zeitgeist of the era. They had studied the texts and histories of anarchism and communism, and along with many Cuban professionals and intellectuals, saw FDR's New Deal as a model for the kind of social contract their society needed to build modern institutions of capitalism and democracy.

The path of armed insurrection began on July 26, 1953, when Fidel Castro, Raul Castro, and 135 other conspirators staged an attack on the Moncada army barracks in Santiago de Cuba, on the eastern side of the island. Their plan was to seize Moncada's weapons and take up arms against Batista. The attack was an unmitigated disaster. Sixty-one participants were killed in action, and of the remaining fighters, over half were captured and/or executed. A small contingent, including the Castro brothers and Juan Almeida (an Afro-Cuban from Havana), managed to escape into the surrounding areas but was soon apprehended and arrested. At his trial, Fidel delivered a speech that would define his view of bringing social justice and a new political order, free of corruption, to Cuba. The suicidal and spectacular nature of the Moncada attack, the power of the speech, and its concluding words, "Condemn me, it does not matter. History will absolve me," put Fidel Castro on Cuba's national political map. Castro and the others were sentenced to varying prison terms (from 7 months to 15 years for Fidel). But by 1955, an amnesty campaign carried out by colleagues, mothers of the prisoners, and supporters of what became the 26th of July Movement successfully pressured Batista to release them. A general amnesty was granted for all political prisoners at the time, including those from the Moncada attack. Soon thereafter, Fidel and Raul fled to Mexico, where in exile they plotted, trained, and recruited supporters for their return to Cuba.

In November 1956, Fidel and 80 men, including the 28-year-old doctor Ernesto "Che" Guevara, landed their small boat, the *Granma*, on Playa Los Colorados, in what is now Granma province, also on the east of the island. As with the Moncada attack, Fidel lost most of his men. The biblically resonant 12 survivors made their way into the Sierra Maestra, where they began their insurgency against Batista. In the 22 months between November 1956 and December 31, 1958, when Batista fled Havana, Fidel Castro and the 26th of July Movement came to dominate the anti-Batista movement on the island, both politically and militarily. But success did not come easily.

In addition to facing shortages of resources and personnel, the 26th of July was not the only game in town. In the wake of Batista's coup, an assortment of revolutionary groups had emerged to challenge the regime, some with more extensive political support and social networks than others. Among the most important was the University of Havana's longstanding student revolutionary group, the Directorio Revolucionario Estudiantil, and its leader José Antonio Echeverría. Echeverría had visited Castro in Mexico City, and between their two organizations there was considerable overlap among the rank and file. But the Directorio's strategy for overthrowing Batista was even more suicidal than the Moncada attacks. In March 1957, joined by another clandestine group associated with Carlos Prío, the Organización Auténtica (OA), the Directorio staged an attack on the presidential palace in Havana in an effort to assassinate Batista and thus bring down his regime. Most of the individuals involved in the palace attack were killed, including Echeverría. In the aftermath, with assistance from the FBI, Batista's repressive forces blanketed Havana with a dragnet of informants, police, and security agents who mopped up most of the Directorio's network. Survivors fled to exile, joined the

26th of July in the Sierra Maestra, and took up arms in the Sierra del Escambray mountain range in the center of the country.

In Oriente province and its capital Santiago de Cuba, another important organization emerged around the leadership of Frank País: Revolutionary National Action. A 22-year-old Baptist school teacher, País had begun to lay down a clandestine network of activists (including some members of the Communist Party's Youth wing) in several cities and towns in Oriente, aimed at carrying out acts of sabotage against the regime. Although País did not visit Fidel during his Mexico City exile, the two corresponded through direct and indirect means. As a result, País agreed to coordinate a series of acts of political violence to coincide with the Granma's landing. The coordination was wildly insufficient to provide enough cover for the Granma forces to flee to the mountains, as intended. But País rapidly took up the mantle of the 26th of July and until his murder at point blank by a Santiago police officer in July of 1957, he was the most important figure responsible for keeping Fidel's new "Rebel Army," the *sierra*, supplied with weapons, men, food, money, publicity, and political outreach.

País and his clandestine network, which came to be known as the urban underground, or the *llano*, were much more than a material rear guard for Fidel. Until the last six to eight months of the insurgency, the lion's share of decisions regarding tactics, strategy, resource allocation, and ties with other opposition groups, Cuban exiles, and the United States was made by País, his colleagues, and successors—Armando Hart, Faustino Pérez, Haydée Santamaría—not Che Guevara, Fidel Castro, or his brother Raul. The balance of power shifted when a general strike in 1958, organized largely by the *llano*, failed. Still, contrary to the revolution's own mythology, which claims victory largely at the hands of the *sierra*, had it not been for the work of the 26th of July Movement outside of the Sierra Maestra during the first 17 months of the insurgency, the final period, when the anti-dictatorial struggle gained unstoppable military and political momentum, would simply not have been possible.

Seeing the Cuban Revolution as much more than the work of a handful of bearded rebels isolated in the mountains with their peasant supporters is critical to understanding how much popular and broad-based support Castro's army possessed when it triumphed on January 1, 1959. Although the military defeat of Batista's army was essential to the regime's collapse, the insurrection also involved a political campaign by the 26th of July movement to establish itself as the leader of a political coalition of armed and nonviolent groups also seeking to overthrow Batista. Although core forces never exceeded more than 200 men under arms for much of the war, the rebel army's military prowess debilitated Batista politically, psychologically, and militarily. Its successes also demonstrated to the other competitors for the presidential palace that Fidel and the 26th of July would likely dominate any post-Batista arrangement. Over time, for the 26th of July's military commanders, soldiers, and rank and file, the guerrilla *foco* came to be cast as the formative experience of the revolutionary, the womb that gestated the "new Cuban man," that near-superhuman individual, free of material wants and bourgeois false consciousness, whom Che Guevara would mythologize and attempt to reproduce throughout Cuban society.

A number of young U.S. citizens also participated in the insurgency, whether taking up arms in the Sierra Maestra and Sierra Cristal, participating in a short-lived guerrilla front in Pinar del Río, or serving as gun runners flying weapons in from New York and Miami for the underground's general strike. One in particular, an ex-Marine by the name of Frank Fiorini, also known by the 26th of July cadre as "Garcia," came to be viewed as a key figure in destroying the strike's chances by pushing for a hard-core militarist approach while also failing to actually deliver most of the weapons the rebels paid him to procure. Fiorini's ties in the United States seemed to extend beyond arms networks. Upon returning from Miami to Havana, he passed a message to the rebels from unnamed individuals said to be laying the groundwork for Vice President Richard

Nixon's presidential campaign. At the time (July of 1958), Raul Castro was holding 42 Americans and Canadians hostage and negotiating for their release with the U.S. consulate in Santiago. Nixon's messengers offered to provide the 26th of July with weapons in exchange for a hostage release deal that would allow Nixon to take credit for securing their release. (Fiorini, whom Cuban intelligence came to believe had been working as an American agent during the insurrection, later worked with the CIA to overthrow Castro, and was involved in assassination plots against him. When Nixon finally became president, Nixon employed Fiorini more directly: Fiorini/Garcia was the same Frank Sturgis who staged the Watergate burglary that would destroy Nixon's presidency.)

Beyond the sociological and tactical importance of military action, the 26th of July deployed a number of nonmilitary resources to survive and ultimately prevail over Batista and the other contenders for power. To circumvent press censorship at home, the revolutionaries cultivated, and manipulated, the U.S. and international media around their cause. They started their own underground press (no e-mail, blogs, or YouTube for their generation) and a radio broadcast, Radio Rebelde, that helped penetrate the censors and amplify the movement's reach and image. To make their case against Batista and ease anxieties about their radicalism, 26th of July leaders and their more buttoned-up supporters among Cuba's professional class actively cultivated the sympathies of members of the U.S. Congress, State Department officials (including staff at the U.S. embassy in Havana and consulate in Santiago), military personnel at Guantánamo, U.N. officials, and important political players in foreign capitals. Fidel himself, and later his supporters, built extensive networks for funds and weapons among Cuban exiles in Miami, Tampa, Chicago, New York, California, Madrid, and Caracas. Beyond the Cuban diaspora, artists and writers performed to raise money for their movement, including the cellist Pablo Casals.

Cuban political history had taught Castro and the 26th of July both the treachery and necessity of big-tent coalition politics. "National unity" became the buzzword for the revolutionaries, but what they really meant was hegemony over the other groups. Competitors sought early in the insurrection to rope the movement into joining a government in exile, and some of Castro's deputies flirted with the idea for the purpose of gaining money and arms. Yet Fidel, Che, and Raul gambled early in the insurrection that their ultimate path to success lay in delaying any such formal structures until they had gained strength on the ground. The resulting tensions between military and civilian players on Cuba's political stage (both in Cuba and in exile), within the 26th of July, and between Castro and other insurgent groups remained essentially unresolved when the revolution triumphed on January 1, 1959.

Likewise, and related to their core conviction to end politics—or *politiquería*—as usual, there was no consensus among the revolutionaries about how they would relate to the U.S. government. Much has been made about one line in a letter Fidel wrote in 1957 casting his ultimate destiny as that of defeating the American Goliath. Likewise, Raul Castro's kidnapping of 42 American and Canadian employees of the Moa nickel mine in eastern Cuba in order to force a halt in Batista's bombing of the Sierra has been interpreted as a gesture pulsing with anti-American gall. But many of Cuba's leading revolutionaries had been educated at American universities; grew up on Hemingway, Cab Calloway, Ivory soap, and Coca Cola; and did not yet imagine, as the outsider Che Guevara may well have, a Cuban future without the United States. Like many Latin Americans, they viewed the United States with a mix of admiration and resentment. That Batista's brutality against his political and militant challengers had been made possible by weapons, political support, and military and police training from the United States was a central part of the movement's public relations campaign in the United States. Because of their own ties with progressive flag officers in the military, Fidel and the others anticipated U.S. attempts to replace Batista with more benign military officers as part of last-ditch third-force options. The revolutionaries also saw the United States as part and parcel of Cuba's institutional deficits, distorted political culture, and economic dependence. Yet when the revolution triumphed, although there was perhaps a desire to challenge the economic status quo and address the issue of dependence, completely extirpating the United States from Cuba was not an explicit, nor really even implicit, part of the 26th of July's goals.

Indeed, Castro's movement generally invoked the rhetoric of social justice, clean government, and independence. At the time, "revolution" did not automatically equal communism. The triumphant rebel leaders expressed their objectives vaguely and in a way that would garner the broadest appeal possible. Thus, once Batista was out of the picture, expectations of what the revolution would become were bound to be confounded.

Batista's departure to exile amid overwhelming rebel support on New Year's Eve of 1958 marked the end of nearly 25 years on the political stage. Over the course of his career, several different Batistas had emerged. First was a young officer, caught in the throws of political turmoil during the 1930s. Second was the Populist leader who during the late 1930s and early 1940s ushered in a social democracy and permitted space for left-wing, including Communist, activists—all consistent with international politics in the era of the Great Depression and the Popular Front during World War II. Finally, as the Cold War hardened to a freeze in the early 1950s, Batista emerged as an anti-Communist strongman, in the same vein as many other Latin American dictators at the time. Above all, he was a survivor and a political animal, one who had helped construct Cuba's liberal 1940 order and helped destroy it 12 years later.

What role did women play in the Cuban insurrection?

It is hard to imagine a more masculine image of revolution than the ubiquitous photos disseminated to the world in early

1959 of the victorious *barbudos:* the rebels with beards, arms in
hand, filthy, exhausted, but euphoric in their victory—a man's
victory. But behind the macho bravado that captured Cuba and
the world's attention were a host of extraordinarily brave and
talented women who made survival and success possible. Many
had been colleagues of Fidel in the early years of the Ortodoxo
party. Others had been followers of Rafael García Barcena, a
University of Havana professor who led a short-lived anti-
Batista conspiracy in 1953. They came from Cuba's aristocracy,
from its professional classes, and from its working class. Some
were educated in the United States and had traveled in Europe.
They and their male comrades consciously took advantage of
the flexibility their gender afforded them. In the most obvious
example, Cuban women transported weapons from one end
of the island to the other by sewing them into the pleats of
their hoop skirts. But transporting the weapons was the least
of their involvement. They raised vast sums of money, whether
selling bonds, coercing taxes from landowners, or prevailing
upon high-value donors and wealthy politicians in the country
clubs of Havana, Cienfuegos, Santiago, or Miami. They also ran
clandestine cells that carried out acts of violent sabotage. Most
prominent among the female partisans of the 26th of July was
Celia Sánchez, a doctor's daughter from the city of Santiago de
Cuba, Oriente province's capital. Sánchez emerged as Fidel's
closest confidant, his chief of staff, his administrative aide,
his accountant, and the revolution's chief document collector.
Another riveting figure was Haydée Santamaría, known as
Yeyé. Raised in a sugar mill town, her brother Abel had been
tortured and killed after the Moncada attacks, and her husband,
Armando Hart (who replaced Frank País after his assassination
as chief of the urban underground), spent most of the insurrection in prison. Yeyé had a knack for convincing Cuba's leading
opposition figures, whether exiled in Miami or Caracas, to
support the 26th of July. After the urban underground's debilitating failure to carry out a general strike in 1958, Fidel sent
her to Miami to rebuild the political, financial, and material

support the movement had lost as a result of the disastrous strike. Her personal interventions with deposed but financially endowed President Carlos Prío succeeded in securing for the Rebel Army a new injection of money and weapons. She well understood the balancing act of preserving the 26th of July's independence while advocating unity among all of the opposition groups and was able to calibrate and leverage her negotiations to the Rebel Army's own battleground successes, especially in the second half of 1958. Vilma Espín, the daughter of the Bacardi rum company's chief counsel, was Frank País's top deputy in the city of Santiago's clandestine network. After his assassination put her own life at risk, she joined the Second Front of the Sierra Cristal, commanded by Raul Castro, who became her fiancé during the war.

The letters and images of these women reveal that they were conscious of their ambiguous positions within the revolution. Some photographs show them smoking in fatigues and berets, evoking the bravado of the hard-boiled, though well-kept fighters that they were. Others, taken after 1959, show them dressed to the nines in lipstick and pearls, donning the latest fashions. In the Cuba of the 1950s, none would have described themselves as "feminist." And while the men whose work they made possible harbored a deep appreciation for their talents, it would take 15 years for the first woman to become a member of the Politburo. Still, many of the revolution's leading women went on to create and lead institutions designed to bring a degree of dignity to Cuban women, whether through literacy programs and job training or to preserve, in the increasingly orthodox institutions of the radicalizing revolution, some space for Cuban arts and culture.

How did race relations figure into Cuba's political development during the prerevolutionary period?

With the advent of the PRC, José Martí and other independence leaders explicitly tied Cuba's struggle for independence to the creation of a new raceless nationality, "with all and for the good of all." "A Cuban is more than mulatto, black, or white," Martí had written in 1893, and so it was within the liberation army, with Afro-Cubans of varying backgrounds participating actively and, theoretically, on equal terms with their white counterparts. In an era where Darwin and the precursors of eugenics were en vogue among biologists, Europeans, and U.S. politicians alike, the Cuban independence movement's strong ideology of "antiracism"—coupled with the leadership of Afro-Cuban heroes like Antonio Maceo—stood in sharp contrast to dominant international attitudes at the time. Yet as with much in Cuba's history, practical realities failed to live up to lofty ideals. Internationally and domestically, qualms regarding black mobilization persisted, and comparisons to Haiti's "black republic" were ubiquitous, sowing fears during and after the war that Cuba was not fit for self-government. To counter such perceptions, especially in the wake of the Platt Amendment and the U.S. occupation, partisans of the independence struggle and other politicians endeavored to promote a "whiter" or "more civilized" face of their movement through its largely Spanish-descendant leadership. But just as often, such biases and racial anxieties were shared by those leaders of the Cuban nationalist collation purportedly charged with upholding Martí's ideals.

The result of such lingering tensions was a pattern of race relations throughout the republican period characterized by paradox and unfulfilled expectations. Universal male suffrage was guaranteed in 1901, making Afro-Cubans active political agents and targets of politicians seeking votes (women of any race would not gain the right to vote until 1934). Afro-Cuban cultural societies and institutions were as embedded in networks of patronage and corruption as other sectors of society. Likewise, a number of Afro-Cuban or mulatto politicians gained prominence in the early years of the republic, such as Juan Gualberto Gómez and Martín Morua Delgado, both veterans of the abolitionist and independence struggles. By the early 1920s, Afro-Cuban dance and music forms like *rumba* and *son* were increasingly seen as symbols of Cuban nationality, inspiring varied interpretations and appropriations by elite intellectuals in a sustained *afrocubanismo* art craze. Afro-Cuban artists like singer Benny Moré and poet Nicolás Guillén became national stars. Indeed, the imposing figure and political career of Fulgencio Batista, himself a mulatto, lent some credence to the notion that Martí's antiracism had not gone totally unheeded in a society that was, after all, more integrated and intermixed racially than its neighbor to the north.

Yet just as Batista's mulatto heritage was a repeated point of suspicion and derision for some of his opponents, Afro-Cubans contended with prejudice, inequality, and even violence throughout the republican period. In many corners of elite society, Martí's writings on race came to be interpreted as a call for racial fraternity rather than equality, a suggestion that carried a strong grain of paternalism. Indeed, a number of well-known Cuban independence leaders argued early in the century that Afro-Cubans owed white Cubans a debt for having sacrificed themselves in pursuit of abolition. Following this logic of fraternity (embraced by not only whites but also some moderate well-to-do Afro-Cubans), any attempt by Afro-Cubans to address grievances by organizing politically along racial lines was seen not only as a threat to the political order but also as, ironically, racist. The consequences of such thinking turned deadly in 1912 when none other than Martín Morua Delgado, the moderate mulatto politician, sponsored a law banning the existence of the Partido Independiente de Color (PIC)—a fringe political party founded by Afro-Cuban veterans disillusioned by continued discrimination and poor economic opportunities. The PIC revolted in response, and was brutally suppressed.

Entrenched racial anxieties appeared in a number of other arenas as well. Over a number of years, politicians used immigration policies to specifically attempt to "whiten" the population, viewing Spanish migrants as more industrious than

Afro-Cuban descendants of slaves. Public opposition to the importation of cheap labor from Haiti and the Antilles by U.S.-owned enterprises, while a focal point of Cuban nationalism and early anti-imperialism, also carried strong racial overtones. Likewise, early artwork ostensibly celebrating Afro-Cuban culture tended to carry its own sense of paternalism, as well as an exoticizing impulse. Eugenics and other pseudo-scientific approaches justifying racist preconceptions of Afro-Cubans' supposedly lesser intelligence and predilections toward depravity made significant inroads among the Cuban intelligentsia, including in the work of renowned anthropologist Fernando Ortiz, remembered more often for his later works celebrating Afro-Cuban culture than his earlier tracts denouncing Santería and other syncretic practices as "witchcraft."

At the day-to-day level, racial borders in Cuba were certainly more fluid than in the United States. Yet Afro-Cubans nonetheless faced innumerable instances of discrimination, both overt and concealed. While nothing compared to the breadth of Jim Crow legislation existed on the island, struggles for access to institutions, facilities, and spaces were a consistent component of Afro-Cubans' quest for fairer treatment. At elite clubs and institutions, the presence of Afro-Cubans was generally proscribed, whether explicitly or through tacit understandings. Thus, even as some Afro-Cubans rose to national prominence and were celebrated by a broad array of citizens (such as well-known musician Bola de Nieve or the boxer "Kid Chocolate" in the 1930s), they were at times denied access to hotels and exclusive restaurants. Likewise, access to jobs across various sectors of the labor market was decidedly more difficult, though not always impossible, for Afro-Cubans—often because of near-constant competition from white immigrants. Where racial prerequisites were officially banned, employers found more indirect ways, such as the dubious qualification of "good appearance," to exclude Afro-Cubans. Labor movements generally welcomed all workers, especially radical unions close to Communists and other leftists. But within their ranks, Afro-Cubans seeking leadership roles occasionally faced an uphill battle against persistent prejudice. Finally, while public schools in Cuba were never segregated, private institutions that acted as feeders into Cuba's elite, frequently run by North Americans, often were.

Interestingly, at the height of civil unrest in the late 1950s, few if any organized Afro-Cuban institutions publicly denounced the Batista regime. In fact, supporters of Batista's government attempted to portray the revolutionaries as antiblack. This does not mean, however, that Afro-Cubans were necessarily less likely than others to support the revolution, as is often thought. Still, the issue of race was not a particularly prominent part of the political program promoted by either the 26th of July movement or any of the other revolutionary groups active at the time. During and after the insurrection, a number of well-known Afro-Cuban figures sympathetic to the Castros urged the new government in public and in private to make discrimination an important social issue under the revolution. By March of 1959, it was clear that the subject would receive pronounced and sustained attention from the new government.

Beyond the realms of politics and economics, how closely intertwined had Cuban and American culture become by the 1950s?

Just as American politics and economic power exercised an undue degree of influence over Cuban society before 1959, so too did U.S. culture make its presence felt across the island, in myriad ways. From boxes of Kellogg's Corn Flakes and Coca-Cola to New York fashions and Ford automobiles, not to mention the ever-growing presence of American tourists, consumer culture for much of Cuba's republican period boasted a decidedly American imprint. In many ways and for many years, the presence of such a significant repertoire of Americana across the island not only was a symptom of the island's political and economic dependence on the North but also subtly reinforced this state of affairs through the power of cultural messaging. How could a youngster enraptured by Hollywood blockbusters of the day not idealize the United States—the land of movie stars, macho cowboy heroes, and victorious soldiers who defeated the Nazis? Likewise, American products were associated and marketed as indicators of modernity and social advancement. United States influences could be more explicitly malicious as well, as in the terrain of race relations, where early years of U.S. occupation provided fuel for racist attitudes toward Afro-Cubans (as well as the creation of the Ku Klux Klan Kubano, or KKKK).

Yet despite the power and reach of U.S. cultural influence on the island, the relationship between U.S. and Cuban culture was not simply one of unilateral domination. In some respects, it was precisely the unfulfilled aspirations for material well-being, efficiency, and progress unleashed by the North American consumption ethic that fed popular support for the revolutionary struggle in the 1950s, ironically contributing to a growing nationalist and vaguely anti-American impulse. But Cuban culture was not exclusively defined by its ties to the North. Spanish and African (as well as more broadly European) influences—whether in literature, art, food, music, religion, or language—remained vital as well, contributing to what Fernando Ortiz called a rich *ajiaco*, or stew, of hybrid practices. Cubans often "Cubanized" U.S. pastimes and products, turning them into something their own, something that most Americans might not even recognize. For example, while baseball became by far the most popular sport on the island, Cubans developed their own distinctive style and traditions surrounding the game.

Cuban culture also profoundly influenced aspects of American culture, despite being seemingly outmatched in size or reach. This was most apparent in the arena of music. Just as American jazz left an enduring mark on Cuban music, inspiring the emergence of big-band mambo in the 1950s, for example,

Cuban rumba, mambo, and cha-cha-cha shaped everything from U.S. commercial kitsch (Perry Como's 1954 hit "Papa Loves Mambo" comes to mind) to avant-garde "Cu-bop" jazz pioneered by Dizzy Gillespie and Stan Kenton. Cuban band leaders like Pérez Prado and Xavier Cugat toured the United States extensively, driving dance crazes across the country. Less known is that a Cuban baseball player of likely mulatto descent played in the Major Leagues well before Jackie Robinson broke the color barrier for African Americans.

In these ways, prior to 1959, Cuban and American culture were deeply intertwined with one another, if not always in equal proportions. Many aspects of these linkages would be attacked in the postrevolutionary period as vestiges of Cuba's neocolonial dependence on the North. Yet even in a context of polarized nationalism and economic isolation at the hands of the United States, cultural ties between the two countries would prove impossible to break entirely.

THE CUBAN REVOLUTION AND THE COLD WAR, 1959–91

DOMESTIC

Why did the Batista regime collapse?

On New Year's Eve 1958, Fulgencio Batista fled Cuba on an airplane full of family, an inner circle of supporters, and allegedly millions in loot from Cuba's treasury. His regime collapsed under the weight of a defeated and divided military, demoralized after years of rural and urban warfare against an ever-growing insurgency. By late 1958, public sentiment against the government, its repressive policies, and, above all, Batista's own abrogation of Cuba's democratic constitution of 1940, had long become widespread. Support for the revolutionaries of the 26th of July Movement and other groups had reached euphoric levels. Loss of support from the Eisenhower administration perhaps provided the final nail in the coffin of Batista's long political career.

What was so special about Fidel Castro?

By the time the revolution triumphed, the 26th of July had become the most dominant political movement among the loosely tied coalition of anti-Batista forces. The Directorio Revolucionario Estudiantil remained active in the Escambray Mountains and enjoyed strong support among Cuban university students. Yet it was the leader of the 26th of July—Fidel Castro—who had clearly established himself as the preeminent and most charismatic hero of the revolution. Upon news of Batista's flight into exodus on New Year's Eve, two important rebel commanders, Che Guevara and Camilo Cienfuegos, arrived in Havana ahead of Fidel to establish control of key military posts. Fidel, meanwhile, hung back in the capital of Cuba's eastern Oriente province, Santiago. It was Fidel who oversaw the swearing in of the revolutionary government's first president, Judge Manuel Urrutia, on January 3, and Fidel who had dinner with the U.S. consul general based in Santiago. Even before he had taken power, as his confidante and personal secretary Celia Sánchez had previously observed to her father, Fidel had already become *nuestro caudillo*, the man with the status, mystique, and, importantly, title (he served as commander in chief of the Rebel Army) to quickly be regarded as the center of new revolutionary power.

Symbolically, Fidel began to consolidate his position during a triumphal nine-day cross-country march from Santiago to Havana. Kissing babies, tussling hair, meeting in every province with the once clandestine leadership of the 26th of July Movement, local politicians, and all manners of supporters, Fidel and his rabble rebel clan basked in the limelight of their triumph and the extensive, uncensored media coverage it received at home and abroad. More important, Fidel used the trek to reinforce the message that the revolution's success and survival required unity—in other words, his own hegemony over all other aspirants then crowding under the tent of revolutionary power.

What did the Communist Party have to do with it all and were the Soviets involved?

The Cuban Communist Party, known at the time as the Partido Socialista Popular (the Popular Socialist Party, or PSP), didn't really get on board the armed revolutionary bandwagon until the middle of 1958, when the Havana leadership sent a few liaisons to meet with Raul Castro and Che Guevara in the Sierra Maestra, including Carlos Rafael Rodríguez, later a vice president of Cuba. A number of writers and intellectuals affiliated with the party supported the revolution's triumph in early 1959, but neither the party leadership nor Moscow played a leadership role of any sort. Indeed, many in the underground opposition viewed the PSP with skepticism or even derision, due to its occasional collaboration with Batista's police forces (driven by realpolitik as well as the PSP's own disagreements with a strategy of insurgency) and its broader alliance with the Batista government of 1940–44. Some party leaders had even served in the cabinet of that administration.

Nonetheless, not long after the triumph of the Cuban Revolution, leaders of the 26th of July and the PSP forged a closer working relationship. This was not surprising, given the established ties of some prominent 26th of July leaders to the party already. Raul Castro himself had joined the Communist Youth earlier in his life and traveled to Vienna and other East European capitals in the 1950s. After 1959, the PSP would become increasingly essential to the revolution's consolidation. Not only would key members provide much-needed technical and organizational skills that the 26th of July lacked, but they would also ultimately provide the link to Moscow that helped Cuba's leaders broker Russian assistance as U.S. economic sanctions set in.

By the middle of 1959, the revolution's first president, Judge Urrutia, denounced the government's radicalization and resigned. The new appointed president, Oswaldo Dorticós, a lawyer from Cienfuegos, had served as the personal secretary to the Cuban Communist Party's secretary general in the 1940s. But particularly in those early moments of revolutionary uncertainty, the budding relationship between the Communists and the revolutionary leadership did not always go smoothly. The party never broke its allegiance to Moscow, and Moscow never fully backed Cuba's support for revolutionary movements abroad, usually regarding such efforts as "adventurism." In fact, by the mid-1960s, further consolidating power would require folding the PSP into the ranks of the revolutionary leadership under an umbrella party and simultaneously putting a stop to what Castro regarded as dangerous sectarian maneuvers by Communist Party stalwarts.

After Fidel took power, what happened to the other revolutionary groups?

It took a few years for the leaders of the Directorio Revolucionario (one of the principal anti-Batista groups competing for influence) to grasp that Fidel and the 26th of July Movement leaders would always regard their organization and its tactics as subordinate to the Rebel Army's military and political leadership. The power struggle between the two groups went on into the early 1960s. By middecade, Fidel had neutralized any challenge the Directorio posed by sending its two top leaders to the Soviet Union as diplomats, the equivalent of political Siberia for an organization that had been the direct victim of prior PSP collaboration with Batista's police and intelligence services.

What did Che Guevara do after 1959?

In the immediate aftermath of the triumph, Guevara took control of the Fortaleza San Carlos de la Cabaña, a Spanish colonial fort just outside of Havana that had become a military barracks and prison. Together with Raul Castro, Che oversaw the rounding up and executions of roughly 160 Batista officers as chief prosecutor for a series of "war tribunals." Like other similar events in Latin America's future, these show trials took place in Havana's main sports stadium and were even broadcast on television. Foreign observers and the international press were alarmed by the revolutionaries' brand of ad hoc justice, as were important sectors of Cuban society, some of which had been supportive of the revolution to begin with.

Yet by and large, the executions not only aroused little popular opposition but in fact also garnered significant support from a Cuban public that had been victimized, traumatized, and perhaps desensitized by the Batista regime's repression over the previous decade. Reinforcing the rationale for revolutionary justice, Cuba's major periodicals, all of which had been heavily censored under Batista, ran an extensive series of reports on the insurgency itself and prominently displayed photographs of Batista's victims, just as the victimizers themselves were being brought to "trial" in the stadium.

After the initial months of 1959, and before his adventures to Africa, Eastern Europe, Asia, and finally Bolivia (where he died in 1967), Che played a major role in Cuba's economy, first as the head of the National Institute for Agrarian Reform (INRA), and later as the president of the National Bank of Cuba. Che was also a leading revolutionary theorist. In particular, he was a strong advocate of the revolution's experiments with elevating moral over material incentives in search of greater worker productivity and the creation of the revolutionary *hombre nuevo* (or new man).

What did the first revolutionary cabinet look like?

When the revolution triumphed, Castro and the Rebel Army enjoyed enormous popular support that spanned race, class, and geography. They were viewed as the embodiment of Cuba's long national quest for unity, independence, liberation from corruption, and an end to dirty politics, or politics as usual (*politiquería*). Fidel's oratorical skills and personal charisma, as well as the sheer audacity of the way in which the rebels defeated the standing army of a U.S.-backed strongman, earned him political credibility and popular adulation. Moreover, because the 26th of July Movement had been so successful at involving professionals, working people, and leading national figures from Cuban civil society inside of its organization, and because the Batista regime of the 1950s had brought such a degree of political malaise to the island, popular demands for deliverance to a new era were quickly concentrated on the figure of Fidel. Naturally, Cuba's insurgent leader took advantage and cultivated this image further.

Fidel also demonstrated early on his strategic political acumen, particularly when composing the first revolutionary government's cabinet. Rather than immediately seizing the highest position in the new government structure, Castro helped select key supporters and potential rivals to high executive offices, and chose instead to wield his significant leverage as commander in chief of the Rebel Army, outside of the cabinet. The prime minister slot, for example, went to a tentative Castro ally at best who had led the Cuban Bar Association, then gone into exile, and spent the late 1950s positioning himself to use the success of the *barbudos* (bearded ones) as a stepping stone to the presidency. The president, Manuel Urrutia of Santiago, a former judge, was a largely symbolic figure. Back in 1957, he had poked his finger in Batista's eye by ruling in favor of several Oriente insurgents, arguing that their rebellion against the regime was constitutional. Almost all other members of the first cabinet came from the ranks of the civilian wing of the 26th of July. Others had collaborated with the 26th of July for years. In sum, the first cabinet was designed to signal to Cuban public opinion that the revolutionaries might, in fact, not be so revolutionary. Many thus expected a moderate, middle-class revolution that might finally restore and implement the progressive tenets of the 1940 constitution, something that Fidel had himself suggested he might do at an earlier point in his long anti-Batista struggle.

Was Castro really a Communist?

The farther in the distance the Cold War recedes, the more this question and its answer take on a musty quaintness. But in the 1960s, in light of the Cold War's polarizing impact on politics within Cuba and Latin America more broadly, the question of

Fidel's political heart was all the rage. In the late 1940s, Fidel joined the Partido Ortodoxo, a political party that primarily defined itself in opposition to the corruption of the Partido Auténtico and its presidential administrations from 1944–52. Fidel associated himself with the Ortodoxos' more progressive wing, whose politics might be loosely associated, in the American context, with those of the New Deal Democrats. Later, after splitting from the Ortodoxos and failing in his 1953 bid to attack the Moncada barracks in Santiago de Cuba, Fidel was imprisoned on the Isle of Pines, where he read a library full of historical, philosophical, ideological, and economic texts, including plenty of Marx. Still, he regarded the Cuban Communist Party (still known as the PSP) as part of the old guard of bankrupt political parties. Fidel rejected its go-slow approach to social change as wishy-washy. By choosing to take up arms against the dictator rather than waiting for the proletarian struggle to emerge organically, Fidel's strategy thus directly opposed not only Cuba's PSP but also Moscow's own preferences at the time.

After 1959, as the revolutionary government's policies increasingly brought it into conflict with domestic and international actors (namely, the United States), Fidel came to need the party, and the party needed Fidel, as described on page 39 ("After Fidel took power, what happened to the other revolutionary groups?"). Once it became clear to him that the United States intended to overthrow the Cuban Revolution, Fidel publicly declared himself a Socialist. Indeed, Fidel made such a declaration just a day prior to the Bay of Pigs invasion while attending the funeral services of those killed in preliminary air strikes designed to cripple Cuba's air force. By July 1961, the 26th of July, the Directorio Revolucionario, and the PSP would merge into one single party, the Organizaciones Revolucionarias Integradas (ORI), or Integrated Revolutionary Organizations. Fidel was the obvious and natural choice for first secretary, who would go on several months later to declare himself not just a Socialist, but a "Marxist-Leninist." In 1962, the ORI became the

United Party of the Cuban Socialist Revolution (PURSC), and by 1965 the organization was again reconstituted as the Partido Comunista de Cuba (PCC), or Cuban Communist Party.

The consolidation of all revolutionary groups under the single unifying tent of the Cuban Communist Party—coupled with the simultaneous proscription of all other organized political voices, Cuba's growing friction with the United States, and the island's expanding ties to the Soviet Union—was certainly seen at home and abroad as a sign of the Cold War times. But the Cuban revolutionaries explicitly and repeatedly related the creation of the Cuban Communist Party not simply to ideological allegiance to the Soviet Union, but rather to Cuba's long quest to secure true independence from imperial powers. More specifically, they argued that political consolidation represented, in essence, an effort to reincarnate the single party created by José Martí in 1892 to help secure Cuban national independence: the Cuban Revolutionary Party. Whatever the obvious gymnastics necessary to equate nationalism and independence with geopolitical alignment with Soviet Communism, Castro and his supporters argued that this strategy was the only way to defend the revolution in the face of American imperial designs.

Yet embracing the rhetorical trappings of Communist ideology did not mean that Fidel was only a Communist. There were domestic and geopolitical reasons for doing so in addition to an ideological common cause. But throughout his half-century in power, as his recent memoir makes clear, Fidel really remained a hybrid thinker, willing to draw from his entire history and experience to interpret events, his response to them, and his efforts to shape them. And as this book addresses later, Fidel acted quite independently of the Soviet Union on more than one occasion.

So, did Communism mean no democracy?

The creation of a one-party Communist state certainly did mean the end of democracy as commonly understood in the West.

For Cuba's new leaders, the liberal democratic order came to be seen as central to Cuba's vulnerability to capitalist exploitation and political control by the United States and Cuba's U.S.-oriented elites. In their view, political parties were the wedge by which the Americans would pry apart revolutionary unity. Ample evidence in Cuba's own recent history bolstered such fears. With the possible exception of several years in the 1940s, Cubans by and large saw their own democratic order and party system as deeply corrupt, self-immolating, and in many cases beholden to foreign interests. Consequently, revolutionary leaders would resist reinstituting the principal tenets of this order. Likewise, restrictions on free speech, the press, and other civil rights were justified as necessary to secure the government's hegemony against implacable internal and foreign enemies. By April 1959, just several months after taking power, Fidel had reshuffled the cabinet and assumed the title of prime minister.

Yet for some early supporters of the revolution, distrust of the old political order did not signify a desire to deviate altogether from Western-style democracy so much as a yearning to reform its ills. Perhaps recognizing this, in February 1959 Fidel had promised to hold elections within two years, arguing that immediate electoral contests would serve little purpose at a time when overwhelming popular support for the revolution was readily apparent. As time passed, whatever lingering hope some may have held for reforming the progressive constitutionalism of the 1940s quickly dissipated, especially as space for dissent in the press and in public was dramatically constricted. By July 1965, the PCC had been created and Fidel was named its first secretary. The one-party nature of the Cuban revolutionary state was thus firmly cemented.

In 1976, a new Socialist constitution was put into place, establishing a quasi-legislative branch called the National Assembly of People's Power—with affiliated regional assemblies as well. Since then, elections at the municipal, provincial, and national levels have taken place every five years, with a president of the National Assembly elected by its deputies. Likewise, the National Assembly deputies are responsible for electing members of the Council of State, Cuba's highest body of executive authority, composed of a president, a first vice president, and several other vice presidents. Between 1976 and 1987, Fidel Castro was elected three times by the National Assembly and the Council of State to be president of the Council of State; during the same period, he was also chosen by the membership of the Cuban Communist Party to serve as its first secretary in three separate party congresses. But for all of those elections, which Cuban loyalists would describe as absolutely democratic and broadly participatory, there was still only one political party, and within that party, Fidel Castro's authority was hegemonic, total, and uncontested. Dissent was tolerated only on a limited basis, and only within the confines of officially sanctioned institutions.

How did the revolution organize Cuban society?

By the end of the 1960s, Cuba's revolutionary government had entirely overhauled Cuban society. Nationalizations early in the decade put sugar mills, oil refineries, utilities, transportation companies, most land, and small businesses into the hands of the state. Sectors with high degrees of foreign ownership or investment were priorities during this process, but all were eventually affected. Housing and other individual properties eventually fell into the hands of the state as well. Meanwhile, discriminatory laws and practices detrimental to black Cubans and women were chiseled away. Health and literacy programs—which soon became signature elements of the revolution's social justice agenda—were directed toward the rural and urban poor, mobilizing hundreds of thousands of volunteers in the process. A land reform, which by subsequent Latin American and previous Asian standards was comparatively modest and systematic, put vast holdings into the hands of the state while leaving plots under 402 hectares in private hands.

In an effort to get away from the island's historic dependence on sugar, the state initially attempted rapid-fire industrialization. Indeed, Guevara, Fidel, and other revolutionary leaders firmly believed that deepening Cuba's revolution required transforming the island's peasants into a rural proletariat. Progressive economists from around Latin America flocked to the island to support this process and institute a top-to-bottom renovation of the economy. Yet with Che Guevara alternately serving as minister of industries, president of the National Institute for Agrarian Reform (in charge of implementing the land reform), and president of the Central Bank, visiting specialists encountered extensive mismanagement and grew frustrated by the chaos. Indeed, Che's philosophical musings about moral incentives for productivity and vague hopes to eliminate the use of currency did little to solve the practical economic problems of the day. Like the economy, the Cuban media gradually came under the complete control of the state as tolerance of dissent diminished in the face of challenges to Castro's rule from within and from abroad. As armed resistance picked up speed in some parts of the country, and as the United States intensified its harassment of the Castro regime, these defensive, conservative impulses were reinforced, making national security and survival the priority. In the lead-up to the Bay of Pigs invasion, Castro famously established Committees for the Defense of the Revolution (CDRs)—neighborhood watch groups tasked with informing authorities of anyone seeming to participate in counterrevolutionary or otherwise suspicious activities. Likewise, mass organizations such as the Cuban Workers Federation and the Federation of Cuban Women—originally conceived as state tools to mobilize great swaths of the population in the absence of defunct political parties and discredited state institutions—gradually became mechanisms of political control. In an already culturally conservative society, the deepening of Communist revolutionary ideology led the government to regard everything from long hair and the Beatles to homosexuality and certain kinds of poetry as counterrevolutionary. Undesirables or otherwise suspicious characters were often sent to various forms of obligatory work duty (including the now infamous Military Units to Assist Production—or UMAP—work camps, operational between 1965 and 1968).

Why did Cubans start leaving for exile?

By expropriating land; nationalizing medium, large, and eventually small businesses; and asserting state control over sugar mills, oil refineries, utilities, and the transportation infrastructure, Cuba's revolutionary government sought to turn upside down the socioeconomic status quo to benefit Cuba's rural and urban poor. It also hoped to uproot those Cubans who, because of their wealth or because of their ingrained habit of looking to the United States as the ultimate arbiter of Cuban affairs, might threaten the revolution's project of national rejuvenation. If the symbol of the Ortodoxo party had been a broom—signifying a desire to clean up corruption—the revolution had embarked upon a full-scale cleansing.

By the end of the 1960s, two significant waves of emigration from the island had already occurred. The first began immediately after the triumph of the revolution and at first included, generally speaking, those individuals and their families most closely associated with the Batista regime. Then, as nationalizations of large-scale holdings and American-owned property set in, other wealthy Cubans as well as some middle-class professionals and technocrats began to depart, settling primarily in Miami. Some had even supported the revolution at the outset, and most believed their stay abroad would only be temporary. By 1962 (when the Cuban Missile Crisis halted the early immigration wave), roughly 200,000 Cubans had left. A second notable wave began in 1965, when Cuban authorities' decision to permit emigration from the port of Camarioca induced confusion and chaos. United States and Cuban authorities quickly agreed to a program of twice-daily "Freedom Flights" between Havana and Miami. A steady out-migration thus continued over the course of the decade, peaking in 1968 immediately following the expropriation of virtually all remaining, and by then almost entirely locally owned, small businesses. At decade's end, what opposition had not been exported into exile was otherwise neutralized, or in jail. Indeed, despite worries about losses of skilled professionals, throughout this period Cuban authorities preferred that those who wanted no part in the revolution leave the island. By the time the Freedom Flights ended in 1973, roughly 260,500 Cubans had sought exile in the United States.

Both the Catholic Church and the U.S. government played instrumental roles during the exodus. In addition to providing liberal visa entry policies for Cuban émigrés, federal authorities offered resettlement assistance and job training programs. The Catholic Church, meanwhile, played a dominant role in Operation Peter Pan (1960–62)—a program through which Cuban families sent their children to live with host families in the United States, again, temporarily most assumed, until which point their parents would be able to join them abroad or it would be safe to return to Cuba. As a result, many families remained divided for decades, and still do to this day.

What kind of backlash was there to the revolution's radicalization?

Events within Cuba between 1959 and 1961 unfolded at a rapid pace, and the depth and density of changes was felt rather quickly as well. With such a dense braid of competing actors and motives, it is enormously difficult to assess whether the "counterrevolution" was homegrown, fomented and funded largely by the United States, or, like many critical turning points in 20th-century Cuban history, a fusion of domestic and international factors. There is no doubt, and now plenty of documentation and oral history records prove, that the Central Intelligence Agency and the White House were absolutely determined to get rid of the Cuban Revolution—first under Eisenhower and then John F. Kennedy and Lyndon Johnson. Yet at the same time, the revolutionaries' determination to completely remake Cuban society was bound to draw criticism and resistance in some corners of Cuba. With such a convergence of interests, the emergence of domestic resistance—drawing on local grievances but supported and amplified by U.S. support—was no surprise.

Resistance emerged from several sources. Within the 26th of July Movement, radicalization provoked charges of communism as early as 1959 among both civilians in the first cabinet and lower ranking field commanders from the rebel army. Notably, Huber Matos, an important rebel commander who had accompanied Fidel on his triumphant march to Havana, twice attempted to tender his resignation that year due to what he saw as the growing Marxist direction of the government. On the second occasion, he was promptly arrested and thrown in jail, where he would ultimately spend 20 years. Cuban authorities maintain that Matos was conspiring with the CIA, attempting to support counterrevolutionary actors. Another rebel commander, Eloy Gutiérrez Menoyo, followed a similar trajectory. Beyond such high-profile cases, alienation spread as well, particularly among those rank-and-file revolutionaries who supported the revolution's quest to bring about a more just society with more independence and local control, but who weren't prepared for a one-party Communist state. Some of these took up arms against the revolution and engaged in political violence. In one notable case, anti-Castro activist and CIA asset Antonio Veciana successfully plotted an operation to destroy the El Encanto department store. Veciana would go on to play a key role in Cuba's internal resistance as the Cuba-based leader of Alpha 66, a paramilitary organization with an exile component in Miami. Disaffected anti-Batista opposition activists affiliated with defunct political parties schemed and plotted, too, winding up abroad or in jail. Perhaps the most active in the anti-Castro armed resistance came from the ranks of the Directorio Revolucionario, some of whom returned to their base in the Escambray Mountains and took up arms.

Particularly between 1961 and 1965, the counterrevolutionaries (seen by their supporters as freedom fighters) were much more than a mere nuisance; they posed a substantial threat to political stability. The newly minted Revolutionary Armed Forces and Cuba's new domestic intelligence services spent much of the 1960s eliminating the so-called "bandits" and quashing their conspiracies. Covert support to these groups from the CIA was crucial, in some cases, to their survival, while ineffectual in others. But just as the Castro revolutionaries had found havens and support from some governments and Cuban exiles sprinkled throughout Latin America, so too did the resistance draw on support not only from the U.S. government but also from the Dominican Republic and Venezuela, where Cuba had set its sights on exporting revolution. Meanwhile, Guatemala, then under military rule, would soon go on to provide the territory on which the CIA would train those who took part in the Bay of Pigs invasion.

What kind of benefits did the revolution deliver and to whom?

Fidel and his revolutionary cohorts believed strongly in social justice and craved to see Cuba's full potential realized after decades of persistent inequality. For them, continued illiteracy, malnourishment, and ill health, especially in the countryside, were unacceptable. They understood the purpose of their revolution to be not only realizing José Martí's dream of full independence but also permitting all Cubans to live with a degree of material and social dignity—albeit dignity, it would turn out, at the cost of political and civic freedoms. Over the first three decades of the revolution, authorities worked to enlist poor and working-class Cubans as stakeholders in the revolution through a number of means. On one hand, they conducted adrenalin-laced mass rallies in Revolution Square, which, in addition to uniting Cubans behind an intense feeling of patriotism, allowed citizens to relish the intangible but unmistakable high of successfully defying the United States.

Yet authorities also focused on enacting real and often dramatic changes in material life, family welfare, and social mobility. In the early years of the revolution, once most residential property was nationalized, rents were dramatically reduced to a fraction of their former rates. Once telephone and electricity and other utilities were nationalized, Cubans likewise paid just pennies for these services. A nationwide literacy campaign brought illiteracy rates to zero within the first few years of the 1960s. Universal education closely followed, with school guaranteed first through sixth grade, then required through the ninth grade, and made available to everyone through technical, university, and graduate levels. Within a generation of the revolution's triumph, the children of illiterate peasants or Afro-Cuban urban poor were graduating with professional degrees.

In healthcare, the revolution initially suffered after Cuba lost many of its medical professionals to early waves of outmigration. Yet, over time, Cuban authorities made primary and preventive healthcare a major priority, investing significant percentages of the national budget to that end decade after decade. Measured by the number of children vaccinated, the rise in life expectancy, improved maternal and fetal health rates, and steady declines in infant mortality, in the period ending with the collapse of the Socialist bloc in 1991, the Cuban Revolution's accomplishments in public health were the envy of the developing world and in fact rivaled those of many industrialized countries.

In the early years of the revolution (as the U.S. economic embargo kicked in but before the Soviet Union started buying most of Cuba's sugar crop or providing a multi-billion-dollar subsidy to the island), authorities employed a system of rationing to ensure equal access to scarce food resources. Beginning in 1962, all Cuban families received the *libreta*, a ration card that guaranteed access to state distribution centers (one can hardly call them stores), which provided the basic basket of rice, beans, cooking oil, sugar, eggs, poultry, meat (in the good times), and a limited array of produce. In addition to the family ration card, once the Cuban state adopted the Soviet central planning model and state enterprises guaranteed full employment (which didn't necessarily mean productive employment), Cuban workers were provided with meals and snacks at their workplaces, only without having to worry about the cash register at the end of the line of the cafeteria. Still, with the combined effects of the U.S. economic embargo and the inherent inefficiencies of central planning, occasional shortages occurred. Likewise, certain products that had previously been readily available (spices, for example) were often in short supply. Thus, while the ration card may have provided a basic amount of food security, it did not cover all needs. Over time, it came to symbolize not only a culture of equality but also one of scarcity and inefficiency.

A better way to tackle the question of who benefited from the revolution's patronage is to scrutinize the regime's criteria for excluding beneficiaries. After exporting, jailing, neutralizing, or co-opting most of its opponents, the question on the table for Cuba's leaders was how to guarantee ideological compliance with the tenets of the revolution—compliance, that is, beyond the basic popular "buy-in" the state could expect if it delivered reasonably on bread-and-butter issues (which it often failed to do). In order to attain, virtually for free, the highest professional education and training, as well as access to privileges associated with their profession enjoyed by peers in the West or colleagues in the Socialist camp, Cuban citizens were required to rigorously demonstrate their ideological loyalty and political reliability. Especially in the period of the Cold War, but certainly thereafter as well, merit was not the only measure necessary for a Cuban young person to enter university and compete for slots in engineering, medicine, biotechnology, the hard sciences, and other top professions. Thus, while the government's claim of providing free universal education is accurate, to qualify for training and practice in the advanced professions, Cubans needed to demonstrate political purity and revolutionary zeal, normally through their membership in a number of mass organizations and multiple references. Notably, however, because membership in the Communist Party or the Communist Youth was highly selective and competitive, it was not necessary to be a party member to land a slot in the coveted schools of high education and training. Likewise, because the need for a well-educated and trained labor force continued to grow, the ideological and institutional blessings were, judging on the steady growth of graduates, easy enough to obtain.

How did race factor into the equation?

As we saw in "Cuba before 1959," pages 1–35, Cuba's earlier wars of independence were complicated by racial uncertainties and broader disagreements over the role of Afro-Cubans in an independent republic. Throughout the prerevolutionary period, questions of race were left largely unanswered and unaddressed by various generations of Cuban leaders.

Fidel Castro and his revolutionaries inherited the latent unrest left by these disappointments. In 1959, Afro-Cubans represented 40% of the total Cuban population. To a certain degree, such statistics should be taken with a grain of salt, as in Cuba, the racial divide was never as stark as in the United States. Then, as now, Cuban citizens came from a wide spectrum of racial backgrounds, combining varying degrees of European, African, Native American (Taíno, Carib), and even Asian ancestries (Chinese laborers had been brought to Havana during the 19th century). Still, even by the 1950s, racial biases remained a prominent, if slightly more understated aspect of daily life in Cuba, unjustly restraining opportunities and conditioning access.

Only a few short months after coming to power, Fidel Castro announced that race was one of the fundamental issues the revolution would have to address. Influenced by previous revolutionaries such as José Martí, whose attempts to build a colorblind Cuban society had fallen short, Castro warned the

Cuban nation that divisions along racial lines would threaten the success of the revolutionary project. In one of his early speeches in 1959, he condemned racial discrimination at both institutional and societal levels, declaring that all Cubans, regardless of skin color, should enjoy equal access to basic necessities and the means to improve their lives.

The revolution thus set out to deliver full equality before the law. It prohibited all forms of discrimination that restricted access to employment and education. Likewise, the government quickly opened the doors of state services to all Cubans. Rapid desegregation and many of the early redistributive economic policies benefited Afro-Cubans tremendously, as they were disproportionately represented among the economically disadvantaged prior to the revolution. After a few short years, the government went so far as to declare an end to racial discrimination.

Indeed, explicit forms of legal discrimination had been eliminated. Yet, even as the revolution undertook these measures, the cultural biases of the previous centuries persisted. Official policies outlawed discriminatory hiring practices, increasing the representation of black Cubans in all sectors of the Cuban economy and labor force. Still, more subtle forms of racism continued, and Afro-Cubans continued to be underrepresented in most coveted professions, particularly within the political leadership, where Afro-Cuban participation was disproportionately low. While the benefits experienced by many Afro-Cubans were significant, the Cuban leadership struggled to address the underlying racism in Cuba that existed on a societal level. In some cases, government policies seemed to replicate older suspicions. Ironically, authorities continued to regard independent black-based organizations as unnecessary in the new egalitarian society created by the revolution. In fact, independent organizing of any kind, let alone independent Afro-Cuban organizing, was viewed as a potential challenge to the regime's own message of unity as well as its quest for hegemony. Such justifications echoed the very same pretext political authorities in prerevolutionary Cuba had used to challenge and contain demands for more equal Afro-Cuban representation.

As Cuba's involvement in African independence struggles expanded, Havana's official silence regarding the persistence of racial inequality at home became more problematic. Beyond Angola and supporting various anticolonial movements on the continent, Cuba played a crucial role in opposing apartheid in South Africa, bringing attention to the issue long before many western governments did. Thus, despite the recognition that racial problems persisted on the island, Cuba earned an abiding level of respect and credibility for its international activism in favor of racial equality, including among African Americans in the United States. As a result, notable African American leaders developed a certain rapport with Cuban authorities that would in the future provide them the space to raise concerns about persistent racial discrimination and exclusion on the island.

In a notoriously patriarchal society, how did women fare under the revolution?

In the early years of the revolution, women emerged as a central part of the state's mobilizing machine. Eliminating prostitution, a trade that had contributed to Cuba's reputation as a brothel and gambling getaway for American tourists, became one of the new government's most important social priorities. Celia Sánchez, Fidel's personal secretary and confidante, oversaw programs designed to provide respectable jobs and educational opportunities for former prostitutes. Yet beyond these initial reforms, and despite U.S. attempts to isolate the island, Cuba's revolutionaries were acutely conscious of the liberation movements exploding all around them, including women's liberation and feminist movements in Europe and the United States. Moreover, Cuban feminism had deep historical roots. Indeed, prior to the Batista period, female activists had played an important part in passing some of the most progressive legislation for women in the Western Hemisphere at the time.

But in the 1960s, Cuban women still weren't exactly ready to burn their bras, and Cuban men were hardly prepared for a feminist uprising. Instead, under the leadership of Vilma Espín, the MIT-trained wife of Raul Castro, Cuba created the Federation of Cuban Women (FMC) in 1960. The FMC became an amalgam of institutions providing job training, education, and counseling for its members. It also helped to educate the broader Cuban public about women's issues. Among the key early messages was that Cuban women who traditionally endured the *doble jornada*—work by day on the job and work at home taking care of their husbands and children—were no longer going to take it. Eventually, such sentiments came to be embodied in the government's 1975 "Family Code," which guaranteed equal rights for women in the home. Over time, the distribution of housework between the genders did palpably improve. Likewise, the legal and cultural space for women to participate more equitably in all affairs of Cuban society—especially in the professional sphere—grew immensely. Women's representation in Cuba's Communist Party rank and file also climbed, as it did in the National Assembly after its creation in 1976. Nevertheless, by the end of the Cold War, a quick glance at the faces of the cabinet, flag officers, and polit-buro members showed that their representation at the highest levels remained disproportionately low, as in many developing and developed countries. As one skeptical insider once quipped, over time, the Federation of Cuban Women proved to be as "feminist" or "radical" as the League of Women Voters in the United States.

What kind of space did the regime allow for intellectuals and artists?

At the time of the revolution's triumph, Cuban arts and letters were widely regarded as among the most sophisticated and cosmopolitan of Latin America. On the eve of the revolution, Cuban musicians had already exerted significant influence on American music, spearheading the spread of Latin jazz, Cu-bop, mambo, and the infectious cha-cha-cha to cities throughout the United States and parts of Europe. Meanwhile, Cuban visual artists such as Wilfredo Lam, along with writers such as Guillermo Cabrera Infante and Alejo Carpentier, mingled as equals among contemporaries in London, Paris, New York, and Mexico City. Indeed, during the 1950s, many of Cuba's most prominent writers and artists escaped the repression and censorship of the Batista years by seeking exile in these very cities.

Paradoxically, the revolution did a great deal to both further develop and stifle this rich artistic and cultural tradition. On the one hand, one of the early objectives of the revolution was to make all forms of culture more widely accessible to all Cubans regardless of social standing or whether they lived in urban or rural areas. To further this end, cultural initiatives established specialized schools for the arts, advanced training programs, and performance groups that would be sent out to Cuba's rural provinces to spread artistic awareness beyond the traditional metropolitan confines of Havana. State-run cultural institutes, like the Cuban Institute of Cinematographic Arts and Industry (ICAIC), were created to disseminate revolutionary culture to the masses. Often, and especially in ICAIC's case, their work generated international acclaim as well.

On the other hand, the early years of the revolution also witnessed intense debates over the fundamental purpose of art and artists within a revolutionary society, as expressions of social/political criticism common in artistic circles came under close scrutiny. In now infamous 1961 remarks, "Words to the Intellectuals," Castro announced the basic criteria for the revolution's cultural policies: "Within the Revolution everything, outside the Revolution nothing." Criticism or social commentary deemed to be "outside" the revolution was to be proscribed. Exceeding established boundaries could result in censorship and, at times, expulsion. Yet the exact boundaries themselves were never entirely clear. In fact, for much of the 1960s, some artists were able to engineer or preserve a significant degree of leeway. The early films of Tomás Gutiérrez

Alea, for example, challenged viewers to think critically about ongoing changes within Cuba's revolutionary society.

Yet at other moments, repression and censorship turned more aggressive. Before becoming widely heralded troubadours of the state-supported, largely prorevolutionary *Nueva Trova* (or New Song) movement, singers Pablo Milanés and Silvio Rodríguez faced ostracism from cultural authorities who viewed their admiration for western artists as symptoms of cultural imperialism. Both were sent to complete compulsory work duty. Later, in 1971, the poet Heberto Padilla and a group of other prominent Cuban writers—all early supporters of the revolution—were arrested for publishing "subversive" work critical of the revolution. The "Padilla Affair" inaugurated a five-year stretch of cultural stagnation, during which the Cuban state imposed a much harsher degree of artistic dogmatism. Today, these years (1971–75) are remembered as the "grey period" of Cuban revolutionary art. (Padilla was released from prison in 1980 and would move to the United States, where he went on to teach at Princeton University.)

The "grey period" and continued repression notwithstanding, within the boundaries established by the revolution, artists and intellectuals have managed to create and maintain a surprising degree of creative space over the years—more space in fact than is permitted in most other sectors of Cuban society. Self-censorship continued to limit instances of crossing clearly demarcated redlines. But into the 1980s, Cuban writers, visual artists, musicians, and filmmakers continued to subtly challenge taboos, creating some of the most substantive and widely spread critiques of Cuban politics and current affairs. These dynamics would only increase following the collapse of the Soviet Union.

How did the regime deal with its adversaries in the exile community?

Among Fidel Castro's many strategic insights, perhaps the most crucial was his understanding that for an island nation 90 miles from the United States, the smartest way to deal with domestic opposition was to export it. Yet Fidel was also well aware of exiles' capacity to use the United States (and other countries, too) to amass money, weapons, and political support against him. Well before the revolution, Cuban émigrés from Martí to Grau to Prío had all used their years in exile as extensions of their domestic political battles. Fidel's 26th of July Movement was no exception to this trend, drawing on a strong supply of foreign supporters throughout the insurrectionary period. Once in power, Fidel stood aside as his domestic adversaries fled the country and accepted the attendant losses of technical and professional expertise. Yet his intelligence services also probed emerging and preexisting networks of Cubans living in the United States to gather information on the activities of exile political organizations.

In the face of ample evidence, Fidel correctly assessed that the U.S. government, principally the CIA, would use Cuban exiles as the front line in a slew of policies throughout the Cold War aimed to overthrow the revolution. Although only a percentage of Cuban exiles came to be directly involved in the most high profile of these ventures—the Bay of Pigs invasion, Operation Mongoose, a wide array of assassination attempts, and violent attacks on Cuban planes, ships, and diplomats—the Miami community's seemingly generalized support for such initiatives fed the regime's antiexile rhetoric and the Cuban population's nationalist outrage. Exiles were labeled *escoria* (scum) and *gusanos* (worms)—in other words, turncoats, traitors, sell-outs. That the Florida and New Jersey state social services, subsidized by the federal government, provided generous resettlement assistance for Cuban exiles, including help with language, job placement, and housing, added salt to the wound.

Still, while the immense majority of Cuban Americans during this period remained hostile to the Castro regime and continued to support U.S. policies of economic and political isolation, during the 1970s, smaller, mostly younger groups slowly began to emerge advocating a different view of Cuba than most exiles who left the island as adults in the early 1960s. Swept up to a certain extent in the aftermath of the student and antiwar protest movements of their generation (during which time the Cuban Revolution remained a potent symbol), some young Cuban Americans—associated particularly with arts and cultural circles—adopted a considerably more positive stance toward the revolution. Others, older and younger, maintained their opposition to Castro, but had resigned themselves to the regime's presence and sought to open a new, more pragmatic chapter of dialogue.

Thus, in the late 1970s, even as militant exile groups—not to mention known terrorists such as Luis Posada Carriles and Orlando Bosch—continued their plotting against the regime (with often devastating consequences, as in the 1976 bombing of a Cubana airlines passenger jet), the stage was set for an opening between Cuban authorities and those sectors of the Cuban American community—still strongly in the minority— disposed to a different approach. In September 1978, Castro invited Cuban exiles to Havana to discuss a number of issues. As intended, the invitation deeply divided the Cuban American community. Indeed, some participants in this *diálogo* became targets, and victims, of extremist exile terrorism; others were blacklisted from jobs in Miami. Those who did participate effectively signaled their eagerness to look past ideology and, in some cases, their own prior counterrevolutionary activism in order to build bonds of reconciliation across divided families. Participants also tended to believe that breaking Cuba's isolation might help improve human rights or secure the release of political prisoners, who still ranked in the thousands. Both family reunification and the fate of political prisoners were explicit items on the agenda.

Whatever the motives or consequences of participation, as a result of the *diálogo,* in 1978 the Cuban government began to allow Cuban Americans to return to the island to visit family members. Though the prospect of returning to the island caused conflict within the exile community, by 1979 over 100,000

Cuban Americans had nevertheless traveled to the island. For the first time, Cuban filmmakers, writers, and artists began to portray delicate and formerly taboo subjects such as divided families, the Cuban diaspora, and the implications of Cuban citizens' growing consciousness that a better material life with more political freedom awaited just across the Florida Straits. In addition, during this period laws were passed stipulating that Cubans who left the island retained their Cuban citizenship, meaning that to this day, those who were born in Cuba but are now citizens of the United States, Spain, or Mexico remain Cuban citizens and are eligible for Cuban passports.

Since the years of the *diálogo,* the Cuban government has sought to sow political divisions within the Cuban American community while sending the signal that for those willing to give up on overthrowing the revolution, for those who just want to see and support their families, visiting home is a neutral act. By contrast, for those few but politically and financially powerful Cuban Americans who held onto the fantasy that they would be able to recover their confiscated properties, let alone the small handful who clung to the pretense that they might resume political and economic control of the island, the consistent message from the Cuban government was always one of total repudiation.

Of course, throughout this period, the majority of Cuban Americans neither fit the caricature of rabid exile counterrevolutionaries, nor were they ready for a full-blown reconciliation. Between active participation in armed plotting and traveling to Havana for talks with government officials lay an immense middle ground. Were they anti-Communist? Of course. Anti-Castro? Without a doubt. Supportive of isolationist policies? For sure. But counterrevolutionary? Well, it depends on the definition. Undeniably, the violent, terrorist actions of some groups and individuals continued to receive tacit and at times overt support from significant portions of the community. Even if they didn't actively campaign in their favor or provide them with resources, some tended to view men like Bosch and Posada

Carriles as freedom fighters and national heroes, following their exploits carefully. More broadly, within the context of Cuba's long history of political violence, it did not seem out of the ordinary or wholly unjustified to attempt to violently overthrow an opposing government viewed as unjust. After all, Fidel Castro had done the same thing. Yet over time, and especially in the 1980s and beyond, most Cuban Americans disabused themselves of the notion that they would ever return to Cuba, settled into American life, and decreased their support for violent action as a result. Increasingly, community leaders looked to the tools of U.S. policy (embargo, isolation, condemnation), rather than direct military intervention or covert action, as the means to voice their continued opposition to the Castro regime's repression of democratic freedoms. Simultaneously, a growing silent majority—though nominally supportive of the embargo and isolation—thought about Cuba less and less, concerning themselves most with advancing within American society. As families set firm roots in Miami and beyond, those individuals who had left the island rarely lost their passion for Cuban politics, but neither their lives nor certainly the lives of their children revolved around an all-consuming anti-Castro vendetta.

How did the revolution handle religion?

At the time of the revolution, Catholicism was the most prevalent organized religion in Latin America, and Cuba was no exception. Yet the Catholic Church in Cuba and the practice of Cuban Catholicism were not nearly as omnipresent as, say, in Mexico, Colombia, or many Central American countries. For one thing, the Cuban clergy was heavily populated by priests rotated in from Spain and the United States, so much so that in 1959 foreign-born priests outnumbered their Cuban-born counterparts. More important, close contact with the United States had fostered the development of a variety of Protestant denominations, and Afro-Cuban syncretic faiths were widely practiced as well.

During the insurgency, clergymen from a number of Christian denominations were sympathetic toward the revolution. Some even took part in or directly supported the revolutionaries' challenge to the Batista order. In 1958, the Catholic Church joined the Conjunto de Instituciones Cívicas, an umbrella group calling for Batista to step down. But after the revolution's triumph, as the government radicalized and the country became more polarized, relations between the new guard and the church soured rapidly. In 1962, the revolution shut down parochial schools, arguing that the church was providing haven to counterrevolutionaries. Many clergymen subsequently joined in the anti-Communist clamor of those whom the revolution was sidelining. Practitioners of Protestant faiths faced similar circumstances. Methodists, Episcopalians, and Baptists had all participated in the anti-Batista insurgency. Frank País, one of the most well-known and beloved figures of the urban underground, remained a devout Baptist until his assassination at point blank by Batista's police. Yet, after 1959, many Protestant churches simply folded in upon themselves. Many were particularly devastated by the closing of all parochial schools, a vocation that had been a mainstay of the Protestant presence on the island for years.

At its base, the revolution's growing aversion to religion was in some sense inevitable. As Cuba drew closer to the Soviet Union, the atheism and anticlerical leanings inherent in traditional interpretations of Marxism naturally compelled a break with organized churches. Yet the actions of Cuban authorities were motivated not just by Marxist ideology, but also by a constant suspicion that independent organizations or organizing of any kind could challenge the hegemony of the state. As a result, as revolutionary leaders consolidated their authority and merged once diverging political and ideological tendencies into the Cuban Communist Party, all religious faiths faced ostracism. Party membership was proscribed for active believers of any faith.

These developments hardly signified that Cubans abandoned spiritual practice and prayer altogether. Catholic and

Protestant churches lost much strength and many resources but were able to retain a sparse yet persistent presence throughout the island. In fact, in later years (roughly the 1970s), and in the wake of the Vatican II reforms and the growing liberationist tendencies in many Christian theologies, some Catholic and Protestant leaders would embark upon a reassessment of their faiths, realigning their readings of the Bible with revolutionary principles of social justice. Some sects were thus slowly able to regain a measure of legitimacy, which would only be fully apparent in the post–Cold War period.

Meanwhile, the practice of Santería and other syncretic faiths remained ubiquitous, not only among the Afro-Cuban population, but also for Cubans of every shade of skin and class origin. Whether through popular imagery, idiomatic expressions, or other cultural references, Santería is as familiar to Cubans as, say, certain elements of Jewishness or Yiddish culture are among secular or Christian America. Syncretic rituals and practices of these faiths had long been fused to forms of Christian worship in Cuban society. Indeed, because Cuba's syncretic religions were more decentralized and lacked the same kind of formal institutional structures and resources of Christian denominations, they were more tolerated than many other faiths. Predictions for the island issued at the end of each year by the Ifa priests or Babalawos of Cuba, Santería's highest religious authorities, remained significant for Cubans across the island, from the party faithful to the most politically apathetic or disaffected.

After the Cold War ended, and the orthodoxy of Soviet-oriented Marxism/Leninism subsided, religious practice came much more into the open, including for Catholics.

Why did the revolution make such a big deal out of sports?

As in many other fields, such as science, the arts, and medicine, Cuban athletes had already established themselves as global competitors before 1959. Yet for the revolution, investment in organized athletics assumed a new level of priority. Cuban authorities devoted significant financial resources to provide high-quality training facilities and competitive leagues. Likewise, as an integral part of primary and secondary education, organized sports became accessible to Cubans of all races.

Whether in boxing, ballet, baseball, volleyball, or track and field, year in and year out, Cuba produced world-class athletes. Their successes not only became potent symbols for the revolution's efforts to foster the creation of a new national identity but also gave the Cuban people a source of pride and accomplishment in difficult times. Of course, as the exclusive terrain of the state, sports also became a tool for coercion and control. High-profile defections at the Olympics, the Pan-American Games, or other international venues—often at the instigation of agents working on behalf of American professional clubs—were a continual occurrence. Nonetheless, especially during the Cold War, Cuban athletes ranked among the best in the world and helped symbolically bolster Fidel's claim that the revolution embodied not only ideology but also a deeply nationalist project. Some Cuban stars, such as the gold medal boxer Teofilo Stevenson or the Olympic volleyball player Anna Fernández Valle, finished their careers in sports to assume prominent roles as public figures at home.

What about Cuba's human rights record during this period?

Throughout the 1960s and much of the 1970s, thousands of political prisoners were jailed in Cuba. Just before the Bay of Pigs invasion, when security was on high alert, the numbers were reported to be over 20,000. By the mid-1970s, they had dropped to between 4,000 and 5,000. The number decreased further when, as a result of the *diálogo* and the Carter-era openings, another 3,000 were released. Later, in 1984, Reverend Jesse Jackson would lead a subsequent initiative in Cuba and negotiate the release of an additional 26 prisoners.

In addition to those political prisoners arrested for conspiring against the state, homosexuals and others deemed to be "anti-social" by Cuba's culturally repressive domestic intelligence service were rounded up and sent to work camps for communist reeducation during the 1960s and 1970s. Although this practice faded out in the mid-1980s, in many ways Cuban society is still struggling to recover from the legacy of state-sponsored homophobia and the overall allergy displayed toward what the regime considered potentially counterrevolutionary behavior. There were isolated reports of torture during the early years of the revolution. By the 1980s, however, torture and extrajudicial executions (all rampant in those Latin American countries of the era ruled by military regimes, or in those where elected governments faced insurgent challenges) no longer formed part of the revolution's repressive toolbox. Conditions in Cuban prisons have ranged widely. Measured by the standards of treatment and the density of the prisoner population, some facilities at the time (when the Soviet subsidy still flowed) compared favorably to U.S. prisons; others were deplorable. Although activist organizations in Miami continued to accuse Cuban officials of poor treatment, on balance conditions remained much superior to prisons in most Latin American countries (although they would decline when the end of Soviet subsidies left Cuba bankrupt). Of course, for those imprisoned on the basis of such dubious and politically motivated charges as "ideological diversionism" or "precrime social dangerousness," debating the conditions they encountered perhaps matters less than highlighting the questionable pretext of their original arrests.

Beyond imprisonment and forced labor for antigovernment activists or antisocial behavior, broader baskets of individual human rights in the traditional western model were constricted as well. Civil and political liberties associated with liberal democracies—the rights to free speech, association, and assembly—were explicitly and aggressively circumscribed by the laws, statutes, and regulations put in place as the revolution institutionalized its control. By contrast, like much of the

Communist world or the global South, Cuba defended a "social" or "collective" conception of human rights—rights to health, education, home, etc. Outside observers were, however, right to doubt why a commitment to social rights precluded respect for individual liberties like free press and free speech. The Cuban state's consistent if not wholly persuasive answer was that while under threat from an implacable enemy, such freedoms (or open internal divisions) risked leaving the country vulnerable to destabilization. As we have already discussed, during this period, numerous intellectuals and artists landed in exile as space closed for public expression that could be construed as counterrevolutionary. Yet others managed to establish, retain, and even expand room for expression, often challenging the orthodoxy of the revolution and becoming adept at cautiously seizing periodic openings of cultural space.

Beginning primarily in the 1980s, some individual dissidents organized and garnered public attention outside of Cuba for their criticisms of Cuba's human rights record. Under Cuban law, any nascent dissident groups were technically illegal unless they applied for and received official permission to carry out their activities. Moreover, the Cuban regime was acutely conscious of efforts by the West (especially the United States) to promote dissident activities against it. Cuba's state intelligence apparatus thus adopted a number of measures to neutralize or discredit these individuals and small groups. First, it generally denied them legal status. Second, it spied on them aggressively. Third, its counterintelligence agents infiltrated their ranks, and at times started their own dissident front organizations. Arrest, jail, public repudiation, and eventually exile awaited virtually anyone in this period who attempted to publicly denounce the regime's human rights transgressions. And because these groups at times garnered significant attention from western governments and media, the government ran publicity campaigns at home and abroad to discredit their claims.

Up until 1991, consistent with its efforts to support dissidents and civil society actors in the eastern bloc countries, as a matter of policy the United States covertly directed financing and other forms of support to bolster some of the early antiregime dissidents. These policies, of course, provided the Castro government with ample ammunition to target its domestic critics as lackeys of imperialism, thus distracting attention from the substance of the dissidents' allegations. By assuming that it could recreate the conditions for revolt that had ultimately contributed to the collapse of communism in Europe—human rights campaigns, independent labor movements, a politically mobilized Catholic Church, economic sanctions, and international isolation—the United States and other countries in the West consistently misread the nature of the Cuban regime's domestic support. Whereas the Socialist bloc populations bristled under a system imposed upon them by the Soviet empire, Cuba's revolution was entirely homegrown. Surely the regime's repressive apparatus, Fidel Castro's personal charisma, and the government's absolute control over politics and public space helped to forcibly hold Cuban society together. Yet it was also true that the Cuban Revolution retained a strong base of domestic legitimacy, based not only on nationalistic pride for Cuba's defiance of the United States, the historic challenger to Cuban independence, but also on marked improvements in the material lives of the majority of Cuba's people. By misreading that cultural context, efforts to promote regime dissidents as the champions of human rights and democracy in Cuba were at best going to deliver some public attention to the revolution's dark side, without ever standing a chance at bringing it down.

Why did King Sugar continue to dominate Cuba's economy after the revolution?

For most of the 20th century, Cuba sold almost all of its sugar exports to the United States under a quota system regulated by the U.S. Congress. The quota guaranteed a major market for Cuban sugar, and prompted significant investment by

American capital into Cuba's sugar industry. It also created dependence on one crop, and relegated a huge part of the labor force to reliance on seasonal work during harvest and planting, but unemployment in the intervening months.

As potent symbols of power and oppression, whether at the hands of the Spanish, the Americans, or local elites, sugar plantations and refineries served as historic focal points for Cuban insurgents of many generations, starting with the 19th-century wars of independence. Thus, after the revolution triumphed, international development economists, Che Guevara, and many other Cubans hoped to rid themselves of the island's sugar monoculture by pursuing rapid industrialization. When the Eisenhower administration moved in Congress to eliminate Cuba's share of America's global sugar imports, prospects for freeing the island from sugar not only grew but also became a potential strategic necessity. No country, however, could possibly wean itself off such a cash cow without sufficient time to develop and build up an alternate focus of economic activity.

As Cuba broke relations with the United States and Washington moved to impose economic sanctions, the Soviet Union stepped in to provide much-needed economic support and trade opportunities. Cubans bitterly watched as continued dependence on sugar became a necessary component of their incorporation into the Soviet orbit. As early as 1960, the Soviet Union had begun purchasing important quantities of Cuba's sugar crop. Seeking to convert the revolution's reliance on sugar into a badge of honor, in 1968 Fidel Castro mobilized virtually the entire Cuban labor force, vast stores of limited machinery, and what managerial expertise remained on the island to attempt a whopping 10-million-ton sugar harvest. The effort failed. Although the country did produce a record yield—over 8 million tons—Castro's costly miscalculation exposed and dramatized what critics among the island's old-school Communists, those in the Soviet Union, and antagonists at home and abroad regarded as his reckless and indeed megalomaniacal belief in the capacity of volunteerism and sheer collective will to perform miracles. More shopworn state bureaucrats regarded such ambitions as delusional fantasies about human nature. Fidel offered to resign in the wake of the humiliation. But instead, the disaster of the 1968 *zafra* (or harvest) prompted a major reorientation of the Cuban economy, with central planning and Soviet-style five-year plans the new coin of the realm. Throughout the 1970s, Cuba fully integrated into the Council for Mutual Economic Assistance (COMECON), an economic organization that linked all members of the Soviet bloc. Sugar production continued, with a guaranteed market now to the east rather than the north. Only after the Berlin Wall fell and the price of sugar dropped to under 6 cents per pound did Cuba begin to dismantle its singular sugar infrastructure.

What were the main economic features of Cuba's integration with the Soviet bloc?

Cuba and the Soviet Union restored diplomatic relations in 1943, and the Communist Party thrived on the island until being suppressed in 1947. Further and fuller repression would follow under Batista's rule. Yet before 1959, trade between the two countries was practically nonexistent. Cuba became a full-fledged member of COMECON only in 1972, but the island began to benefit from Soviet largesse beginning in 1960 when, as discussed on page 68 ("Why did King Sugar continue to dominate Cuba's economy after the revolution?"), Moscow began purchasing part of Cuba's sugar crop. Indeed, between 1965 and 1970, the Soviet Union agreed to purchase over 24 million tons of Cuban sugar. As the decade progressed, the Soviet Union began providing Cuba with discounted oil (which Cuba was then allowed to resell on the world market for profit) as well as supplying the island with a wide variety of mechanical parts that could no longer be obtained once the U.S. embargo had gone into effect in 1960. Cash inflows, food, weapons, and manufacturing equipment gradually started to arrive as well.

Once the 10-million-ton *zafra* exposed the Cuban government's economic and managerial incompetence, Castro
and the revolution's leadership, with help from leading and
long-time Communist Party members such as Carlos Rafael
Rodríguez, took a deep breath and jumped into the deep end
of the Soviet bloc pool. Over the course of the 1970s, central
planning and five-year plans replaced the management-by-
personality approach of the previous decade. Soviet financing
fueled hundreds of industrial initiatives, such as the repair/
modernization of sugar mills. Military assistance in the form of
advisers, training, and weapons flowed liberally as well. Moreover, thanks to Soviet largesse, thousands of Cubans received a
higher education and/or technical training in the eastern bloc.
By the mid-1970s, it was estimated that Soviet-funded projects accounted for 10% of Cuba's total GNP, and by the end of
the 1980s, the annual Soviet subsidy had reached between $4
billion and $6 billion according to most estimates.

What was "rectification"? How did Fidel and Raul Castro view the prospect of market reforms in the 1980s?

Soviet-style planning gave Cuba a modicum of stability, and
Soviet aid ensured a modest but reliable standard of living.
Nevertheless, the fact that productivity had become disasso-
ciated from Socialist values grated on the sensibilities of the
Castro brothers. For Fidel, whose legendary antipathy for the
market inspired his belief that the Cuban "new man" (or *hombre
nuevo*) should toil for the common good, Cuba and Cubans had
settled into complacency at home. For Raul, whose more pragmatic side cringed at the inefficiency and waste of the island's
burgeoning bureaucracy, stagnation risked diminishing the
revolution's staying power. On April 17, 1986, Fidel gave
a blistering speech in which he denounced the lethargy of
Cuban workers, the pettiness of Cuban bureaucrats, the
beginnings of a real corruption problem, and the notion
that material incentives could somehow, as under the Soviet

playbook, suffice to sustain the revolutionaries' zeal. Cuba, he said, was not like the other Soviet bloc countries, and the Cuban people were capable of more. A process of "rectification" would ensue, aimed at recovering the zeal of the 1960s while pushing the party, government bureaucracies, and Cubans on the street to work harder, better, and more efficiently.

At the same time, however, Raul Castro, who had built Cuba's Revolutionary Armed Forces into a well-run, disciplined, and highly trained institution, began, undoubtedly with the tacit agreement of his brother, to sniff around capitalist economies to see how some of their fundamentals could be adapted to the Cuban context. As Cuban troops returned from southern Africa beginning in 1988, the Cuban military started to put its toe into the economy. Raul Castro and others, including Fidel protégé Carlos Lage, sent several hundred military officials to business schools and management training programs abroad—mostly in Europe and Canada. Soon, the revolutionary leadership introduced a *systema de perfeccionamiento empresarial,* or "system of enterprise perfection." This rhetorical mouthful was code for an experimental program that, over the next several years, would bring capitalist business practices to about 3,000 state enterprises, many run by the military. Indeed, with the military on the verge of undergoing a major downsizing in its budget, troop levels, equipment, and role abroad, increased involvement in the economy would help the institution become self-financing over the next 10 years. During the same period, Cuban officials returning from visits to Russia were starting to utter the words *glasnost* and *perestroika* as reforms unfolded in Moscow. Some did so welcoming the prospect of change. Others feared it. But Fidel smelled the pending Soviet collapse and regardless of the ideological purity that drove his rectification campaign, he also perceived, as did Raul, that Cuba should not permanently keep its eggs in the Soviet basket. However strong the scent of imminent dissolution, neither of the brothers had planned for what was to be the most severe external economic and existential shock the island would face since the 1959 triumph and, shortly after, the 1962 Cuban Missile Crisis.

Who was General Arnaldo Ochoa and why was he executed?

General Arnaldo Ochoa was among the most highly decorated and widely revered officers of Cuba's Revolutionary Armed Forces. After first fighting against Batista in Cuba's own insurgency, throughout the 1960s, '70s, and '80s, he took part in Cuban internationalist missions across Latin America and Africa, including in the Congo, Ethiopia, and two tours of duty in Angola. In June of 1989, Ochoa was slotted to take command of Cuba's Western Army when he was arrested. He was executed the following month. Several other high-ranking officers in the Ministry of Interior (including the minister himself) as well as the minister of transportation were also arrested during the same period, with three sentenced to death.

The basic charge was corruption, but not your everyday black-marketeering or low-level theft. Instead, Ochoa and others were accused of engaging in a level of misconduct that, in the view of the Castro brothers, the Council of State, and the military tribunal responsible for the trial, threatened to inflict irreparable damage to Cuban national security. The basic outlines of the story are as follows. Two Ministry of Interior officials, twin brothers Patricio and Tony de la Guardia, had been granted considerable latitude to set up dummy corporations in order to thwart American economic sanctions. Each, in collaboration with Ochoa, abused the terms of their mandate. Ochoa, while in Angola, had become involved in ivory and diamond smuggling along with Patricio de la Guardia, also stationed in Luanda. Funds earned from this illicit trade were then funneled through Tony de la Guardia's office at the Ministry of Interior. Tony de la Guardia had also begun to use his Ministry of Interior cover to start cutting deals with the Colombian drug cartels. Ochoa and one member of his staff abetted these transactions.

According to close U.S. government observers as well as the Drug Enforcement Administration, Fidel and Raul Castro were entirely unaware of the drug trafficking. Indeed, for Cuba's senior leadership, such a scandal jeopardized the revolution's reputation, exposed its senior officials to blackmail, and risked confirming an association between the Cuban government and drug smuggling that some in the United States had long attempted to establish. Speculation soared that Ochoa's arrest and execution were a smoke screen to quash a charismatic officer's attempts to build an independent power base within the Armed Forces and possibly beyond. Yet by all accounts, the trial, which was broadcast live and transcribed into published proceedings, established a detailed history of the illegal activities countenanced by Ochoa and the others. Of course, those convinced that the whole episode was nothing more than a political show trial would never be satisfied with such explanations. Abroad and in Cuba, most came to regard the affair as an instance of the regime, for the first time since the early 1960s, recognizing and taking severe, unpopular steps to eliminate an internal threat tied to the external arena. In its aftermath, the Ministry of Interior was restructured and placed entirely under the command of Raul Castro, then the minister of the Revolutionary Armed Forces.

U.S.-CUBA

Was there ever a chance that the United States would react well to the Cuban revolutionaries?

The short answer is no. Protagonists of the Cuban Revolution, as well as those who contended with its consequences within the U.S. government, thoroughly embodied the histories of their countries and the international environment in which those histories unfolded. To have risen above the national, bilateral, or geopolitical moment in which the Cuban Revolution emerged would have required dozens, maybe hundreds of individuals to have made thousands of decisions in defiance of type, circumstance, and sheer political instincts.

Even before Batista fled and Fidel arrived in Havana—as early as 1957, in fact—the Eisenhower administration, especially the State Department, had come to the conclusion that most of the revolutionaries who had not already fled to exile were far from the country-club set of Cuba's political elite on whom Washington and the U.S. embassy in Havana had come to depend. Nonetheless, many U.S. authorities downplayed or dismissed their beards and berets, their fiery rhetoric, and, most dramatically, their willingness to challenge established authority and economic power with violence. Instead, most American officials watching Cuba from afar chose to believe in the continued relevance of more traditional Cuban political actors as well as the abiding ability and right of the United States to manage Cuba's domestic politics for its own ends.

During much of the insurrection, exiles from the Ortodoxo and Auténtico parties, and later from the 26th of July Movement itself, lobbied the State Department and Congress to cut off Batista. An arms embargo was finally imposed in March of 1958. But cutting off Batista and taking a position of nonintervention—which everyone but Batista himself still saw as tacit support for his regime—was a far cry from embracing the revolution. Sure, there were some in the CIA who were rooting for Fidel and the Sierra Maestra rebels, and the American consul in Santiago was particularly sympathetic, even helpful. In light of the gruesome symbolism Guantánamo has acquired in the 21st century, it seems a quaint note of history that in the 1950s Americans and Cubans working on the base provided a network of money, arms, and intelligence to Cuban revolutionaries. A handful of Americans joined the rebels; larger numbers contributed financially to their efforts. And the media, especially Herbert Matthews of the *New York Times*, clearly had a sympathetic view of the revolution at its birth. Yet on a much more fundamental level, the revolution's quest for independence and its strong grain of nationalism cut directly into the

United States' traditional patronage of Cuba's economy and domestic politics. Indeed, given the degree of influence that the United States exerted over Cuba's domestic politics and culture, once Fidel triumphed, a clash with Washington on some level was perhaps a foregone conclusion. In the last days of 1958, the Eisenhower administration explored a handful of "third force" options—civil-military juntas, reformist officers from the military, etc.—but Washington was too late. By then, Cubans had become too energized by the dazzling heroism of the revolutionaries to accept any half-baked measures hatched out of the U.S. embassy or its military mission on the island. Once the rebels were in power, the United States woke up to the revolution's profound implications. As Cuba radicalized, Washington became both an object and an instigator of that radicalization.

How much weight did U.S. economic interests have in driving the two countries apart?

At the start of 1959, American investment in Cuba totaled over $1 billion, much of it concentrated in the sugar and nickel industries. North American firms (subsidiaries of U.S. companies) employed nearly 150,000 Cuban citizens across virtually all sectors of the economy. Prior to 1959, 59% of Cuba's exports went to the United States and 76% of its total imports came from the U.S. market. More to the point, Cuba exported over 50% of its annual sugar harvest to the United States, supplying roughly one third of total U.S. sugar imports. To say that Cuba's economic fate was strongly tied to its northern neighbor is an understatement; the two countries were conjoined at the hip. For a government with nationalist pretensions, Cuba's economic dependence on the United States was an obvious and natural target of early reforms.

Between 1959 and 1961, relations between the United States and Cuba progressed from mutual suspicion to clear and reckless rupture. Economic grievances and successive waves of nationalizations played a key role in this deterioration. The cycle began when the Castro government provocatively asked U.S.-owned oil refineries to process Soviet crude in June 1960. United States officials were incredulous. Although the companies themselves were willing to accommodate the request, the State Department put its foot down. As a result, the Cuban government nationalized the operations of Esso (Standard Oil), Texaco, and Shell (the latter a U.S. subsidiary of the larger multinational conglomerate). In retaliation, the United States enacted its previously conceived plan to cancel Cuba's sugar quota. Other nationalizations and expropriations followed until the month of November, with the United States ratcheting up its own retaliatory measures as well, culminating in a partial trade embargo by October 1960.

When all was said and done, Cuba had expropriated over 300,000 acres of U.S. property, all U.S.-owned tobacco enterprises, all U.S. banks, and all other U.S. business interests. Cuba offered compensation pegged to the often undervalued claims the companies had filed in their most recent tax returns. Some companies accepted, others did not, but most received insurance payments to cover their losses. Meanwhile, in addition to building its own progressive program of sanctions against the Cuban regime, the United States set up a claims commission designed to eventually compensate American corporate claimants.

In short, nationalizations, agrarian reform, expropriations of private property, Soviet trade delegations, weapons deliveries from the eastern bloc, and Castro's vituperative and crowd-pleasing rhetoric all deeply alarmed national security managers in Cold War–era Washington. In another place and time, the United States may have been able to accommodate Cuba's new reality while still opposing some of its policies. In fact, several of Cuba's revolutionary changes—particularly the agrarian reform—might later have been seen as modest and ultimately manageable measures. But at the height of the Cold War, a hardened and visceral anti-communism—supported by the clear antipathy of Eisenhower and later Kennedy toward Cuba's leaders—reigned supreme.

What really happened when Castro visited Washington in 1959?

In April 1959, barely four months from his victory march across the island, Prime Minister Fidel Castro traveled to Washington, D.C. Diplomatic relations had grown tense, but had not yet reached a point of rupture. Castro was accompanied by a plane-load of ministers, bankers, and economists, most of whom had planned to meet with officials at the IMF, the World Bank, and other institutions in search of loans and assistance to support their plans for modernizing Cuba's economy. But by the time Fidel and his delegation had arrived in Washington, perhaps pushed by Che and Raul, as some historians have suggested (or perhaps because their recommendations confirmed Fidel's own instincts), Castro instructed his delegation to politely listen but neither ask for nor accept a dime from Washington or the multilateral institutions it controlled. This decision may well explain Fidel's frame of mind when he arrived for a meeting with Vice President Nixon, after being snubbed by President Eisenhower.

Nixon's meeting with Fidel has become legendary. In subsequent years, both Cuba and the United States looked back on the encounter as a barometer of a souring and soon-to-be-broken relationship. Nixon spent three hours with Fidel. Publicly taking a hard line toward Castro, he privately, in a now public memorandum of conversation, concluded that the Cuban leader, while having the potential to rise to leadership throughout Latin America, was either enormously naïve or under the control of Communists but nevertheless someone the United States should undertake to shape and control. Fidel, in full beard and fatigues, dutifully explained the revolution's project to Nixon at length, but it was a dialogue of the deaf. Days before the meeting, the National Security Council had already begun drawing up plans to prevent the revolution's consolidation. Within a matter of months, Eisenhower would instruct the CIA and the State Department to move much more aggressively against Castro. By March of 1960, shortly after the first Soviet delegation led by Deputy Prime Minister Anastas Mikoyan arrived in Havana, plans to cut off Cuba's sugar quota were already under way. At the same time, Eisenhower authorized planning for the Bay of Pigs invasion, and CIA deputy director Richard Bissell by August 1960 decided to use the U.S. mafia to try and assassinate Castro as part of the invasion plan, while also drawing up a spate of covert operations, including plans for industrial sabotage and political destabilization against the island. In presidential debates that year Congressman Jack Kennedy would harangue Vice President Nixon for being too soft on Castro. By the time JFK was elected president in November 1960, the CIA was already quite far along in training an exile force to invade the island and install a new, more compliant pro-American government.

Why did the Bay of Pigs invasion fail?

In January 1961, the United States severed diplomatic relations with Cuba. Before leaving the Oval Office, President Eisenhower and his CIA chief Allen Dulles briefed incoming president John F. Kennedy on their plans to deploy an invasion force of Cuban exiles to overthrow Castro.

The plan had been drawn up under Dulles's watch by Richard Bissell, a career CIA officer credited with crafting the covert operation that successfully overthrew Guatemalan president Jacobo Arbenz in 1954. Soon after coming to power in 1951, the left-leaning Arbenz enacted a bold agrarian reform, attempted to tax the wealthy, legalized the local Communist Party, imported weapons from the eastern bloc, and even challenged the U.S.-owned United Fruit Company's legendary dominance of Guatemala's agricultural industry. (At the time, a young Argentine, Ernesto Guevara, was living these events firsthand while married to a member of the Guatemalan

Communist Party, the PGT.) Such policies earned Arbenz the ire of Washington. Yet even the staunchest proponents of intervention in Guatemala were surprised by the relative ease with which a democratically elected, reform-minded Latin American government was toppled. Faced with a coordinated campaign of psy-ops, antigovernment propaganda, and threats of economic retaliation, the Arbenz government quickly fell apart when a group of well-trained, well-armed, and externally supported opponents challenged its authority. To add insult to injury, the United States had also successfully foiled the Arbenz government's attempts to import military supplies from the eastern bloc to arm its own defense.

Arbenz, who like a generation of Latin American left-leaning leaders wanted to bring a measure of modernity to his country's institutions and dignity to its population, may well have wanted Guatemala to remain genuinely neutral in the East-West conflict. Yet for Washington in 1954, especially in America's historic sphere, neutrality was as good as full-blown communism. By comparison to Arbenz, Fidel Castro not only moved much more aggressively against his own country's political and economic elite but also more boldly challenged U.S. property interests and Washington's presumptive hegemony over Cuban affairs. By March 1960, Eisenhower had signed a comprehensive CIA plan to overthrow Castro: By early 1961 on the eve of the invasion, Cuba could hardly have been regarded as neutral in the East-West conflict.

Events in Guatemala left the Eisenhower- and Kennedy-era CIA with several mistaken assumptions about Cuba. Most important, they believed that domestic political support for Fidel Castro could be as easily manipulated—and weakened—as it had been in Arbenz's Guatemala. Though there were some analysts and covert ops agents in the CIA who understood the difference between the two countries, at the center and top of Washington's national security circles, one little Latin American country was really no different than the other. Bay of Pigs planners assumed that what popular support Fidel did command would collapse once the Cuban public was presented with the *fait accompli* of a U.S.-backed provisional government sent to establish order. Thus, in addition to training its Cuban exile intervention force, known as Brigade 2506, in the months leading up to the April 1961 invasion, the CIA endeavored to stoke a climate of chaos and uncertainty on the island using antiregime propaganda and sabotage. The operation began on April 15 with strategic bombings of Cuba's air force to eliminate Castro's ability to strike the invasion force from the air. These were followed two days later by an amphibious landing, and the Kennedy White House and Cuban exile leaders—many of whom had fought against Batista and joined Fidel's first cabinet—erroneously believed the end of the Cuban Revolution was imminent.

If the first mistake—underestimating Castro's domestic political support—was strategic, the second was related, but tactical in nature. Almost nothing about the U.S. role in the operation was covert, and little about the invasion a surprise. Fidel had begun to deploy intelligence networks in Cuba to keep an eye on potential adversaries as soon as he took power. Within the exile community as well, the Cuban government certainly had its intelligence assets. Penetrating these circles turned out to be not so difficult, and became a skill that Cuba would hone over succeeding decades. Press reports of a growing, "covert" invasion group being trained in Central America (Guatemala and Panama to be precise) had been circulating for months. Indeed, long before the invasion began, the buzz in Miami, Washington, New York, and Central America had grown deafening, giving Castro time to put the country on alert, mobilize his army and air force, arrest suspected subversives, and quickly defeat the exile invasion force once it arrived. Castro's victory was helped by the fact that the Bay of Pigs, 202 km to the southeast of Havana, was a most inhospitable and overexposed place to stage an amphibious landing; Brigade 2506 members had to make their way through a virtually impenetrable mangrove swamp onto beaches covered with sharp coral shards, several hundred yards from the protective cover of trees. Moreover, at the last minute, Kennedy canceled a second preliminary air strike once the press caught wind of the pending invasion and a round of air cover to accompany the second day of the invasion was botched. Yet even if the invasion plans hadn't been so mismatched to actual conditions in Cuba, and even if the exile force had benefited from sustained air cover, it is doubtful they would have triumphed. Because the Cuban Revolution maintained broad support on the island, the fundamental conditions that allowed Fidel Castro to prevail over the invading exile force were far more a product of Cuba's revolutionary national identity at the time than the blunders of the invasion itself.

In the end, the few U.S. voices of skepticism about the invasion plan were right on the mark. When privately asked by President Kennedy what he thought about the plan, former secretary of state Dean Acheson (then in his 70s) responded, "Are you serious? It doesn't take Price-Waterhouse to figure out that 1500 Cubans are no match for 25,000 [the number of soldiers Cuba's army was thought capable of rapidly mobilizing from an army of 200,000 in immediate response to the invasion]."

Of the 1,511 total number of exiles who landed in Cuba on April 17, 1961, just over 100 were killed by Cuban forces; 1,214 were held prisoner until their release in time for Christmas in 1962. Their freedom was secured after tough negotiations in which Kennedy envoy James Donovan pledged to send $53 million in U.S. foodstuffs and medicines to Cuba.

After the invasion fiasco, did the United States continue covert operations against Cuba and how did the United States involve Cuban exiles?

Covert operations against Cuba continued in one form or another over the succeeding two decades. The 1975 Church Committee interim report, for example, presented evidence that the CIA was specifically involved in at least eight attempts to assassinate Fidel Castro between 1960 and 1965. Cuban government sources, meanwhile, put the total for assassination attempts by individuals and entities receiving support from the U.S. government in the hundreds. In the lead-up to the Bay of Pigs, both the CIA and the U.S. military had cultivated a number of Cuban exile paramilitary and covert operatives. These ties did not simply end with the failure of the invasion, however; they continued for a generation. In the 1960s, Operation Mongoose, a sabotage and destabilization campaign carried out on the island with the blessing of Robert Kennedy after his brother's assassination, involved Cuban exiles as a key resource. The political relevance of Cuban exiles as a potential alternative government to Fidel, however, receded the longer he remained in power.

As time passed, exiles did not forswear their opposition to the Castro regime, but most slowly gave up hope of returning to Cuba, choosing instead to restart their lives as productive and peaceful American citizens. For the U.S. government and the popular media, their stories served as a continual foil for the merits of the Cold War struggle against communism and reinforced America's own immigrant mythology. A small sector of the exile community, however, continued to promote violent action against the regime and received substantial support, not only from the U.S. intelligence establishment but also both tacitly and sometimes more overtly within their own community. There is some debate over exactly how organically tied to the CIA and other U.S. government agencies these small armed exile groups remained in the 1970s. In 1976, a handful of disparate groups formed an umbrella organization, Coordination of United Revolutionary Organizations (CORU). Among its leaders were two already notorious anti-Castro operatives with ties to the CIA, Luis Posada Carriles and Orlando Bosch. Both men were enlisted to carry out acts of sabotage against the Cuban government, and both became known in U.S. and Cuban intelligence circles as the intellectual authors of a terrorist plot (not explicitly a CIA operation, although evidence shows the agency was aware of its likelihood) that successfully blew up Cubana Airlines Flight 455 heading from Cuba to Barbados in 1976, killing all 73 on board, including the entire membership of the Cuban National Fencing Team. Individuals and groups associated with Posada, Bosch, and CORU kept up their violent conspiracies against the Cuban regime well into the 1990s, including several foiled plots to assassinate Fidel Castro. Yet they also internationalized the scope of their activities. During the 1970s, some collaborated with Latin American dictators and with the United States to support Operation Condor, a covert campaign waged by several Southern Cone military regimes to suppress left-wing, pro-democratic, and/or human rights activists, primarily through assassination, torture, and kidnapping. Others helped supply and possibly train the Contras in Central America during the 1980s. However, although men like Posada continued to operate in an anti-Communist underworld, over time the U.S. government shifted away from the armed exile groups as a viable tool of policy, as the political arena of special interest politics increasingly became the focus of Cuban American anti-Castro activism in the 1980s.

What was the Cuban Missile Crisis?

On October 22, 1962, John F. Kennedy appeared on national television to announce that the Soviet Union had placed nuclear missiles in Cuba. Kennedy's dramatic revelations, based on CIA reconnaissance photos of the missile sites, which Ambassador Adlai Stevenson later presented to the United Nations, came in the midst of the most dangerous "13 days" in the history of the world. Kennedy announced a naval blockade of the island and warned against the consequences of a "worldwide nuclear war in which even the fruits of victory would be ashes in our mouths."

After the Bay of Pigs, Castro had become entirely convinced that the United States would stop at nothing to destroy the revolution. Khrushchev, for his part, wanted to test Kennedy's mettle and provide a psychological and strategic balance for the deployment of U.S. missiles aimed at Russia from American bases in Turkey and Italy. To create time for a deal to be struck for the removal of missiles and to avoid nuclear war, the United States set up a naval blockade around the island to prevent further deliveries of Soviet material. Although Cuban authorities digested the move as an act of war by American imperialism, much more was at stake than the fate of a tiny island. Between October 22 and October 28, the White House and the Kremlin played their strategic cards. Militaries in both countries agitated for strong action, ranging from quarantine to air strikes on the American side to the authorization of Soviet forces on the ground. For his part, Fidel, believing that a massive attack on Cuba was imminent, wrote to Khrushchev that such an event would be a prelude to a direct American strike against the Soviets, one which the Soviets might preempt by firing their missiles first. Tensions reached their highest when the Soviets shot down a U-2 spy plane over Cuba on October 26, the most dangerous day of the crisis.

Ultimately, by the end of October, the Soviets and Americans cut a deal with one another through back channels, leaving Havana sidelined. Without informing Cuba of their plan, the Soviets agreed to withdraw their missiles in exchange for a U.S. promise to remove its missiles facing the Soviets at a U.S. base in Turkey (though part of this deal was the understanding that the Turkey removal would follow several months later and never be discussed as a concession made by the United States). Another key component of the understanding was Khrushchev's demand with respect to U.S. actions toward Cuba. In a formal letter to Kennedy, the Soviet premier had demanded that the United States sign a formal accord at the United Nations, to "respect the inviolability of Cuban borders, [respect] its sovereignty," and not "interfere in [Cuba's] internal affairs." Moreover, the letter demanded that the United States not "permit [its] territory to be used as a bridgehead for the invasion of Cuba, and restrain those who would plan to carry [out] an aggression against Cuba, either from U.S. territory or from the territory of other countries neighboring to Cuba." In his response, Kennedy did acknowledge and seem to accept the basic principle that the United States would not invade Cuba. Nonetheless, just as the Soviets probably never intended on fully complying with their commitment to on-site inspection, so too did the United States interpret its pledges as nonbinding. Indeed, no international agreement was ever signed at the United Nations or elsewhere, and nowhere did Kennedy explicitly or formally renounce any and all efforts to undermine the Castro government. Moreover, the United States and the Soviets simply ignored the Castro government's own "Five Points" demands for preventing such crises in the future: an end to economic sanctions, an end to covert activities, an end to all air attacks, an end to all flights over Cuban airspace, and the return of the Guantánamo naval base.

For the world, the end of the crisis brought enormous relief. For Kennedy, it was a moment of tremendous political and geopolitical strength. Indeed, Kennedy's success at forcing the Soviets to withdraw the missiles went down in history as a major piece of the Camelot lore, reinforcing an image of heroic masculinity and strategic brilliance. The Soviets, too, could claim victory with the eventual American withdrawal of missiles from Turkey. But Fidel Castro was devastated to find himself but a tool in the Cold War, left without a voice in the conflict's resolution. To Fidel, the episode was a replay of the 1898 Treaty of Paris, when Cuba's independence fighters were not permitted to participate in the final negotiations that set the conditions for Spanish withdrawal and the beginning of American primacy in Cuba. Moreover, just as Cuba's formal independence ushered in decades of humiliation at the hands of U.S. economic and political forces, Fidel didn't trust that a vague commitment from the United States to respect Cuba's sovereignty would give his country any protection. In his view, one empire had traded Cuba's security for a bigger set of rewards from another empire. Continued covert operations well beyond 1962 suggest that Castro had a point. Initiatives like Operation Mongoose, which began before the Cuban Missile Crisis and may well have goaded Cuba into accepting the missiles, and covert operations afterward offered ample evidence that the Americans remained intent on destabilizing the revolution. Yet as a matter of state policy, the United States did sit on its hands and watch as the Soviets gradually expanded their presence on the island with investments, advisors, military bases, and listening posts over the next two decades.

How did U.S. attempts to overthrow Castro play inside of Cuba?

The increasing clarity with which the United States was seeking to unseat the Castro regime provided the context for, if not directly motivated, a number of domestic measures within Cuba that further radicalized the revolution and increased the Cuban government's authority over its citizens. Weeks before the Bay of Pigs invasion took place, for example, Castro armed a new national militia and also created the Committees for the Defense of the Revolution (CDRs), neighborhood watch groups organized block by block in order to sniff out counterrevolutionaries who might be collaborating as a rear guard with an invading force and their imperial backers. The invasion itself only prompted a further radicalization of the revolution's rhetoric, driving Cuba's leaders closer to the Soviet sphere. A day before the Cuban exile–led Brigade 2506 landed on Cuban shores, Castro officially declared that the Cuban Revolution was Socialist in nature. Later that year, Fidel went a step further, declaring that he himself was a Marxist-Leninist.

Within Cuban society, U.S. plots had differing but complementary effects. Despite the exodus of a sizable Cuban exile population, Fidel and the revolution were enormously popular in the early 1960s. The Bay of Pigs invasion, as well as subsequent covert operations to undermine Castro's rule, did far more to bolster the revolution's popular status than to sew domestic discord and doubt about its viability. Moreover, the nationalist backlash that such plots incited perhaps inclined the Cuban population to more willingly accept the logic for such intrusive mechanisms as the CDRs. Although it cost money and lives for Cuba to resist American schemes, the rampant and relentless hostility of the United States strengthened support for Fidel and allowed him to justify domestic repression and growing ties with the Soviet Union as requirements for national survival against an implacable enemy.

What was the scope of U.S. economic sanctions?

As described on page 76 ("How much weight did U.S. economic interests have in driving the two countries apart?"), by October 1960, following successive nationalizations of U.S. property and business within Cuba, the United States had implemented a partial trade embargo. This policy remained in place until the fall of 1961, when the U.S. Congress passed the Foreign Assistance Act, prohibiting U.S. aid to Cuba and authorizing the president to create a "total embargo" on all trade with the island. By February 1962, the United States had indeed imposed a complete economic embargo with the single exception of licensed sales of food and medicine (an exception that lasted until the mid-1960s).

Once the full embargo went into force, American companies were banned from investing on the island, purchasing Cuban goods, or even importing goods from other countries that contained Cuban material. Cuba likewise could no longer buy American products nor could Cuban citizens invest in the United States. Cuba's and Cuban citizens' holdings in U.S. banks were frozen. In early 1963, Americans were also prohibited from traveling to the island directly from the United States or engaging in any commercial or financial transactions with Cuba. Meanwhile, only Cubans wishing to seek political refugee status could enter the United States legally. This changed, however, with the passage of the 1966 Cuban Adjustment Act, a landmark law that granted all Cuban migrants the right to "adjust" their status to that of U.S. permanent resident after residing one year within the United States.

The effect in Cuba of the embargo was felt almost immediately. After all, for the first 60 years of the 20th century Cuba's economy had been almost completely integrated with that of the United States. In addition to selling most of its major export crop (sugar) at a subsidized price to the American market, Cuba's agricultural, manufacturing, telecommunications, public health, water, energy, and transportation infrastructure was constructed almost exclusively with American-made parts. Although Cuba could theoretically replace parts and buy products outside of the United States, the embargo banned Cuba from purchasing products that contained more than 5% of U.S. content. Thus, as American companies merged and consolidated with companies around the globe over time, it became harder and harder to find parts for Cuba's pre-1959 infrastructure that were free of U.S. content. Soviet replacement parts practically never served as adequate substitutes, leading to the inevitable degrading of Cuba's infrastructure.

Throughout the 1960s, the combination of haphazard, often chaotic, and centrally planned economic policies instituted by the Cuban government could never compensate for the financial, economic, and infrastructure cost of U.S. sanctions. To get around the embargo, not only would Cuba place its economic fate in the hands of the Soviet Union by the 1970s, but it would also develop extensive networks to circumvent American sanctions through dummy import-export companies in third countries, especially in Latin America.

How successful was the United States in isolating Cuba in the 1960s and into the 1970s?

In addition to severing its own bilateral relations with Havana, the United States endeavored to gather multilateral support in its early efforts to isolate and undermine the Cuban regime. The principal diplomatic swipe took place at the Organization of American States. Venezuela and Colombia joined the United States in an initial effort to, in effect, suspend Cuba's membership at the OAS in 1961, breaking diplomatic ties with the island that year and calling for a follow-up meeting the following January (1962). At that session, two thirds of member states voted to exclude Cuba from the organization. Though many Latin American governments had strongly opposed the Bay of Pigs invasion and other U.S. attempts to unseat Castro, they were amenable to this U.S.-led initiative due to their own anger at Cuba for fomenting domestic unrest in other countries of the region. Moreover, in those days the United States called the shots at the OAS. The punitive resolution also declared that Marxist-Leninism was incompatible with the inter-American system. Fourteen of the twenty-one member countries supported the resolution, with six abstaining (Argentina, Bolivia, Brazil, Chile, Ecuador, and Mexico) and one (Cuba, naturally) opposing. Pressure from the United States did not stop there. In 1964, the American delegation to the OAS would compel a vote on a resolution requiring all member states to break diplomatic and trade relations with Cuba. Only Mexico refused.

With the dawn of the 1970s, however, Cuba began making significant inroads in its attempts to break the hemisphere's U.S.-led policies of isolation. Independently, Latin American countries such as Chile (under the Socialist government of Salvador Allende), Argentina, and Peru reestablished some form of diplomatic and/or commercial relations with the island. Canada, meanwhile, helped to mount opposition to embargo restrictions on U.S. subsidiaries in third countries. Likewise, the U.S. Congress and business communities began to express an increasing disposition toward improving the bilateral relationship with Havana. Eager to maintain executive privilege over foreign policy, in March 1975 Kissinger signaled that the United States would stand back were the OAS to lift its collective diplomatic and commercial embargo of the island. Privately, he also expressed his willingness to lift restrictions on the trade of U.S. subsidiaries with Cuba. These moves took place as secret negotiations between U.S. and Cuban representatives (see page 92, "What's the story behind the Kissinger/ Ford secret diplomacy with Cuba in 1974?") were unfolding, but still inconclusive.

Traditionally, Kissinger's more flexible approach to Cuba is described as part of a global pursuit of détente, certainly en vogue at the time. Overlooked is the regional component. Thus, while possibly trying to give a boost to bilateral dialogues (soon to be constrained by the imminent discovery of Cuban involvement in Angola), Kissinger was perhaps equally as interested in the practical geopolitical benefits of policy liberalization within the Western Hemisphere, where countries were already individually breaking the terms of collective sanctions anyway, seeming to openly flout U.S. prerogatives. Indeed, by permitting subsidiary trade and standing back as the hemisphere pursued greater engagement with Cuba, Kissinger hoped to remove the practical difficulties that contentious and extraterritorial policies caused for U.S.-Latin American relations generally.

In July of 1975, the OAS—with tacit U.S. support—did vote to permit member countries to renew diplomatic and trade relations with Cuba as each country saw fit. Less than a month later, just as U.S. intelligence agents were starting to become aware of the Cuban presence in Angola, the United States nonetheless removed its ban on subsidiary trade with the island. As a result, after an effective dry spell of 10 years, Cuba was able not only to resume trade and economic ties throughout the hemisphere but also to purchase goods produced by third-country subsidiaries of American companies. American enterprises quickly took advantage. Indeed, by the beginning of the 1990s, American companies primarily in the pharmaceutical and agricultural sectors were selling about $700 million a year in U.S. products to Cuba.

What's the story behind the Kissinger/Ford secret diplomacy with Cuba in 1974?

Henry Kissinger's pursuit of détente with the Soviets under Presidents Nixon and Ford played out on several fronts around the globe, and Cuba was no exception. In November 1974, Kissinger deployed a handful of close deputies to initiate a series of secret meetings with Fidel Castro's emissaries. During discussions over the course of 10 months, both sides addressed issues ranging from the decolonization wars in Africa (though without specific reference to Cuban involvement in Angola, as this was not initially known to the United States), to the Puerto Rican independence movement, to the state of U.S.-Soviet relations and Cuba's own revolutionary trajectory.

On the specific question of the prospect for the United States and Cuba to restore trade and diplomatic relations, the talks ultimately stalled. American participants claim that Cuba's increasingly public involvement in Angola's postcolonial civil conflict made further progress impossible. The Americans, however, initially and incorrectly saw Cuban involvement in Africa as directly responding to Soviet prerogatives, assuming that Cuba lacked the independence to move closer to the United States. Unsure of Cuba's intentions, reluctant to draw the public spotlight on the issue during a presidential campaign season, and generally tepid about making Cuba a high priority on the Ford presidency's to-do list, the U.S. side gradually lost interest in further talks.

Fidel Castro later acknowledged that making nice with the Americans was not a priority of Cuban foreign policy at the time. Cuba's leaders had learned to live without the United States, were receiving a healthy Soviet subsidy, and believed they had much more to gain geopolitically by aiding decolonization struggles in Africa than by reverting to the more docile role the Americans had likely envisioned for the revolution. Notably, Kissinger's negotiators made clear to Castro's envoys that the United States had no designs on Cuba's domestic arrangements. In other words, these foreign policy realists were prepared to accept Cuba's one-party state as well as its Socialist economy and human rights problems if doing so could unhinge the island from its Soviet dependence and thus deny the Soviets their base in the Western Hemisphere.

How did Jimmy Carter's administration approach Cuba?

Jimmy Carter's campaign and presidency sought to distinguish itself from the previous era of hard-nosed realpolitik by making the cause of human rights, especially in the third world, the centerpiece of his foreign policy. Like his predecessors, Carter did not place a high priority on Cuba. Nonetheless, moving toward better relations with Havana was consistent with the administration's tough stance toward Latin America's many right-wing and military rulers, dictators whose pursuit of "dirty wars" against suspected subversives (often with prior U.S. support) entailed human rights abuses far worse, systematic, and brutal than those in Cuba. The new approach toward Cuba was also consistent with his broad philosophy that the United States should pursue civil relations even with hostile countries, including North Korea and Syria. By this time, influential voices in the Democratic Party had begun to call for a new policy toward Cuba. Moreover, a fresh approach seemed politically doable, as Cuban Americans had yet to organize themselves into a lobbying or campaign finance force of any significance. Internationally, Canadian Prime Minister Pierre Trudeau was reaching out to Cuba as well, visiting the island at the end of January 1976. Notably, Cuba remained disposed to move toward normalization despite several setbacks, namely, the dramatic bombing of Cubana Airlines Flight 455 in October 1976, perpetrated, CIA and FBI sources reported, by former CIA asset Luis Posada Carriles and Orlando Bosch, both Cuban exiles.

With Carter's approval, and under the lead of Secretary of State Cyrus Vance, U.S. diplomats met with their Cuban counterparts to hash through a number of outstanding bilateral issues that accumulated over the years. The explicit intention was to establish a framework and a process for ultimately restoring trade and diplomatic relations. In contrast to the 1974–75 period, there was nothing secret about the Carter-era talks. Nor was it a secret that by 1976 Cuba had sent over 30,000 troops to Angola, let alone that it supported insurgencies in Central America and played host to thousands of Soviet military advisors and intelligence installations at home.

The meetings established a boundary line defining each country's territorial waters in the Florida Straits and the Gulf of Mexico and placed back on the agenda antihijacking agreements Cuba had suspended after the bombing of the Cubana flight. The first academic exchange program, between Johns Hopkins University and the University of Havana, started at this time. Significantly, in 1977 the Carter administration lifted the travel ban, allowing large numbers of Americans to visit the island for the first time since 1961, including for tourist purposes. And the two countries opened "Interests Sections" (one step short of a full embassy) in each other's capitals, sending "chiefs of mission" to provide diplomatic representation.

Although the sting of Cuba's foreign policy exploits initially seemed to fade as a thorn in the American side, human rights violations—most graphically dramatized by the thousands of political prisoners in Cuba's jails—did capture Washington's attention. The State Department let it be known that the fate of the political prisoners could well determine the pace of potential reconciliation between the two countries, and at least for a time, Havana seemed prepared to play ball.

At this time, Jimmy Carter also lent his support to what came to be known as *el diálogo* between a small segment of the Cuban American community and the Cuban government, described on pages 36–125. Concurrently, and parallel to Carter's decision to lift the travel ban on American citizens, the Cuban government granted permission for émigrés to return to the island and released 3,000 political prisoners, the biggest single gesture of this sort since the revolution had taken power.

The move gave the State Department political cover to advance the bilateral agenda; showed a flexible, pragmatic side of the Cuban government; and, in a politically and economically cost-effective strategy, allowed Havana to export its long-standing internal enemies rather than keep them in jail serving sentences of multiple decades to life. But one dimension neither the *diálogo* nor the official talks settled was a joint system for managing the all but relentless pressure not from political prisoners, but from Cuban citizens searching for a way to leave the island.

Although significant progress had been made, the Carter administration was not entirely unified on the merits of a further opening with Cuba. Individuals in Havana and Washington closest to the process understood perfectly that despite opening the Interests Sections, establishing territorial boundaries, and releasing political prisoners, they had only just begun a long process of negotiation. There was still the matter of Guantánamo, the uncompensated claims of American companies who lost their properties, and the even more difficult issue of the Soviet presence on the island. By 1979, the international climate circumscribed the likelihood of a further opening and strengthened hard-liners in the Carter White House who opposed rapprochement with Havana. Not only had the Carter presidency become weakened by the Iranian hostage crisis and the Soviet invasion of Afghanistan, but also more Cuban troops were flowing into Africa, Fidel Castro had assumed leadership of the Non-Aligned Movement, and the Sandinistas had succeeding in ousting the Somoza regime in Nicaragua. Under such circumstances, individuals in the Carter administration, notably his national security advisor, Zbigniew Brzezinski, and his deputy for Latin America, Robert Pastor, lobbied against a further opening with Cuba. With the resignation of Cyrus Vance as secretary of state, meanwhile, the State Department's Cuba initiative was left without a senior-level protector. More broadly, détente had come under attack by a new coalition of Republicans and anti-Communist Democrats who attacked Carter's foreign policy for being too soft in the 1980 presidential election season. Carter's early moves to restore diplomatic relations, end the trade embargo, and improve human rights in Cuba were ultimately thwarted.

What was the Mariel boatlift?

By early 1980, Jimmy Carter was fighting with Ted Kennedy for the Democratic presidential nomination and deflecting a heavy barrage of attacks from the GOP. Republicans argued that his geopolitical weakness had not only allowed the Iranian revolution to jeopardize American interests and the strategic balance in the Middle East but also given the Soviets space to get away with a nuclear buildup that threatened NATO allies in Europe. Closer to American shores, Castro's communism seemed to be once again stoking the flames of revolution in Central America, Carter's opponents contended, and revealing the limits of the White House human rights agenda. Not surprisingly, in such an environment, Cuba failed in its efforts to secure U.S. approval for an annual quota of entry visas for Cubans wishing to migrate north.

Indeed, prior to 1980, migratory pressures within Cuba had begun to grow. Cuba's economy suffered under a stagnant centralized bureaucracy, declining workforce motivation, the lingering effects of the 1979 world spike in oil prices, and continuing U.S. economic sanctions. While the visits of tens of thousands of Cuban exiles and American citizens to the island during this period provided some much-needed economic relief, they also exposed Cuban citizens to new ideas, perspectives, and realities, provoking many to reevaluate their own society and question the government's vilification of the United States and Cuban exiles in particular. As a result of this combination of factors, for many Cubans, revolutionary zeal was on the decline.

By March of 1980, a handful of Cuban citizens had already smuggled themselves into foreign embassies in search of asylum. The Peruvian embassy was one target, and the

Peruvian government was not at the time disposed to return the intruders to Cuban authorities. Later that month, when several Cubans crashed a bus into the gate of the Peruvian complex and provoked a violent incident with Cuban soldiers, Fidel responded by removing all police protection from the embassy grounds. Within 48 hours, over 10,000 citizens had taken refuge inside the gates.

An initial airlift for the asylum seekers negotiated multilaterally only lasted four days, after which point Castro suspended the flights, accusing the United States of using the exodus for political purposes. Yet Fidel remained conscious of the pressure-cooker environment in Havana at the time and sought to rid himself of a much larger base of potential opposition. Thus, when Carter suggested he would open America's doors to those Cubans willing to leave, Castro readily took him up on the offer, announcing that all Cubans who wanted to leave the island could do so, and that Cubans in Miami would be welcome to come to the port of Mariel, west of Havana, to pick up their relatives. Within a month, over 40,000 Cubans had left the island in the largest exodus since the early years of the revolution. Upward of 80,000 more departed before the crisis was resolved, bringing the total number of emigrants close to 125,000.

The Mariel boatlift was the first time in which substantial numbers of Afro-Cubans and working-class citizens had participated in a mass exodus. As such, it significantly changed the racial and class mix of Cubans in Miami. Importantly, Fidel took advantage of the moment to export not just the disaffected working poor; among the *marielitos* were also criminals Cuba released from its jails and, it was alleged, patients released from its mental institutions. In addition to recovering their family and friends, Cuban exiles with boats at the port of Mariel were often forced to take on unknown individuals as passengers, including some of the released criminals. Sympathetic to the initial asylum seekers at the embassy, but overwhelmed by the scale of the exodus, establishment Miami was noticeably worried about its capacity to handle the influx. When surveying the humanity arriving on his shores, the mayor of Miami quipped a memorable and derogatory insult: "Fidel has just flushed his toilet on us." But it wasn't just the municipal and social services of South Florida that bore the effect of the new refugees. Local officials outside of Florida, such as a young governor of Arkansas named Bill Clinton, soon found their jails populated by Cubans with criminal records, many of whom were prepared, quite literally, to torch the prisons to win their freedom.

Although the Mariel exodus exposed the discontent of wide sectors of the population with the Cuban regime, at the same time the absence of a bilateral migration agreement had left the White House vulnerable to the whims of Fidel Castro. In the end, Castro knowingly foisted an unwanted influx of migrants on to the United States at a time when the economy was reeling and Carter was already in deep political trouble. In this way, Carter's vacillation and fundamental misreading of Cuban domestic politics helped deliver Ronald Reagan the White House in the 1980 election.

Why did Reagan toughen up U.S. policy toward Cuba?

Ronald Reagan's presidency revived the Cold War. The Soviets became the "evil empire," their satellites the cause of subversion, and third-world conflict a product of a monumental ideological struggle rather than the result of cumulative grievances exploited or exacerbated by the superpowers. Liberating Cuba from Soviet clutches and purging Castro's communism from the island was at the center of the Reagan administration's policy of "rollback" in Latin America. Reagan's Latin America hands, from the neoconservative Elliot Abrams at the State Department to Constantine Menges at the National Security Council, believed that resisting Communist encroachment in the hemisphere vastly outweighed the moral kudos the United States might gain from supporting the broader international human rights agenda. In the spirit of Jeanne Kirkpatrick's pragmatic defense of U.S. ties to authoritarian (as opposed to totalitarian) governments that were aligned with U.S. interests, Latin America policy under Reagan would continue ties with South America's anti-Communist military regimes (such as that of Augusto Pinochet in Chile), move aggressively against the leftist insurgency brewing in El Salvador, and unleash a major effort (first covert, then not so much) to overthrow the Sandinista government in Nicaragua.

Opposition to the spread of the Cuban model (however false such comparisons might have been) offered intrinsic reasons for the Reagan White House to overhaul both Kissinger's realism and Carter's idealism. Naturally, then, Cuba's support for revolutionary struggle in Central America, just a three-hour plane ride from Miami, made a crackdown inevitable on the country that Secretary of State Alexander Haig described as the "source" of Communist subversion in the region.

What did Reagan do to crack down on Cuba?

During Reagan's two terms in office, the White House enacted a number of bilateral measures to tighten the screws on Cuba. Reagan made it more difficult for Cuban diplomats to enter the United States, reinstated the travel ban that had been lifted by the Carter administration in 1977, and authorized harsher enforcement on third-party countries trading with Cuba. In one arena, migration, Reagan attempted to move forward with direct negotiations, in an effort to avoid the repetition of the Mariel crisis. Yet when the administration backed the creation of Radio Martí, a Voice of America broadcast aimed at liberating Cuba from Communist clutches by bypassing the Cuban government's control of the media, what tentative arrangements had been worked out were left by the wayside. More broadly, U.S. authorities also launched a healthy dose of psychological warfare aimed at convincing Cuba of possible direct U.S. military action against them, a prospect that had substantially diminished over the previous decade, if not longer. In addition, the Reagan White House was really the first presidential administration since the Eisenhower years to make the U.S. Congress a central tool of active efforts to undermine the Castro regime. Between 1981 and 1988, a bipartisan coalition of legislators appropriated funds for a mix of covert and overt operations. Some involved support for dissidents, along the lines of the anti-Soviet, prodemocracy civil society groups the United States was then supporting in Eastern Europe, especially in Poland and Czechoslovakia; others involved stepping up radio propaganda broadcasts beamed at the island. At the same time, like previous administrations, the two governments sent senior representatives to meet—this time in Mexico City and again with few results—to sound one another out on Central America, the still unresolved issue of migration, and Cuba's activities in Africa.

Who was Jorge Mas Canosa?

Jorge Mas Canosa (1939–97) was born in Santiago de Cuba. After participating in anti-Batista activities as a student, he left the island in 1960. He soon joined the 2506 Brigade and was scheduled to take part in the Bay of Pigs invasion, but his decoy boat never deployed to the island. Shortly after returning to the United States in June of 1961, the CIA sent him for training in paramilitary counterinsurgency techniques at Fort Benning, Georgia. Like many exiles of his generation who became involved in early counterrevolutionary activities, overthrowing Fidel Castro became his lifelong mission, even as he took on the "only-in-America" trappings of achievement as a businessman and a family patriarch. Many in his cohort harbored the fantasy that a violent overthrow was always just one violent attack or assassination attempt away. Declassified FBI files clearly track Mas Canosa's financial and legal support for those directly involved in terrorism against Cuba during the 1960s (including Luis Posada Carriles). Cuban government and other sources likewise claim to have documented his continued support for such activities later in life. Yet Mas

Canosa became a legend even more for his acutely honed sense of American politics. With a skill set that went way beyond violent conspiracies, he is the individual most clearly responsible for the birth and success of the Cuban American National Foundation (CANF), the most effective and formidable Cuban American lobbying organization in the United States, from its founding in 1981 until the end of the 20th century.

How did the Cuban American National Foundation emerge?

While the Cuban American National Foundation was largely the creation of Jorge Mas Canosa and a number of other Cuban exiles, the Reagan administration offered substantial help in conceptualizing its purpose and modus operandi. Reagan and his team came to office with their hearts set on unseating Castro but also understood that they would need some help with the Democratic-controlled Congress to move aggressively. Richard Allen, Reagan's first national security advisor, recommended that Mas Canosa and his colleagues closely study the American-Israel Political Action Committee (AIPAC, an organization of American Jews that lobbied Congress for policies that support Israel). By using AIPAC as a model, Allen advised, Cuban Americans could build an organization that would transform Cuban exiles from mere proxies for the U.S. government into citizens with a legitimate stake in their country's policy toward their homeland. Very quickly, and with a wide open door from the administration, CANF became a membership organization with a donor base drawing on contributions of as little as $5 from pensioners in Hialeah to hundreds of thousands of dollars from wealthy scions of the exile community in South Florida, New Jersey, and elsewhere around the country. Under Mas Canosa's charismatic and often intimidating leadership, CANF lobbied Democrats and Republicans alike while launching aggressive public and media advocacy campaigns on behalf of the cause of liberating Cuba from Castro's clutches. A public action committee, or PAC, was also formed to reinforce

CANF's lobbying activities with campaign finance contributions on both sides of the aisle. By the end of Reagan's second term, CANF could claim responsibility for making the views of the Cuban American anti-Castro hard line, then the majority of the community, strongly felt in Congress and in the executive branch. Legislative victories—such as Radio Martí and new funds for advancing the cause of human rights and democracy in Cuba—would not have been approved were it not for the new political, financial, ideological, and media space that CANF came to occupy over the course of the 1980s.

At various times and from various corners, CANF has been accused of supporting or helping to organize violent plots against Fidel Castro or the Cuban government. Luis Posada Carriles even at one point told the *New York Times* that he had received direct assistance from Mas Canosa and CANF for some of his activities, though he later claimed he had deliberately misinformed the paper. The CANF leadership has routinely and repeatedly denied any such charges, yet it is unmistakable that Mas Canosa and Posada had some relationship. Not only was Mas Canosa involved in supporting Posada's work long before the foundation of CANF, and not only did they know each other at Fort Benning, Georgia, but it has also been widely reported, for example, that Mas Canosa, as head of CANF, helped to orchestrate Posada's eventual escape from Venezuelan custody in 1985 (where he had been imprisoned on charges related to the 1976 Cubana Airlines bombing). Other individuals associated with CANF, such as its current president Francisco "Pepe" Hernández and former board member José Antonio Llama, have also registered long records of voicing support for violence to unseat Castro (although Hernández has renounced violence more recently).

What is Radio Martí?

The creation of Radio Martí in 1983 is also credited largely to the activism of Jorge Mas Canosa. Inspired by Radio Swan (the

Bay of Pigs–era broadcasts aimed at softening the Cuban population in the lead-up of 1961 invasion) as well as Radio Free
Europe and other Cold War instruments of U.S. public diplomacy, Radio Martí was intended to provide Cubans on the
island with everything from news about the world to the truth
about their own repressive government, and, it was implied,
a source of inspiration to overthrow the communist regime.
Named for the Cuban liberator and independence champion José Martí, the prospect of such a broadcast produced
a firestorm of protest from the Cuban government. Authorities in Havana were not only incensed at the ratcheting up of
propaganda but also were perhaps even more angered by the
appropriation of Martí's name. Mas Canosa and CANF, with
support from key congressional allies from Cuban American
districts in Florida and New Jersey, passionately made the case
for Radio Martí in the U.S. Congress. In its first year of funding,
the program received $10 million (with $7.7 million allocated
for the following year) through the Voice of America. Voice of
America began recruiting Cuban exiles to produce the broadcast. By the end of Reagan's two terms in office, Radio Martí
had become an established but not especially effective feature
of U.S. policy toward Cuba. And for a time, Cuban listeners
could tune in to an array of fairly generic news about Cuba,
Latin America, and world events, as well as *telenovelas*, horo-
scopes, and even recipes. The Cuban government ranted and
raved about the broadcast, questioning its name and its legality,
but after recovering from its annoyance at the concept eventually succeeded in blocking the signal.

Radio Martí may not have unhinged the regime's grip on
Cuban public opinion, but it did become a source of employment for Cuban exiles and, over time, the political fiefdom of
Mas Canosa, where jobs and titles were doled out in exchange
for ideological compliance. As a result, what even its critics
describe as initially a surprisingly professional broadcast given
its political aims grew into a propaganda tool with not a whit
of dispassion or neutrality. The broadcast came to offend not

only the Cuban government but also many of the professionals within the Voice of America. By 1987, Mas Canosa began to float the idea for a TV Martí, and Congress appropriated $16 million for its launch in 1990. By 2007, U.S. taxpayers had contributed over $500 million to radio and TV broadcasts that few if any Cubans actually hear or see.

CUBA IN THE WORLD

Why did Fidel, Che, and the other revolutionaries think they would succeed in spreading revolution in the third world?

The Cuban Revolution burst onto the world scene just as wars of decolonization were sprouting all over Asia and Africa. Simultaneously, many Latin Americans were discovering that their own political independence, though won in the previous century, had not brought the liberty, equality, and fraternity promised by the American and French revolutions, models upon which many early independence struggles were based. In such an environment, Cuban revolutionaries came to believe that their own triumph over an *ancien régime* coddled by an imperial power and held together by an entrenched elite and complicit military could be reproduced elsewhere. Moreover, the Cubans believed that the specific model they had pioneered—a guerrilla *foco* capable of dealing a military, psychological, and political defeat to the established order— could be adapted to local conditions across the hemisphere, if not the world. High on their victory and pulsing with youthful hubris and macho bravado, the Cuban revolutionaries eagerly embraced the nation-building myth Guevara had helped author. Despite the complex set of circumstances, dynamics, and actors that paved the way for the Cuban Revolution to come to power, Guevara focused on the guerrilla as the crucial centerpiece of any revolution, dependent perhaps for material support from other political actors and supporters, but largely unencumbered by the need to practice real politics, build coalitions, or otherwise create a domestic and international strategy to reinforce a largely isolated and vulnerable armed challenge to the status quo.

When the Cuban revolutionaries looked at the world in the early years of the 1960s, they saw extreme poverty, racial discrimination, underdevelopment, and injustice. Civilians such as Foreign Minister Raul Roa or President Osvaldo Dorticós sought a middle course between quasi-colonial dependence upon the United States and rigid alignment with the Soviet bloc. But they also derived from Cuba's experience the firm conviction that violent revolution might be the only path that could successfully deliver the independence and self-determination that anticolonial movements around the world were seeking, whether under Ho Chi Minh in Vietnam, Patrice Lumumba in the Belgian Congo, or Ahmed Ben Bella in Algeria.

What were the basic objectives of the Cuban Revolution's foreign policy?

During the first three decades of the revolution, Cuba's leaders endeavored to align their foreign policy with their view of the strategic, economic, ideological, and political objectives of a revolutionary country forging a new national identity. Two overarching dynamics were critical during this period. First, the global context of the Cold War and the extent to which Cuba came to be seen, rightly or wrongly, as a Soviet proxy definitively shaped the conditions for, reactions to, and implications of the lion's share of Cuba's international activities. Second, Cuba's foreign policy was tied closely to its domestic politics. Even as they were acutely aware of the international setting in which they functioned, Cuba's revolutionary leadership, military and civilian, viewed their internationalism as the existential sine qua non of national independence.

The chaotic exuberance, polarization, and radicalism of Cuban domestic politics during the early 1960s were part and parcel of a broader vision. Revolution at home was not sufficient. True revolutionaries were equally committed to liberation for others facing oppression around the globe. Of course, such passions led Cuba to the ostensibly contradictory position of rigorously defending its sovereignty at home from U.S. aggression while also arguably undermining the sovereignty of other states. Nonetheless, the revolutionaries were convinced that their cause was just and that the governments they challenged required fundamental, revolutionary change. Any accusations of hypocrisy were forcefully, if clumsily, denied. Even in the 1970s, as Cuba consolidated its institutions, settled into a rhythm of central planning, and became fully integrated into the Soviet economic system, Cuba's authorities managed to support liberation struggles in Central America, southern Africa, and beyond with cash, training, and troops—with or without Moscow's blessing. The 1980s tempered Cuban ambition to some degree. With the Soviets weakened by a costly arms race and bogged down in the empire-smashing war in Afghanistan, and with Ronald Reagan moving aggressively to roll back the revolutions Cuba supported, including its own, Cuba began to more strongly emphasize proper state-to-state relations. With the island's population and political class increasingly aware that ideology and revolution alone weren't going to pay the bills, Cuban authorities looked to expand trade and commercial ties beyond the Soviet bloc.

Whether framed as international solidarity, social justice, or third-world liberation, over the course of the Cold War, Cuba's foreign policies left three critical and lasting legacies. First, through its activism abroad, Cuba demonstrated— primarily to the United States, but also to the Soviet Union— the firm nature of its declaration of independence from its colonial and semicolonial past. Of course, Cuba never fully achieved independence, having become reliant on Soviet patronage. Yet at the same time, Havana's independent action in the foreign policy realm carried an important demonstration effect, effectively warning both Moscow and Washington not to toy with Cuba. Second, Cuba's international exploits helped tie a new national identity at home to a noble social project abroad; international missions became a huge part of revolutionary Cuba's national consciousness and garnered for the island tremendous international support in far-off corners of the world. Third, to a large degree, Cuba believed its Lilliputian brushfires around the globe could help tie down the American Gulliver. With displays of power hard and soft, Cuba showed up in global hotspots from 1959 to the closing years of the Cold War.

Where was Cuba's foreign policy focused during the early years of the revolution and how did Che Guevara fit into the mix?

Throughout the 1960s, Cuba supported revolutionary states, assisted revolutionary movements, and built ties with the Communist and non-Communist Left all over the world, but especially in Africa and Latin America. Che Guevara was a key figure in many of these endeavors. Indeed, while the iconic and now aggressively commercialized portrait of Che may define Cuba around the world today, it was the man himself, not the image, who trekked across the globe to spread revolution with the backing of Cuba's considerable security and intelligence forces. As discussed elsewhere, following the revolution, Che quickly became the model and principal philosopher behind the creation of "the new man" in Cuba, a "new man," incidentally, who was committed as much to social justice abroad as at home. In the early 1950s, Guevara had traveled throughout Latin America, witnessed Arbenz's fall from power in 1954, and eventually made his way to Mexico, where he met Fidel. It was no surprise, then, that the native Argentine interpreted the Cuban Revolution through an internationalist lens. Thus, despite a brief stint attempting, miserably, to run Cuba's economy, Guevara early on developed a keen interest in taking the Cuban Revolution global, with the ultimate objective of bringing it home to Argentina. He and other Cuban leaders were in near-continuous contact with revolutionaries and reformers from a wide variety of countries, searching for windows of opportunity and potential avenues for collaboration.

A few examples provide a window into the breadth of Cuba's activism from the earliest days of the revolution's triumph. In Venezuela, where Fidel's supporters had raised cash and weapons in the late 1950s, Cuba armed and trained a short-lived insurgency led by Marxist rebels who had been cut out of the political deal that removed dictator Marcos Pérez Jiménez from power in late 1959. In the Dominican Republic, Cuba backed an abortive 1959 invasion by revolutionaries fighting against the dictatorship of Rafael Trujillo, a long-time ally of Batista during and after his tenure in power. In Nicaragua, Cuba provided cash and later weapons and training to rebels who would later go on to found the Sandinista movement fighting against the dictator Anastasio Somoza. Guevara himself was most closely involved in an effort to train and arm the Argentine "People's Guerrilla Army" following the conclusion of the 1962 Missile Crisis. After crossing into northern Argentina from Bolivia, the rebel force was betrayed, surrounded, and wiped out before their native son and presumptive leader could join them. Cuba also provided advisors and inspiration to armed revolutionaries in Panama, Guatemala, Peru, and Colombia.

In general, early revolutionary exploits in Latin America proved unsuccessful. Local Communist parties by and large continued to resist the guerilla strategy supported by the Cubans, just as Cuba's own Communist Party had done until late in the island's insurrection. Che and Fidel also looked to Africa as a possible new front. The revolutionaries' interest in Africa began before 1959, when, for example, they followed the exploits of the Algerian war of independence against the French with close interest. Once in power, Cuba sent weapons and advisors to support the Algerian National Liberation Front (FLN) and provided medical assistance, schools, and training for wounded Algerian independence fighters. After the country secured its independence from France in 1962, Fidel pledged support for Algerian rebel leader Ben Bella's new government, sending Cuba's first mission of doctors abroad as well as weapons and military advisors. In exchange, Algeria later in the decade provided Cuba with a logistics base outside of Algiers for training and equipping Latin American revolutionaries.

Fed up with slow progress in Latin America and frustrated with his work on Cuba's economic policies, between 1964 and 1965 Che became Fidel's emissary (a role he had relished in previous trips to Russia, China, Eastern Europe, Asia, and Africa) on a new swing through much of the African continent, becoming the first high-level Cuban official to visit Sub-Saharan Africa. At the time, Belgium's and Portugal's colonial empires were on their last legs, and the continent seethed with the activity of various national liberation groups, often supported by states that had already achieved independence. After first visiting Algeria, Che then traveled to Mali, Congo-Brazzaville (known today as the Congo), Guinea, Ghana, Benin, and eventually Dar-Es-Saalam, in present-day Tanzania, a hub for African national liberation movements. Importantly, during these trips—particularly during his stops in Brazzaville and Dar-Es-Saalam—Che also met with a variety of independence leaders from such countries as Cape Verde, the Congo (later Zaire, and currently the Democratic Republic of the Congo), Angola, Mozambique, and Guinea-Bissau. Just as he and others before him (José Martí and Simón Bolivar) had envisioned a united American continent, Che promoted the concept of African unity at a time when anticolonial struggles had focused independence leaders on the home-front rather than a continent-wide effort. Che's reception in that context was decidedly cool. Yet Che did commit to sending instructors to support rebels in the Congo (Zaire), where nationalist leader Patrice Lumumba had recently been assassinated. Very quickly (likely because Che and other leaders had already set their sights on the Congo as fruitful terrain), this commitment would evolve into Cuba's first major deployment abroad. Over seven months in 1965, Guevara, along with over 100 Cuban troops and advisors, mounted a venture in the jungle to establish a successful guerilla *foco* in the Congo, an effort that Guevara would later describe as an "unmitigated disaster."

Following the failure of the Congo operation, Che would eventually make his way back to Cuba. But Cuba's involvement in Africa did not cease. In 1966, Cuba began sending a small numbers of troops, doctors, and teachers to Guinea-Bissau to aid rebels fighting for independence from Portugal. The Cuban presence there was decisive to the rebels' eventual victory against the Portuguese in 1974. In 1965, Cuba likewise began training Angolan rebels in Agostinho Neto's MPLA, one of three forces that, less than a decade later, would scramble to take power as the Portuguese left Luanda.

With the ultimate goal of bringing his revolutionary struggle to his native Argentina, Che had refocused his attention on Latin America, with Bolivia the destination for a new and, as it turned out, the final revolutionary campaign for Che. To set the stage, in January of 1966, with the United States already deeply enmeshed in Vietnam, Cuba had played host to what came to be known as the Tri-Continental Congress. Bringing together left-wing activists and revolutionaries from across the globe, the conference established Havana as the hub for anticolonial third-world armed leftist movements and leaders, and the global intellectual class that supported them. In his principal address to the conference, Fidel endeavored to tread a delicate line, voicing Cuba's belief in the necessity of (and its disposition to support) armed revolution while also strongly echoing the Soviet Union's more conservative message of "solidarity." Nonetheless, by embracing armed revolution, just as the 26th of July had against Batista, Cuba had unmistakably challenged the Soviet Union's preference that revolution be pursued through the toil and trouble of local Communist parties working in broad front politics. Although by this point Che and Cuba had already come up against the real-world limits of transplanting Cuba's revolutionary model to other continents and cultures, Che was not dissuaded and had already disappeared to prepare his new venture in a country where at least 60% of the population was indigenous and spoke little if any Spanish.

Disguised as an innocuous and balding middle-aged professional, and with a fake Uruguayan passport, Guevara arrived in Bolivia in the fall of 1966 to lead a group of two dozen rebels (mostly Cuban, with nine Bolivians) into southeastern Bolivia. With very little understanding of the "objective conditions" for revolution in Bolivia at the time, Che, with Fidel's support, unilaterally decided to try his revolutionary hand in Bolivia against the objection of the local Communist Party. As a result, he earned enemies not only among Bolivian and U.S. security forces but also within the Bolivian Left, whose leadership was able to eliminate whatever shallow popular support Che hoped to establish for his guerilla operation. Intelligence gathered from two captured supporters of Guevara's Bolivian guerilla band confirmed his presence in the country to Bolivian security authorities. Some also claim that leaders of Bolivia's Communist Party, in addition to undermining the guerilla operation itself by impeding recruitment efforts, supplied key intelligence about the operation to the army. Either way, several months later, with the help of local peasants in the rebels' zone of operations, the CIA, Green Berets, and Bolivian military forces tracked down a physically sick and materially depleted Guevara, executing him on October 9, 1967. Days later in Havana, over 1 million Cubans filled Revolution Square, where Fidel's eulogy launched Che to the status of hero, martyr, and even saint.

The United States tended to see Cuba's international activism as necessarily a proxy for Soviet challenges. Yet as these various cases show, Cuba often defied Moscow's preference for a gradualist approach to revolution. Nor was Che Guevara acting in accordance with Chinese interests, as some of his detractors would accuse in the context of an ever-widening Sino-Soviet split. Despite Che's admiration for some aspects of Chinese communism and his successful diplomacy with China on behalf of the Cuban government in the early 1960s, Cuban foreign policy by design remained by and large entirely independent from both the Soviet Union and China throughout this period.

How did Latin American governments react to Cuba's armed internationalism?

Although Cuba began its support for revolutionary movements in two continents in the early 1960s, Fidel also kept a door open to establishing some kind of equilibrium between Cuba's internationalist goals and the possibility of reaching a modicum of stability with the United States. Months after the Bay of Pigs invasion, Che Guevara met secretly with Kennedy speechwriter Richard Goodwin while both were in Punta del Este, Uruguay, for a meeting of the OAS. Together with Venezuela and Colombia, the United States was pushing to impose multilateral sanctions on the island. Nonetheless, Che, with Fidel's consent, in so many words let Goodwin know that Cuba might be willing to temper its domestic and international radicalism in exchange for a live and let live policy from the Americans. Not surprisingly, the offer got little play back in Washington, and the OAS regardless moved forward to approve a resolution suspending Cuba's membership from the organization. By 1964, as Cuba expanded what Latin American countries considered interference in their domestic affairs, a nearly complete consensus developed at the OAS, where member states approved a new resolution requiring all member countries to break diplomatic and trade relations with Cuba. Scarcely paragons of democracy at the time, most Latin American states complied with the OAS mandate, but managed to maintain modest commercial ties with the island.

Mexico was the one country to take a decidedly different and independent approach to Cuba, refusing to abide by the OAS mandate. From the time of the Mexican American War to the birth of the Mexican Revolution in the early 20th century, Mexico's deeply ingrained nationalism was tinged with suspicion and distrust of the United States. As the standard bearer of this legacy, the ruling Partido Revolucionario Institucional (PRI) remained wary of its neighbor to the north, even as it deepened economic ties across the border. Important, too, were the deep ties already between the Cuban Revolution and Mexico dating back to Castro's exile and training there in the 1950s. As a result of these dynamics, Mexico opted to maintain diplomatic and commercial ties with Cuba, and the PRI built institutional ties with Cuba's Communist Party. Yet there was a practical benefit to this arrangement as well, both for Mexico and Washington. In return for Mexico's display of respect, Fidel vowed not to give money, weapons, or training of any kind to the domestic armed Left that emerged to challenge the PRI's increasingly authoritarian rule. Privately, LBJ's administration and its successors took advantage of Mexico's open-door policy to Cuba (as well as its ties to Moscow), with the U.S. embassy in Mexico City becoming a major listening post to keep tabs on the Cuban military, track Soviet weapons shipments, and collect other kinds of intelligence, sometimes directly and other times from Mexico's own security institutions and diplomats.

Despite its isolation from the OAS, which Cuba characteristically came to wear as a badge of honor, the island actively courted membership in regional organizations focused on specific issues such as economic development and subregional groupings in the Caribbean, for example. Beginning in the 1970s, most OAS members bucked the 1964 resolution and over the course of two decades restored diplomatic ties with Cuba, especially after the OAS, with American support, lifted its formal ban on member states opening relations in 1975. In some cases, Cuba came to be seen as a valued diplomatic partner in the region. Colombian officials, for example, eventually sought Cuba's assistance in negotiating an end to its virulent insurgencies.

How did Cuba's presence in southern Africa evolve?

Throughout the 1970s and 1980s, Cuba provided troops, advisors, security personnel, doctors, teachers, and other professionals to some 17 countries on the African continent. But it was in Angola where Havana took a strategic stand that would redraw the geopolitical map of the region. In 1974, Portugal announced that it would definitively withdraw from its colonies in Africa by the end of the following year. Among Angola's independence movements, the race was on for control of the country's capital: Luanda. Contending factions included Agostino Neto's MPLA; the FNLA, later supported by China; and a third group, UNITA, supported by South Africa and the CIA. Castro's ties to the anti-imperialist, Marxist Neto dated to 1965. Despite taking Luanda by the fall of 1975, the MPLA remained relatively weak. With Neto's support, and without consulting the Soviets, Castro deployed the first wave of some 500 Cuban troops to reinforce the MPLA. Following the direct intervention of South African troops soon after, Cuba sent an additional 650-man battalion of Special Forces in what became known as Operation Carlota. With their assistance, the MPLA was able to turn back the South African/UNITA/FNLA advance and gain international recognition as the legitimate rulers of newly independent Angola. Now with Soviet support, more assistance and thousands more Cuban troops and advisors openly followed. Cold War tensions thus elevated substantially as Angola's civil war continued well into the next decade. The CIA and South Africa continued to back UNITA's Jonas Savimbi, indirectly with money and arms and directly with its own forces. Yet Cuban troops weren't just staving off rebel factions; ironically, despite the island's continuing rivalry with the United States, they also found themselves guarding Chevron oil refineries operating in MPLA-controlled areas of the country.

In 1987–88, Cuban and MPLA forces defeated South Africa and UNITA at the battle of Cuito Cuanavale, a major turning point in the war, which led South Africa's white minority to stand down in Angola (as it had earlier in Mozambique, where Cuban troops were also present) and also grant independence to neighboring Namibia. Negotiations mediated by the United States between Angola, Cuba, and South Africa subsequently secured the withdrawal of Cuban troops from the region by 1991. The Angolan civil war would not formally come to a close until 2002, following the death of UNITA leader Jonas Savimbi.

Between 1975 and 1991, over 300,000 (and over 400,000 according to some estimates) Cubans had served tours of duty in southern Africa, whether as soldiers, teachers, doctors, or advisers. The exact number of deaths remains a closely held secret. On his last visit to Africa in 1998, Fidel was greeted not just as a rock star, but as a friend, father figure, and veritable savior. Cuba also was a staunch supporter of the African National Congress, which led the fight against apartheid. At his presidential inauguration in 1994, Nelson Mandela famously thanked Fidel Castro, telling him, "You made this possible" (his whisper was unintentionally picked up by a microphone and broadcast to the world). Mandela may have been speaking to Fidel himself, but his words were directed at every Cuban, for whom the southern Africa experience was a source of personal, national, and, in the case of those families who lost relatives, bittersweet pride.

What was Cuba's role in the Horn of Africa and the Ethiopia/Somalia conflict?

Cuba's role was extraordinarily confusing. First, in the 1960s, Cuba supported Somalia and helped train Eritrean cave-dwelling rebels fighting against the U.S.-backed emperor of Ethiopia, Haile Selassie. Then, when Selassie was overthrown and replaced by a radical Marxist, Mengistu Haile Miriam, Fidel during a 1977 visit to the country determined that the new Ethiopia shared a common vision with Cuba and cut off support to the Eritreans. Still, Somalia's government under Siad Barre was also Socialist and backed by the Soviets. Barre had designs on Ethiopia's swath of the Ogaden Desert, where many Somalis live, and built up forces to take some territory. But more than just a territorial grab, the move reflected a current in Somali thought that envisions one day uniting Somali people living in Somalia, Ethiopia, Kenya, and Djibouti. When Mengistu threw out the Americans, he asked Fidel for support to stave off the Somali encroachment. After an unsuccessful attempt to prevent a conflict between Somalia and Ethiopia, Cuba sent 15,000 troops to Eritrea, and the Soviet Union sent another 1,500 advisors. Together with Ethiopian forces, they beat back a now U.S.-backed Siad Barre in the Ogaden.

Whereas in southern Africa Cuba looked to be independently supporting a number of initiatives—the ANC in South Africa, Namibian independence, and the anticolonial movement with the most legitimate claim to power in Angola—in the Horn of Africa Fidel literally seemed to be throwing Cuba's support all over the map as Ethiopia and Somalia rapidly shifted their own alliances from west to east and east to west. Cuba's involvement in the Horn also came at a time when the Cuban economy had already become entirely dependent upon the Soviet Union, and Cuba was already fighting against South Africa, a U.S. proxy. Thus, by the end of the 1970s, Cuba's critics could plausibly argue that the rationale for détente with Havana and its claim to lead the Non-Aligned Movement in 1979 were both jeopardized by Cuba's association with Soviet policy in Africa, and later elsewhere. Why, or even whether, Cuba's primary interest was to act as a Soviet proxy—the Soviets certainly didn't see it that way—is perhaps less important in the long term than assessing Cuba's legacy in Africa for the Cuban Revolution. Through that lens, Cuba's African policy during the Cold War projected the Cuban people, the Cuban military, and the revolutionary project itself onto the global stage. With African descendents comprising a significant percentage of Cuba's own population, the Africa years did much to expand conceptions of Cuban national identity beyond the mestizo imprint left by

Spain's ruling class. Moreover, Cuba's forays in Africa broadened its international importance well beyond Cuba's historic role as a colonial outpost or second-tier player in the American, or even the Soviet, shadow.

How did Cuba's foreign policy in the Middle East evolve?

As if Latin America and Africa weren't enough, Cuba also extended its reach into the swirl of pan-Arab, nationalist, and decolonization struggles of the Middle East. On one hand, Cuba cultivated diplomatic and commercial ties with secular nationalist states from Egypt and Syria to Iraq, Libya, Algeria, and Israel. On the other, Cuba provided support to the region's nationalist liberation movements—whether Palestinian, Yemeni, or Moroccan, for example. As early as 1959, while visiting Algeria, Che and Raul visited Cairo, seeking weapons from Gamel Abdel Nasser, who later denied a request to provide assistance to Che in the Congo in 1965. Also in 1959, an American-trained officer in the Cuban Armed Forces who would later play a critical role in repelling the Bay of Pigs invasion, José Ramón Fernández, went to Israel seeking weapons. Like Nasser, Israel demurred but offered diplomatic and economic ties to the revolutionary government.

Cuba and Israel initially shared a similar zeitgeist. Both were new countries embattled in their own neighborhoods, both were guided by a socialist-agricultural ethos, and both were equipped with battle-hardened military and intelligence establishments. But Cuba's aspirations for a starring role in the Non-Aligned Movement, its anti-imperialist ties with Fatah and the PLO, and its deepening Soviet ties ultimately threw the island into direct conflict with Israel. With the outbreak of the Yom Kippur War in 1973, Cuba broke diplomatic relations, sending troops and tanks to the Golan Heights in Syria. At the UN and other international forums, as well as within the state-controlled press at home, Cuba came to routinely condemn Zionism and Israel, echoing the third-world anti-Israel drumbeat of the era. Cuba also began providing training, weapons, and refuge to the PLO. Yasser Arafat and a number of PLO leaders, including today's president of the Palestinian National Authority, Mahmoud Abbas, visited Havana, where the PLO had established what was described to visitors as its "embassy" well before the Palestinian National Authority was even a thought. Cuba parlayed its support for the PLO and its hostility toward Israel into support from an array of Arab states, especially at the United Nations and of course within the Non-Aligned Movement.

In a more low-key fashion, Cuba sent doctors to Jordan and Baghdad in the 1970s and early 1980s. Though Cuba avoided taking a position on the Iran-Iraq war, it did condemn Saddam Hussein's invasion and attempted annexation of Kuwait (it opposed, however, the UN's authorization of American-led action to repel the invasion). Havana enjoyed proper diplomatic ties with Tehran even while reaching out to the Iranian People's Party (IPP), a group plotting against the government of the Shah. After the 1979 Iranian Revolution, Castro broke with the IPP and cultivated cordial ties with Ayatollah Khomeini despite his virulent anti-Communism. Saudi Arabia's tight alliance with the United States did not dissuade Cuba from sending out feelers to the Wahabi kingdom. But especially in the 1980s, when the Saudis helped Reagan arm the contras in Nicaragua, Cuba's entreaties received a cold shoulder.

While Cuba and Israel have never restored diplomatic relations, informal ties did later expand to some degree. Retired Mossad agents and a number of other Israeli businesspeople, for example, invested in Cuba's citrus and fishing industries, while members of Cuba's Jewish, scholarly, and artistic communities traveled to Israel and vice versa. Quietly, Cuban and Jewish authorities also worked together to help Jewish Cubans immigrate to Israel. These low-key ties evolved despite both countries' rhetorical adherence to their traditional positions: Israel is one of a handful of countries that still votes "no" to Cuba's UN resolutions condemning the

U.S. embargo; Cuba condemns Israeli actions in the West Bank, Gaza, or Lebanon.

Until the end of the Cold War, Cuba associated itself with secular nationalist states and armed political movements. In the Middle East, this meant that Havana's policies often dovetailed, as in Africa, with those of the Soviet Union. But especially in the case of the PLO and also with respect to Israel, the premium Havana placed on independence from great power control when possible meant that its foreign policies were first and foremost an expression of its own national identity as a radical revolutionary state.

How did world events shape Cuba's relationship with the Soviet Union?

Cuban-Soviet ties began to deteriorate in the mid-1980s. The collapse of the Berlin Wall in 1989 and the withdrawal of Soviet financial and military support by 1991 ended nearly three decades of a relationship that had, over the years, been tentative, tense, suspicious, annoying, and utterly unnatural. On one hand, Soviet economic and military support gave Cuba the boost it needed to pay for massive social programs at home while conducting a global foreign policy. Rhetoric of Socialist solidarity and internationalism gave the impression, at least superficially, that both countries shared a common vision for the third world. Yet, on the other hand, the island's Soviet dependence was fundamentally at odds with the revolution's anti-imperialism and Cuba's quest for national independence. This was no secret, not to Fidel, Raul, and the lion's share of Cuba's senior policy officials or among leading intellectuals and the Cuban public.

Other than the end of the Cold War itself, there were three international events that most clearly dramatized the complexity for Cuba of its alliance with the Soviets. The first was the 1962 Cuban Missile Crisis, during which Fidel was prepared to take the world to nuclear war to defend his revolution, but was then cut out of the U.S.-Soviet talks that brought the crisis to its end. He never took to heart Kennedy's commitment to the Soviets to no longer interfere in Cuban internal affairs, and his armed forays into Africa and Latin America in the 1960s had the effect, if not the direct objective, of demonstrating Cuba's independence from Moscow.

Che's death in 1967 began to give Fidel pause. Three years later, the dramatic 1970 failure of the 10-million-ton harvest illuminated Cuba's inability to build an alternative Socialist model at home, reinforcing the island's increasing insertion into the economic orbit of the Eastern bloc. Yet it was the Soviet invasion of Czechoslovakia in August 1968 that marked the second major international turning point for Cuba in its relationship with the Soviet Union. Until then, Cuba had established its bona fides as a leading voice of international solidarity and revolutionary struggle in the third world. Fidel and Che sought to embrace those elements of Soviet power and ideology that could benefit their goals, all while attempting to keep some political distance and independence from Moscow's power and power structures. Alexander Dubcek's departure from the rigid Soviet model during the spring of 1968 introduced a more democratic approach to socialism, with more space for individual rights and expression. The Soviet military invasion that summer was widely condemned by Socialists and the Left around the world. Yet two days into the military occupation of Prague, Fidel Castro appeared on live television not only defending Moscow's actions as a necessary response to western aggression but also criticizing Prague's short-lived reforms. Outside supporters heavily criticized Cuba's apparent prostration before its Soviet benefactors. Nonetheless, despite this embarrassment, and even as Cuba undertook a wholesale adoption of Soviet economic, political, and ideological institutions in the 1970s, its aggressive defense of revolution and independence in southern Africa—independent of Moscow's approval—helped Havana recover some measure of credibility.

By the end of the decade, Cuba's assumption of the presidency in 1979 of the Non-Aligned Movement had the ring of legitimacy. Revolutionary movements in Latin America were again on the rise, Cuban troops and advisors were all over Africa, and in the Middle East Cuba had associated itself with the radically cutting-edge cause of Palestinian liberation from "Zionist imperialism," as Israel was commonly described. In Afghanistan, Havana had recognized the leftist and pro-Soviet government established in Kabul after a 1978 coup. But when the Soviets invaded the country in December 1979 both to oppose a dissident faction of the ruling party that had taken power and to prop up a friendly government in the wake of an expanding civil war, Castro was again compelled to square the circle of his third-world independence with his Soviet dependence, publicly supporting the invasion as a necessary defense against American designs on Central Asia (by the time of the invasion, the CIA had been covertly providing assistance to *mujahideen* rebels). Cuba's defense of the Soviets was particularly embarrassing in light of Cuba's assumption of the Non-Aligned Movement presidency just three months prior. In the middle of what would become the most consequential and ultimately defining east-west conflict since the Cuban Missile Crisis, Cuba again found itself not only in the dark on Soviet plans to invade but also in the difficult position of chairing an organization whose member states, while professing nonalignment, were divided over whether to tolerate or oppose the Soviets' imperial transgression.

As in Africa, Cuba's support for revolutionary insurgencies and states in Central America blazed the trail for what was a comparatively modest Soviet involvement in America's historic sphere. American strategists, however, never really grasped Havana's capacity to make its own foreign policy decisions, seeing in the Sandinista triumph an obvious example of Soviet manipulation, if only by Cuban proxy. In fact, content with its Cuban beachhead, the Soviet Union had seen little need to challenge the United States in its sphere of influence once again, although Moscow would provide moderate support to the Sandinista regime once in office. Yet again, in lending significant support to the Sandinistas, Fidel and company could hardly be accused of simply doing Moscow's bidding. In fact, with the Soviet economy deteriorating and the Afghan conflict weakening Moscow geopolitically, by the end of the 1980s Fidel and Raul Castro harbored little expectation that the island's fate could be reliably left to Soviet whims. Direct signals from the Soviets to the Cuban leadership confirmed as much.

What were the key features of Cuba's involvement in Central America and the Caribbean in the 1980s?

Revolutionary movements in Nicaragua and El Salvador differed from one another in many ways, and the character of the governments they fought to overthrow differed as well. But in both cases, it appeared to Cuba that armed action was necessary to force open political space. Yet in a part of the world where the United States had vowed never to permit "another Cuba," whether a nationalist insurgency could ever again obtain and maintain total state power was an open question.

In Nicaragua, where the United States had previously worked to quash the anti-imperial efforts of Augusto Cesar Sandino in the 1920s, the Somoza family had been in power with U.S. support since 1936. Famed for kleptocratic impulses and overseeing a dynastic spoils system, Anastasio Somoza, president since 1967, leveraged his corrupt and brutal U.S.-trained security forces to maintain power. Though Nicaragua was much more underdeveloped than Cuba had been under Batista, Fidel and other well-known Cuban revolutionaries believed it to be ripe for successful armed struggle. Beginning in the 1960s, Havana provided cash, training, weapons, political advice, and safe harbor to the Sandinista National Liberation Front (FSLN), a movement led by hardened revolutionaries with support among modernizing sectors of the business class.

When the Sandinista revolution triumphed in the summer of 1979, the victory was savored by an array of Cubans as a sign that Che's dream of expanding revolution in the Americas had not been for naught.

El Salvador was much different from Nicaragua, principally because by the 1970s the shades of a political party system had begun to emerge. Nonetheless, El Salvador's economy, based on coffee and other agricultural products, was controlled by the legendary "fourteen families," who simultaneously oversaw the country's major institutions: its political parties, its military and security forces, and its relationship with the United States. Moreover, after Brazil and Cuba itself, El Salvador was home to one of the longest standing Communist parties in the hemisphere and had a history of peasant uprisings and repression dating back to the 1930s. By the end of the 1970s, an array of armed revolutionary groups and democratic, left-leaning political parties had given up on the ballot box, working to fundamentally alter El Salvador's political and economic landscape.

In both Nicaragua and El Salvador, the United States had long established itself as the principal and most important outside power, offering the benefits of military, security, and economic assistance in exchange for domestic peace and acquiescent foreign policies. The insurgency in El Salvador and the revolutionary triumph in Nicaragua upset this arrangement. In El Salvador's case, the Reagan administration funded and armed a $1 billion counterinsurgency effort, which included the services of at least 55 military advisors supporting the Salvadoran police, military, and, indirectly, local death squads. In Nicaragua, the centerpiece of Reagan's rollback policy in Central America, U.S. authorities helped to arm the Contras, some of whose leaders had fought with the Sandinistas but later lost out in the posttriumph power struggle.

Havana was well positioned to advise the revolutionaries in both countries not only on how to take power but also how to keep it. Unlike his own radical overhaul of Cuba, Fidel Castro advised Nicaraguan leaders such as Daniel Ortega and Tomás Borge not to unnecessarily antagonize the Catholic Church. Moreover, he encouraged them to maintain a mixed economy, work with the business community, and generally keep space open for the coalition of political actors that had helped the FSLN overthrow Somoza. But critically, Castro also knew the importance of establishing a monopoly on the use of force. His advisors helped the Sandinistas put together a new armed forces from scratch, as well as new police and intelligence services. On the social front, a steady stream of Cuban health and education teams flowed throughout the country, while Cuban techno-crats and managers helped design and carry out an ultimately stalled agrarian reform more modest in scope than Cuba's own. As the Reagan administration started training and arming the contra, Cuba stepped up its own efforts to counteract the U.S. destabilization campaign and urged the Sandinistas to resist. By 1989, however, Nicaragua's population was exhausted by nearly a decade of economic sanctions, psychological warfare, and counterinsurgency. Under American-led duress, Ortega agreed to permit presidential elections that year. Fidel regarded this concession as risking political suicide, and Ortega's loss to newspaper heiress and American darling Violeta Chomorro confirmed Havana's skepticism. This defeat, coupled with the collapse of the Soviet bloc and a wave of democratic transitions in South America, reinforced Fidel's belief that Cuba was ulti-mately better off solidifying its ties in the hemisphere through traditional diplomatic and commercial means.

The Salvadoran case was different. Fidel had played a major, if not definitive role in unifying five different armed groups into what ultimately became, in late 1980, the FMLN, the national liberation front named for a Salvadoran communist peasant organizer of the 1930s, Farabundo Martí (no relation to Cuba's national independence hero). Joined by a grouping of left-leaning political parties, the FMLN launched an offen-sive in 1981 that brought the country to a military stalemate by

1989. As with Nicaragua, Cuba provided training, weapons, financing, and a safe place for rest and rehab for Salvadoran guerrillas. Fidel's message of political unity within the revolutionary ranks and, ultimately, his behind-the-scenes role in peace talks were central to the Salvadoran Left's capacity, and the United States' willingness, to bring the government of Alfredo Cristiani to the negotiating table in 1991–92.

THE CUBAN REVOLUTION
AFTER THE COLD WAR,
1991–2006

DOMESTIC

How did the collapse of the Berlin Wall and dissolution
of the Soviet bloc affect Cuba?

Between 1989 and 1991, the rapid cascade of events that brought down Communist regimes in the Soviet Union and Eastern Europe delivered economic, psychological, geopolitical, and, some would say, nearly existential shocks to the Cuban system. Cuba had closely and skeptically watched the introduction of *glasnost* and *perestroika* in the late 1980s, and many young Cuban students on scholarship in Moscow, East Berlin, Dresden, Prague, and Warsaw had even lived the openings and subsequent political shifts directly. Closer to home, ideological tides were shifting as well, as both Cuba and the United States played constructive behind-the-scenes roles in the peace processes bringing an end to guerrilla insurgencies in Central America. Simultaneously, Cuba watched with horror as the Sandinistas in Nicaragua agreed to an election, and then lost it to the U.S.-backed candidate. All of these developments, coupled soon thereafter with movement in the U.S. Congress to tighten the embargo via Democrat-backed legislation, placed a shadow over celebrations of the 30th anniversary of the Cuban Revolution.

Nevertheless, although Gorbachev himself had visited Cuba in 1989 amidst a great wave of change, the new post–Cold

War reality did not really set in for Cuba until 1991. That year, following a series of meetings with U.S. Secretary of State James Baker, Gorbachev announced that the Soviet Union would end its $4 billion to $5 billion annual subsidy to the Cuban economy and begin withdrawing its advisors and troops from the island. This declaration kicked off the darkest period in Cuban revolutionary history. Just as in 1962, when Kennedy and Khrushchev cut a deal to end the Cuban Missile Crisis without consulting Fidel, the Americans and Soviets had once again excluded the Cuban side in their negotiations, deciding unilaterally to remove the Cuban thorn from their diplomatic sides in a move that had everything to do with global politics. If the Cuban Revolution's survival was put in jeopardy as a result of cutting off Castro, so be it, from Moscow and Washington's perspective. Without the Soviet subsidy and with Cuba's ties to Eastern Europe jeopardized as COMECON collapsed, Fidel had much more to worry about than a blow to his sense of propriety or pride. Feeding roughly 10 million people and holding the revolution together was Castro's new and urgent challenge.

How did Cuba adapt at home to the loss of Soviet subsidies and global realignment brought by the Cold War's end?

With the loss of the Soviet subsidy, the Cuban government recognized very quickly that nothing short of the revolution's survival was on the line. Facing a virtually overnight external shock that would cause the economy to contract by 34% between 1990 and 1993, Fidel declared that the island was entering a "Special Period in Times of Peace." This seemingly innocuous euphemism translated into devastating consequences. Government agencies were forced to sharply cut back social services, and Cubans saw the material conditions of daily life they had grown accustomed to over three decades precipitously deteriorate. Most dramatically and politically dangerous, food and electricity rapidly fell into very short supply. Rations that could once be supplemented by goods in state-run stores suddenly were cut; surpluses of anything disappeared. Cubans lost weight, became malnourished, contracted diseases like neuropathy from vitamin deficiency, and had to manage electricity blackouts of 12 to 15 hours at a time, often with only an hour or two of power daily to take care of basic needs. Gasoline vanished; cars and buses disappeared from the streets. The island's infrastructure, which had slowly shed its dependence on U.S. parts and technology, fell into further disrepair and decay as Soviet bloc and other western imports became either unavailable or too costly.

With such widespread economic devastation, the Communist collapse created a small window of breathing room in which the Cuban leadership allowed the introduction of changes that began, in limited but still significant ways, to reflect a new international reality. In 1992, for example, the National Assembly of People's Power approved a new constitution to replace the Soviet-era 1976 document. Four features especially demonstrated an awareness that the era of the Cold War and Soviet patronage had ended. First, the 1992 constitution disavowed the formerly atheistic nature of the Cuban state by recognizing the freedom of religion. Religious belief, therefore, was no longer an impediment to Cuban citizens wishing to hold elected or appointed office. Second, references to Soviet-style ideology and language regarding Marxism-Leninism and the Communist Party were significantly toned down; emphasis was given to the Cuban Communist Party as the party of national unity in the spirit of Jose Martí more than Vladimir Lenin. Third, the new constitution made some gestures—albeit far short of a full-scale "transition"—toward the decentralization and expansion of popular participation. Cubans would now vote directly for their People's Power representatives not only at the municipal level but also at the provincial and national levels. The constitution also allowed for a modicum of competition: Ballots could include a choice among a slate of candidates, albeit all members of the Communist Party, instead of just a choice of one candidate selected by the party. Fourth, in order to begin creating an improved investment climate, the new constitution explicitly recognized the ability of foreign joint ventures to legally own property. In the same period, Cuba would officially declare that all sectors of the economy—save public health, education, and the armed forces—were open for foreign investment, including, in theory, from Cuban Americans. And in 1995, the state would approve a new and complementary foreign investment law, one that provided greater security and incentive to invest in Cuba. The state was still required, however, to own a majority share of any joint venture.

Amidst these juridical changes and the legal, ideological, and political space they helped to open in Cuba, diplomats, economists, scholars, writers, and artists within the framework of party-approved institutions began to probe more directly—though not without some constraints—what Cuba could learn from debates in South America and Eastern Europe about societies in transition. Topics of great interest and intellectual fervor included the role of the state, the scope of civil society, the relationship between the two, and the role emerging for NGOs (some Cuban-based and international organizations were allowed to operate on the island during this period). Finally, and most important because of its impact on Cubans' daily lives, Cuba's intelligentsia fiercely discussed how to successfully reform the economy and the implications of any proposed reforms on the island's overarching Socialist framework.

Why didn't the regime collapse?

Speculation, especially outside of Cuba, that the revolution could not possibly survive the Soviet collapse began in 1989. Expectations of an imminent collapse only increased during the darkest years of the Special Period after the Soviet subsidy disappeared in 1991 and the United States tightened the embargo the following year. Books predicting Castro's "final hour" hit the stands. Yet even as domestic and international conditions seemed to point clearly toward change, and even when in the summer of 1992 blackouts were nearly permanent and genuine hunger ubiquitous, the regime did not collapse.

The answer to this puzzle is both simple and not entirely obvious. In essence, the island's government did not fall because the Cuban Revolution was not imposed by outside powers; it was homegrown. Even though Cuba came to rely for its economic lifeblood on its integration into the Soviet bloc, its political and ideological roots were nationalist, and deeply felt. Even amidst growing skepticism and frustration, made apparent during a 1994 riot in Central Havana known as the *maleconazo* and the concurrent *balsero* refugee crisis (see page 141, "What caused the 1994 *balsero* refugee crisis?"), many Cubans felt a sense of lasting ownership of their revolution that temporary allies in the Eastern bloc never felt, at least not as deeply. When the Soviet Union disappeared, Cuba was exposed and vulnerable on the material and security front, but the country also breathed a collective sigh of relief to no longer depend for their survival on an ideological and geopolitical taskmaster with whom they shared little cultural, political, geographic, or spiritual affinities. Thus, even in the context of terrible and debilitating material deprivation, leading Cuban thinkers embraced the opportunity to chart their own course and helped to usher in a period of enormous creative thinking. Fidel Castro's personal leadership and charisma during this time cannot be underestimated as a factor in Cuba's defiance and survival. Although he did personally oppose a more aggressive set of economic reforms that others in his cabinet, including his brother, supported, many Cuban people looked to Fidel, and not at the time to other political leaders, for solace and inspiration. It was through his ubiquitous presence that many Cubans, even as some of their neighbors receded into apathy or left for good, continued to see the revolution as a set of ideals in which they personally had a stake.

What were the regime's economic reforms, and why were they so limited?

Economic reforms adopted out of sheer survival instincts unfolded in three different iterations between the end of the Cold War and Fidel Castro's illness in 2006. But the most important window into the scope and limits of Cuba's economic reform process was the period between 1991, when the first shock hit, and 1995–96. In these later years, it became clear that Fidel Castro and the hard-liners in the party leadership would do only the minimum necessary to guarantee the revolution's survival, for fear that economic opening would be an invitation to the revolution's enemies in Miami and Washington to undermine internal unity.

Although in the early 1990s Cuban economists based at party-affiliated think tanks and institutions debated a wide variety of potential economic openings, both in terms of scope and pace, their debates took place clearly within the framework of how to preserve the fundamental tenets of Cuban socialism. Equality and inclusion, with the state playing the role of guaranteeing the basic welfare of Cuba's citizens, remained at the center of the discussion. What changed was the introduction of the notion, virtually anathema until then, that the market— the free market, the capitalist market—might actually be a tool Cuba could somehow harness in the interests of socialism and social welfare. This discussion was approached in what can only be described as a gingerly manner, because even in the direst circumstances of the early 1990s, Fidel never let anyone forget his profound allergy to the profit, accumulation, avarice, and social inequality inherent in the market. Yet, there were others close to Fidel, like his brother Raul, or the man who came to be known as the economy czar, Carlos Lage, who understood that some experimentation with the market might actually save the revolution from the dire potential consequences of Fidel's penchant for orthodoxy.

By 1994, Cuban authorities had implemented the bulk of an economic reform program designed to help Cuba adapt to the new global environment. Among the first steps, Cuba opened up farmers' markets where growers were allowed to sell their produce directly to Cuban consumers. Cuban state farms were also converted to cooperatives, and authorities somewhat relaxed the regulations governing the *acopio*, the state collection and procurement system linking agricultural producers to consumers. Together, these measures increased food production and allowed citizens to fulfill basic necessities at a time when the ration system could not do so.

The government also legalized the possession of the U.S. dollar. Cubans with relatives abroad, predominantly in the United States, had taken to receiving dollar remittances to supplement their woefully inadequate state salaries. Thus, the dollar had become the growing black market's currency of preference, although holding foreign currency was still a crime punishable by law. By legalizing possession of the dollar in 1993 and allowing it to operate alongside the traditional Cuban peso, the Cuban central bank may have tacitly acknowledged the power of the black market, but it was also able to mop up at least some dollars circulating in the underground economy. It opened *casas de cambio* where Cubans could exchange pesos for dollars and vice versa, and it opened special "dollar stores" with western consumer goods and some locally produced hygiene and food items largely unavailable in peso-only shops or through the ration system.

To spur economic activity, the government authorized citizens to engage in limited private activities, commonly referred to as "self-employment" or *trabajo de cuenta propia*. Under these reforms, Cubans were permitted to sell their skills in about 200 categories of basic services: repairs, taxi driving, personal hygiene, and the like. An important subset of these activities was oriented more explicitly, but not exclusively, toward the growing tourism industry, a key focus of a renewed foreign investment strategy. Cubans were permitted to open *paladares* (small restaurants located usually in the homes of the families who owned and operated them) as well as *casa particulares* (bed and breakfasts), renting out rooms to foreigners by the night, week, or month. By design, all of these transactions would take place in dollars, with the expectation that the government would be able to capture some of the revenues for state expenditures through taxes and other fees. Yet state mechanisms for taxing the self-employed encountered public resistance, and many owners did their best to avoid regulations. As a result, in a decade of tiny steps toward private enterprise, the self-employed sector would experience a roller coaster of relative flexibility followed by crackdowns on their operations.

Despite these limited small business and agricultural reforms, the scarcity of money and other resources during the Special Period caused a significant degree of material hardship. City dwellers noted a decline in pet ownership and cats and dogs; many speculated hunger had become so dire that desperate Cubans sought protein wherever they could find it. The search for food occupied a huge portion of each family's daily life, creating havoc in productivity and disenchanting many Cubans—especially a younger generation—with the promises of the revolution. At the same time, such scarcity inspired a number of practices that can only be described as ahead of their time for developing countries. Beginning in the early 1990s, urban gardens sprang up all over Cuban cities, from Havana to Santiago. A cuisine centered largely around pork, beef, and poultry was forced by circumstances to shift to soy, an unwelcome entry into Cuban culinary habits, but also seafood, an export that few Cubans, other than those who could afford lobster, really knew what to do with. Rice, beans, and bread remained staples, but over the course of the 1990s and into the 2000s, more fruits, vegetables, and fare for the omnivore returned to the diet. Public education campaigns extended from how to cook and eat in the Special Period to how to stop smoking, drink less, and—as the economy recovered and weight gain replaced weight loss—get enough exercise. Although Cuba remained heavily dependent on imports for its food, as the world price of sugar in the 1990s steadily dropped, the government actively shrank Cuba's sugar industry and reduced the amount of land dedicated to sugar cane. Though many anticipated and argued forcefully for a transformation of sugar-producing land to that for the production of edible foods, Cuban agriculture, with some important exceptions of ventures into organic and specialty produce for export, failed to adapt to the island's new circumstances.

What kind of foreign investment began in Cuba, what consequences did this investment bring to the island, and how did authorities respond?

Another key component of Cuba's economic reforms was the pursuit of foreign investment to stimulate ailing industries and renew the activity of others. Cuba's new joint venture law—known as Law No. 77—created the framework for a limited but still economically significant level of foreign investment to come into the island (under $4 billion between 1994 and 2004). The Cuban government was extremely leery of allowing too rapid of an opening and, despite declaring that all but a handful of sectors were open to foreign participation, only welcomed foreign capital in a limited number of them. As with other reforms, Cuba's new "openness" to foreign investment was contingent on these investments taking place in a regulatory and financial context the Cuban government could directly control. Cuba's tourism, mining, energy, telecommunications, and biotechnology industries, along with tobacco, rum, citrus, and fishing, were the primary sectors open to foreign investment, with capital from Spain, Canada, France, the UK, Germany, Brazil, Israel, Italy, and Mexico among the first to enter. Under Cuba's employment laws, companies requiring Cuban labor were prohibited from directly hiring Cuban workers; instead, they were and are still today required to purchase Cuban labor from a state institution in dollars. Cuban workers are then paid in Cuba's less valuable domestic currency. Such practices have drawn criticism for depriving workers of direct payment or autonomous collective bargaining power. Over time, however, some pay structures allowed for Cubans to be paid partly in domestic currency and partly in dollars or other foreign currencies (although under-the-table, illegal tips in hard currency were also still widespread in many workplaces). As a result, many highly skilled Cuban professionals started to abandon their state jobs—doctors, nurses, professors, engineers—in search of employment in the foreign sector, a trend that fundamentally reinforced the public's negative and skeptical views of the government's antimarket economic orthodoxy.

The resurgent tourism industry was perhaps the most significant target of foreign investment. Beginning in the early 1990s, Cuba's tourism officials began planning for a total of 10 million visitors per year, with an eye eventually on the American market. But in the interim, Canadian, European, and, more recently, South American, Chinese, and Japanese tourists flooded the island's beaches, colonial cities, and cultural and architectural attractions. With significant Spanish and other European investment in the construction of new hotel chains and all-inclusive resorts, the industry soon became Cuba's top earner of foreign exchange, along with remittances, mining, and medical services. But it also catalyzed a surge in prostitution and all manner of hustling (of black market cigars, rum, and other products) from Cubans—often with professional degrees—who found it easier, if also degrading, to make a real living with these activities. At times, Cuban authorities and society reacted with horror at the spectacle of teenage prostitution, and cracked down. At others, anecdotal evidence suggests that authorities turned a blind eye, tacitly recognizing that prostitution and the black market go hand in hand with tourism, especially in environments of scarcity and strong state control. Still, in an effort to shelter some visitors from these practices, authorities began prohibiting Cubans themselves from going to beaches and hotels designated for foreign tourists, a practice that earned the resentment of Cubans at home and accusations of "tourism apartheid" abroad. Seen in historical perspective, the resurgence of tourism was certainly necessary economically but also deeply ironic. After all, in the 1960s, the revolution had sought to wipe tourism off the map, seeing the industry as an outpost of the American mob and a disparaging sign of the island's neocolonial status.

During much of this period, the Cuban military assumed a predominant role in overseeing and administering those sectors of the economy most attractive to foreign investors. In the wake of the Cold War, facing sharp budget cuts and a slackening international profile, the Ministry of Defense gradually evolved into the strategic and financial hub for the island's tourism, real estate, sugar, and other agricultural industries. Much of this was accomplished through state-administered umbrella companies like Gaviota, CIMEX, and Cubanacan—all coordinated by the Business Administration Group (GAESA), headquartered at the Ministry of Defense. Often, flag officers retired to comfortable sinecures managing these enterprises. Technocrats from Cuba's best schools were then recruited to oversee the finances and travel abroad seeking investment. To provide one example, Gaviota, the youngest and fastest growing of the military-run state enterprises, today controls 20% to 25% of Cuba's hotel rooms in partnerships with foreign companies. By the end of the 1990s, the Cuban military had become self-financing and its economic involvement helped generate a political power base for Raul Castro and his closest deputies.

Foreign investment might have saved Cuba's economy from imminent collapse. Yet with abysmally low state wages, a thriving dollar-denominated black market, and only 30% to 40% of the Cuban population with access to remittances from family members abroad, the inequality Cuba had long sought to ameliorate, if never fully eliminate, reappeared as a noticeable societal ill. The Cuban government's decision to strictly limit the amount of foreign investment that would enter Cuba, as well as U.S. pressure against foreign countries and companies considering Cuba as an investment, only aggravated the problem by preventing a broader slate of capital flows from bringing benefits to a wider range of the population. Yet although many Cubans were frustrated with the unequal terms and restrictions of Cuba's limited opening to the market, they, like Fidel Castro, also feared that a wholesale opening would only further undermine the revolution's commitment to social equality and the revolution's legitimacy. With Cuba's enemies in Washington and Miami preaching the virtues of open markets, globalization, and the Washington Consensus, often as part and parcel of their vision for the island's future, it was easy for government officials to capitalize on popular fears of dislocations from rapid market openings and circle the nationalist wagons in defense of a continuing, dominant role for the state in the island's economic affairs. After over 30 years of an ethos of equality and social justice, Cubans across the island bristled at the prospect of inequality even as they participated in black-market activities that drove its growth.

The government eventually halted any push toward further reforms. Moreover, in the early portion of the new millennium, as Cuba's international economic position began to benefit from an environment of rising commodity prices as well as growing external support from Venezuela (see page 138, "Did Cuba attempt to emulate any other economic models in this period?"), the state reasserted a degree of control over those sectors that had seen substantial liberalization. State enterprises were banned from operating in dollars and were required to switch to the CUC in 2003 (a parallel currency to the dollar with no international value, created in 1994 to boost the island's dollar-driven economy). The peso-CUC exchange rate, and before that, the peso-dollar exchange rate, hovered in the area of 25:1. Likewise, new measures required the Central Bank to approve all hard currency transactions by state enterprises. In part to stem the tide of corruption, officials, members of the military, and state administrators were barred from participating in self-employment schemes, while employers and workers in the tourist industry faced greater restrictions on their interactions with guests and their ability to accept hard currency gifts/tips. New licenses for *paladares* and *casas particulares* were dramatically curtailed, with existing license holders facing increased taxes and restrictions on their activities.

Did Cuba attempt to emulate any other economic models in this period?

Throughout the 1980s and 1990s, Communist regimes in former Soviet bloc countries, Russia, China, and Vietnam as well as authoritarian governments in South America began shedding the trappings of statism to varying degrees and ends. In such an international context, it was only natural for observers abroad and some scholars on the island to begin asking what lessons Cuba might draw from the various transitions occurring beyond its shores. But Cuba's path throughout the 1990s remained a hybrid one, with small concessions to private enterprise and pockets of foreign investment combined with significant public sector investments in health, education, and infrastructure. All the while, state payrolls didn't pay workers enough to get by and certainly didn't provide incentives for the kind of productivity that Cuba's faltering industries desperately needed. Although Cuba did not and has not emulated any particular model, its leadership, economists, scholars, and population as a whole are not unaware of the alternatives. All of the top senior government officials traveled during this period to Asia, Europe, and Latin America, as have Cuban economists, scholars, and the managers who run the military's umbrella businesses. Why, then, didn't Cuba embark on bolder reforms? According to many of those elite Cuban officials who most closely studied transitions abroad at the time—some of whom may have even been sympathetic to more ambitious changes—because of its size (tiny), its proximity to the empire (but a sneeze away), and the designs on its riches by some eager exiles, Cuba after the Cold War did not have the luxury to retain one-party control while opening the economy, as in

Vietnam, for example. Moreover, a barrage of studies funded by the U.S. government or conducted by Cuban American economists abroad spun out scenarios for various transition models Cuba might undertake, also placing regime officials on the defensive. By this time, a shrinking faction of the increasingly diverse Cuban American community genuinely aspired to reclaim economic, let alone political control of the island. Yet with backing from such companies as Bacardi and support from old-line families whose former properties were being developed for the growing tourism industry, Cuban American legislators continued advocating increasingly aggressive U.S. policies over the course of the 1990s, some of which resulted in new laws to help exiles recover nationalized property and block foreign investment on the island. These dynamics, combined with the opposition by senior Cuban officials to opening the door too quickly (including, most important, Fidel himself), meant that the political and ideological breathing room necessary for broader economic liberalization in Cuba just wasn't in the cards. As the Cuban government saw it and as the Cuban population was keenly aware, the threat and lure of the United States was a constant reminder of the potential consequences of instability on the island. Control over property and economic activity was the heart and soul of the island's future. Cubans off the island understood these stakes as well.

How did artists manage to pull off such a cultural boom in the 1990s?

A convergence of factors—both internal and external—inspired Cuba's cultural boom at the time. Artists benefited from additional state resources and support, greater room to maneuver and create, and increased market demand (particularly abroad) for Cuban artistry.

With the onset of the Special Period, the cultural sector, accustomed to receiving resources from the government, found itself cut off. The first years of the economic crisis witnessed a drastic reduction in the variety and number of books published, theater and cinema productions, television programs, and other cultural activities. After recovering from this initial shock, cultural organizations and individual artists discovered that as the government lost the capacity to support them, it simultaneously lost some of its capacity to control their art. Thus, despite continuing self and external censorship, artists were able to push the boundaries like never before, touching on themes (migration, exile, and the state's economic ineffi-ciencies) previously considered taboo (while others remained unmentionable). Starting in the early 1990s, the government also opened up aspects of the cultural sector to partnership with foreign companies, making financing and resources more readily available for Cuban artists. Joint ventures between Cuban artists and foreign investors became common, espe-cially within the film and music industries. Indeed, the films of Cuba's well-known and internationally renowned Institute of Cinematographic Arts and Industry (ICAIC) may not have survived without foreign partnerships. Likewise, well-known (and politically reliable) Cuban artists and musicians were granted greater freedom to travel abroad, tour internationally, partner with foreign companies, and keep a handsome portion of the earnings for themselves.

Externally, a number of dynamics drew attention to the island's cultural production as well. In the wake of the Cold War, Cuba became not only one of the last remaining Commu-nist regimes on earth but also one of the few to resist broader economic liberalization. As a result, during a decade where globalization was a buzzword and the spread of global mass commercial culture was celebrated by some intellectuals and denigrated by others, Cuba became a kind of historical artifact, seeming to echo or reinforce idyllic visions of a decommercial-ized past. Such conceptions fueled not only a significant portion of Cuba's draw as a tourist destination but also a renewed attraction to Cuban artists and music. Moreover, beginning in 1987, a crack in the U.S. information embargo opened up when Congress passed what came to be known as the Berman amendment, for Congressman Howard Berman of California. Crafted to protect the First Amendment rights violated by the ban on American travel to Cuba, the new law allowed Americans to import "informational material," interpreted as not only printed material but also any form of creative expression, including music, visual art, sculpture, etc. These liberalized cultural exchange policies under the Clinton administration, coupled with the growing power of digital technology, increased access to a veritable treasure trove of past and present Cuban art that had by and large not received significant Western attention. Perhaps the most prominent example and indeed the catalyst for Cuba's cultural boom abroad was the Buena Vista Social Club, a collaboration of Cuban musicians; American ethnomusicologist, musician, guitarist, and composer Ry Cooder; and later, German filmmaker Wim Wenders. The resulting album and documentary became international sensations, spawning a resurgence of traditional Cuban *son* music throughout Cuba, the United States, and the world, and helping to breathe new life into the work of once towering musicians who had all but disappeared from public view. A quite different but equally important example was the growth of Cuban rap music during this period. Even in Cuba, where access to digital technology, music equipment, and (later in the decade) the Internet remained extremely limited, the globalization of culture could not be stopped as Afro-Cubans were inspired by American hip-hop to create their own local interpretation of the urban art form, strongly criticizing the re-emergence of racism during the Special Period as well as voicing a wide variety of economic, social, and political complaints. To varying degrees, the state has sought to support, suppress, or co-opt this diverse movement.

What caused the 1994 balsero refugee crisis?

By the summer of 1994, three years into the Special Period, seemingly endless rolling blackouts, food and water shortages, deteriorating health conditions, and a decaying infrastructure, combined with the absence of adequate mechanisms to manage migration from Cuba to the United States, brought social tensions into acute relief. Not since the 1980 Mariel boatlift had public discontent been so high. That July, a group of Cubans hijacked a tugboat seven miles outside of Havana harbor. Rather than stopping the boat and arresting the hijackers, however, the Cuban coast guard chased it down and used high-pressure fire hoses in an attempt to impede its movement, an incident that ultimately resulted in the sinking of the boat and the deaths of 41 on board. The political damage of this episode left a legacy: The Cuban regime would no longer attempt to impede illegal attempts to leave the island, unless the United States (where liberal immigration laws and the presence of the Cuban American community implicitly beckoned Cubans to risk their lives at sea) would sign an immigration agreement providing for safe and legal migration between the island and U.S. territory.

A number of other boat and ferry hijackings followed. Migration pressures were clearly on the rise. Then, in August, a small riot broke out in a working-class neighborhood of downtown Havana. At least several hundred rioters—mostly young men, hot, hungry, and with no viable way to make a living—aimed their ire directly at the government's failures and directly at Fidel himself. The riots didn't last long, and no one was really hurt: Fidel Castro himself showed up not long after police arrived on the scene, and the event ended almost as quickly as it began. But it offered a palpable view of the anger and frustration pulsating through Cuba at the time. Clearly, the government needed an escape valve to let off some of the steam.

As in 1980, the Cuban government announced that it would not get in the way of those attempting to leave. Moreover, authorities made it clear that they would hold the United States responsible for failing to provide a safe mechanism and reliable number of visas for those Cubans wishing to migrate. Innovation and desperation carried the day. In boats at first, then in wide varieties of floating vessels made of inner tubes, wood, and even the shells of abandoned cars, increasing numbers of Cuban *balseros,* or "rafters," began departing for Florida, eventually by the thousands. Their plight inspired art, literature, poetry, and, ultimately, tragedy. Although nearly somewhere between 35,000 and 40,000 Cubans eventually made it to the United States—either directly or after being picked up by the U.S. Coast Guard and interned at Guantánamo for a time—no one knows exactly how many people who left the island perished at sea. Beyond the cost in human life and the disruption to Cuban families and society, the *balsero* crisis forced the United States to negotiate migration agreements with Cuba that remain in effect to this day, guaranteeing a minimum of 20,000 visas annually for Cuban citizens to migrate to the United States safely and legally (details of the agreement are on page 165, "How did the United States and Cuba resolve the 1994 refugee crisis?").

How did the Cuban health care system fare in this period?

Health care remains one of the revolution's flagship achievements and is recognized as such not only by Cubans themselves but also by governments, international organizations, and poor citizens around the world who have directly benefited from Cuba's global health policies. Keeping the population healthy in the aftermath of a significant blow to the economy was essential to sustaining the revolution's social contract. Thus, even as the budget for the armed forces was slashed permanently, budgets for health care recovered and even began to show modest increases as Cuba moved beyond the darkest years of the Special Period. But budgets don't really tell the whole story; priorities do. Cuba's health care system is based on primary and preventive care, with front-loaded investments going to maternal, infant, and child health. A system of neighborhood or family doctors makes access to such basic care readily available. By the late 1990s, after recovering from the initial blow to the entire population's nutritional intake, the revolution was able to devote more money to its primary care system and increase the training of new health care professionals, both from Cuba and other countries around the world—even young medical students from the United States.

Nonetheless, the deprivation, emerging inequality, neglect, and corruption evident in the rest of Cuban society during this period also crept into the health care system. Access to doctors remained relatively easy, but it became harder and harder to find pharmacies with medicines to fill their prescriptions. Likewise, with the consolidation of global health care multinationals and the U.S. embargo's ban on imports of products with more than 5% American content, finding parts to replace mammogram, radiology, and cancer treatment equipment, for example, was no easy task. Neither was finding appropriate substitutes for U.S. patented drugs. Loopholes in U.S. law for sales of medicine and medical products made little appreciable difference because of the licensing, on-site verification, and politics involved. Especially during the dark days of the early 1990s, performing surgery with the help of generators during blackouts, and often with reused equipment, presented a number of risks. Hospitalization brought its own set of challenges, many of which persist today. Patients were required to bring their own bedding, food, and hygiene products with them. Staffing, when reliant solely on peso salaries, became increasingly unpredictable, and depending on the hospital administrator, conditions in Cuban hospitals ran the gamut from the gleaming, first-rate institutions depicted in Michael Moore's 2007 film *Sicko* to dilapidated, decayed facilities lacking resources.

Likewise, as dollars and foreign tourists became a part of Cuban life, the health care system sought to capture the new market. Health tourism grew, with visitors from Latin America especially coming to Cuba for specialized care, paid for in dollars. Often the best health care facilities and resources were reserved for these hard-currency carrying visitors. Top

Communist Party leaders also tended to have access to health-care sites with more ample resources, leading many critics of the Castro government to denounce the practice of what they called "health care apartheid."

Despite these challenges and missteps, Cuba continued to send its health care professionals to remote parts of nearly every continent around the world on humanitarian missions (as it would memorably do in Pakistan after the 2006 earthquake and Indonesia after the 2004 tsunami), where they were effective at providing relief services and flying the flag of Cuba's humani-tarian ethos. With about one of every three Cuban doctors working overseas, Cuban medical professionals rank among Cuba's most lucrative sources of human capital, with countries paying for their services in hard currency (with only a portion of the fees going to Cuban doctors themselves) or providing another hot world commodity in exchange. Most notably, in the case of Venezuela, the government of Hugo Chávez has benefited from the assistance of more than 20,000 Cuban physi-cians in exchange for subsidized supplies of oil to Cuba. Like-wise, since 1996 South Africa has paid the Cuban government to supply physicians to hospitals across the country in response to the flight of many of its own doctors in the postapartheid era. On the street, Cubans occasionally complained that so many of their doctors were being sent abroad.

Nonetheless, not only did the health care system on the island hold together during this trying period, but also today Cubans are far less likely to suffer malnutrition, malaria, or other typical third-world afflictions than they are medical prob-lems common in developed countries, such as heart disease (with the occasional but always rapidly contained outbreak of dengue fever). On the global stage, Cuba's health care record remains undeniably strong. Indeed, according to UNICEF's reporting on the status of the world's children, Cuba's infant mortality rates—at 5.3 deaths per every 1,000 births—are lower than any other country in the Americas except for Canada. Life expectancy on the island, at nearly 78 years, is on par with that of the United States. Similarly, Cuba's records on immunizations for children and maternal health are among the best in the developing world and are virtually on par with (and sometimes superior to) many countries within the developed world. Today, Cuba spends 43% of its national budget on health, education, and social security.

How did Cuba cope with HIV/AIDS?

The Cuban state has become well known for intruding upon the private choices of Cuban citizens, but the bedroom has eluded its reach. It is not uncommon for married and single men and women to have multiple partners, a practice potentially conducive to a rapid spread of HIV. The conventional but unconfirmed wisdom in Cuba is that HIV/AIDS arrived on the island as Cuban soldiers returned from Africa at the end of the 1980s and early 1990s. The first case was diagnosed in late 1985.

The Cuban government has implemented a number of programs to successfully contain and combat the spread of the disease, especially important as the tourist industry grew and authorities tacitly recognized the resurgence of prostitution. Even before the first Cuban case was diagnosed, in 1983 health officials launched a nationwide AIDS education program. Cuba also began investing in awareness and prevention programs, which are fully subsidized and readily available to all its citizens. Other strategies, including the controversial practice of isolating all patients diagnosed with the virus (suspended in 1993), received sharp criticism from some for being draconian, despite their effectiveness in containing the spread of HIV/AIDS.

A combination of quarantine and mandatory testing helped contain HIV rates in Cuba close to 0.5% in the 1990s, and AIDS-related deaths totaled 1,300 between 1991 and 2006. Compare this to the broader Caribbean, where HIV infection rates are among the highest in the world (at 2.3%), second only to sub-Saharan Africa (9%). By 2005, Cuba had 6,782 confirmed cases of HIV, and less than 2,800 cases of full-blown AIDS. In the Dominican Republic, by contrast, a country with a significantly smaller population than Cuba, as many as 77,000 people currently have HIV, with on the order of 6,000 to 7,000 patients dying of AIDS each ear. With neighboring Haiti, the contrast is even starker, with AIDS killing 30,000 people every year. The UN has recognized the extremely low infection rate in Cuba and in 2006 hailed the island's program as "among the most effective in the world." Notably, in Cuba only 29 children have become infected with HIV in the past 20 years as Cuba has effectively prevented mother-to-child transmission of HIV, mainly due to the government's universal provision of antiretroviral therapy, which became broadly available in 2001.

In the late 1990s, Cuba's pharmaceutical labs also developed a generic HIV test kit, exporting it for sale and as donations to developing countries around the world. At home, massive public education campaigns helped create the space to begin addressing homosexuality as a fact of life rather than as a forbidden and historically repressed component of Cuban society and culture. Furthermore, Cuba's provision of openly accessible therapy has led fewer HIV-positive women to seek abortions than in the past, effectively addressing one of the difficult social challenges that often accompanies the disease.

How did human rights fare more generally during this period?

Those looking for the end of the Cold War to transform Cuba into a western liberal democracy were sorely disappointed. Organized opposition parties and groups remained proscribed, free speech and assembly continued to be repressed, and, although their numbers had vastly diminished, political prisoners still languished in Cuban jails. (By the end of the 1990s, the number of political prisoners hovered in the range of 200 to 300.)

From the perspective of the Cuban government, the Reagan administration's strong effort to press the issue of human rights on Havana and the world was politically motivated and deeply hypocritical in light of U.S. support for right-wing military regimes in Central America and elsewhere at the time. During the 1990s, and beyond, Cuban academics and officials within state-sanctioned institutions did actively discuss the topic of human rights, with some quietly pushing for greater openings. Yet with liberal western states in Europe, North America, and Latin America—Cuba's new trading partners—gradually embracing the international human rights agenda, Cuba's claim to exclusive sovereignty over its internal matters became a much tougher sell. As coalitions of international NGOs, Cuban American organizations, and foreign governments shined a spotlight on human rights violations in Cuba, sorting through the who's who and what's what of the issue became increasingly difficult, polarized, and ideological. In addition to calling attention to abuses, human rights groups from the United States and activists from former Soviet allies like Poland and the Czech Republic, as well as their governments, began actively channeling greater resources, some from U.S. federal agencies, directly to Cuban human rights activists on the island. Cuba's dissidents faced an impossible position. They lacked resources and the means to communicate with the broader Cuban public, tools that foreign support could theoretically provide. Yet in light of decades of American attempts to unseat the regime, receiving funds from external sources (or simply the perception of being willing to do so) cast a pall of suspicion over their activities, leading to accusations that they were mere lackeys of foreign interests. As a result, Cuban activists found it difficult to build domestic legitimacy—especially when they were perceived to be close to the U.S. government or those Cuban Americans perceived to have adopted the ethos of human rights only to position themselves to benefit from the revolution's collapse.

The Cuban government has offered a variety of responses to outside pressure and foreign support for internal anti-regime opposition activities. At times, the regime has infiltrated existing dissident groups; at others, authorities have simply ignored them. Additional tactics include public attacks (conducted by state-organized mobs in what are known as *actos de repudio*, or "acts of repudiation") as well as more subtle forms of harassment, such as spying on dissidents themselves, their family members, and others suspected of receiving foreign government and/or Cuban exile largesse. Yet old-fashioned jailings and mass arrests, while certainly not as frequent as, say, in the early years of the revolution, did not disappear entirely. In March of 2003, for example, human rights activists were dealt one of their most significant blows since the end of the Cold War when authorities arrested some 75 independent journalists, prodemocracy organizers, and other dissidents. In what became known as the "black spring," Cuban officials targeted those individuals allegedly collaborating with or receiving funds from the U.S. government, Cuban American groups, and/or international organizations agitating for more democracy and human rights. No such widespread action has occurred since.

Of course, repression and intimidation alone are not what keep dissident movements on the island weak and disorganized today. For reasons explored elsewhere in this chapter (see page 129, "Why didn't the regime collapse?"), despite profound popular disillusion, the Cuban Revolution does retain domestic sources of legitimacy that limit the extent to which dissident activists might gain a foothold. Outside actors supporting nascent human rights/dissident groups in the hopes of recreating Poland's Solidarity movement or Czechoslovakia's Velvet Revolution may very well be chasing unrealistic dreams. Still, the repressive tactics and human rights violations of Cuban authorities keep small remaining groups isolated and off-balance.

What was the Varela Project and what is its significance?

In the last 15 years, one outspoken and internationally well-known government critic has navigated Cuba's difficult domestic terrain more successfully than any other: Oswaldo Payá, leader of the Christian Liberation Movement. Payá's work focused on a little-known provision of the 1992 Cuban Constitution, Article 88, that allows citizens to introduce initiatives to be voted on through a national referendum, so long as they collect at least 10,000 signatures of registered voters in support of the proposed initiative. With a host of organizers, Payá set about drafting a petition of sorts, calling for five fundamental reforms: democratic elections, free speech, free enterprise, free assembly, and freedom for political prisoners. Inspired by Father Felix Varela, a 19th-century priest who advocated for Cuba's independence from Spain, they called their initiative the Varela Project. All the while, Payá never too firmly embraced U.S. or European supporters, although they certainly embraced him, rather too tightly.

In 2002, Payá presented 11,000 signatures backing the Varela Project to the National Assembly of People's Power in Cuba, coinciding with former president (and human rights champion) Jimmy Carter's historic trip to the island. After meeting with Payá, Carter gave the Varela Project his full endorsement during his uncensored and nationally televised speech at the University of Havana. In response, the Cuban government held its own referendum, in which Cuba's population was compelled, tacitly if not overtly, to vote overwhelmingly—with 8 million votes—in favor of declaring the irrevocable nature of Cuban socialism and amending the constitution as such.

The Varela Project is significant for a number of reasons, but not necessarily for its success. Payá's referendum proposal went nowhere in the face of the Cuban government's own dramatic response. Nonetheless, Payá was perhaps the first activist to attempt, on a wider scale, to use the legal means of the Cuban state to express profound opposition to the lack of democracy in

Cuba. And the Cuban state, rather than blatantly repressing the initiative, was compelled to instead overwhelm it with its own counterproposal. Because of the attention that Carter's visit had brought to Payá, and because Cuban authorities at the time still hoped for a marginal improvement in the bilateral relationship with Washington, they could not afford a repressive incident. Just a year later, though, when circumstances were different and international attention not focused on Cuba, the regime would arrest over 40 Varela Project organizers (though never Payá himself) during the "black spring." Nonetheless, despite this delayed repression, at the time of Payá's proposal, and even subsequently, the government tacitly recognized that the general sentiments of the Varela Project could well have been shared more broadly, including among some working within the regime's officially sanctioned institutions. This, too, perhaps muted the government's response to some degree.

Moreover, despite vituperative rhetoric from some Cuban officials denouncing Payá as a foreign agent, most were well aware that Payá's tactics of working "within the system" had earned him the ire of traditional exile hard-liners as well as hawks in the U.S. government hoping to avoid any kind of negotiated transition in Havana. Indeed, although his group allied itself with the Christian Democrat International, a network of socially conservative, free-market political parties, many of Payá's proposals attracted adherents of social democracy as well. In addition to opposing aspects of U.S. policy (calling on the United States to "de-Americanize" the Cuba issue), Payá supported the role of the state in providing health care and education, and consistently spoke of the need for reconciliation.

The regime's ability to quickly organize a counterreferendum demonstrated its prowess at mass mobilization and cooptation. Likewise, the government's targeting of Varela Project activists the next year signaled an abiding willingness to repress dissent. Yet, by 2005, subtle signs that the regime was indeed tuned into and worried about popular discontent began to surface in public. In November of that year, Fidel acknowledged in a speech that the revolution could cause its own demise, and without ever using the term *human rights,* Cuba's top leadership initiated a public dialogue about the kinds of conditions and practices the government would have to amend if it wanted to save the revolution. These discussions would only accelerate after Fidel Castro's illness sidelined him in 2006. The Varela Project was in no way directly responsible for this coming to terms. But because it articulated some criticisms of the regime that were shared within respected state institutions, and because it did so without appearing to be as much a tool or creation of outside actors as other dissident initiatives, the decision by the regime to allow the Varela Project to survive, even in a very low-key way, may have foreshadowed, if only by a matter of timing, the public's eagerness for and the government's capacity to manage a wider public debate about the revolution's future without risking counterrevolutionary upheaval.

What kind of space did the regime permit for intellectuals, especially those involved in debates over economic reform?

Beginning with the onset of the rectification process in 1987 (see page 71, "What was 'rectification'? How did Fidel and Raul Castro view the prospect of market reforms in the 1980s?"), and compounded by the collapse of the Soviet Union, the Cuban government began opening up certain sectors of Cuban society to increased debate. The economy emerged as the natural and most critical topic as Cuba faced the loss of its Soviet/Eastern European trading partners. The question was not whether or not to implement a program of substantial economic reform, but how and how fast. Yet even though the regime allowed harsh criticism of the government's economic failures to emerge during the course of these debates, the parameters of the discussion were significantly more constricted when it came to possible solutions for the country's economic shortcomings. The fundamentally

Socialist character of the island would be preserved, with the state as the critical arbiter of economic affairs.

Beyond strictly economic themes, written arguments and critiques of Cuban politics, society, and culture—again, all within the framework of socialism—appeared with increasing frequency in state-run literary publications. Indeed, some Cuban scholars refer to the period between 1993 and 1995 as a sort of "golden era" for Cuban intellectual freedom. Civil society networks and NGOs not directly affiliated with state umbrella institutions were allowed to operate with greater freedom as long as their activities remained largely apolitical and were not associated with opposition activism. Yet after 1995, this increased space was curtailed, with authorities strengthening restrictions on Cuban NGOs, specifically on those that partnered with international, especially U.S., organizations. This fluctuating pattern of relative degrees of openness and retreat has characterized revolutionary Cuba throughout its history and continues to this day.

A number of Cuba's most well-known intellectuals, initially with the protection and support of senior Communist Party officials, tested the limits of permissible economic and political critiques. Some tentatively explored elements of the West's concept of civil society, supporting greater autonomy for established organizations linked to the state as a way of broadening democratic channels in the making of public policy. Others developed proposals for major reforms of the Cuban economy, all while retaining the Socialist character of the government. But by 1996, the key institutions housing these debates were purged. Individuals most closely associated with ideas for reforming the state, all Communist Party members, landed in other posts, some in Havana and some abroad.

How did space for organized religion evolve during this period?

As described on page 127 ("How did Cuba adapt at home to the loss of Soviet subsidies and global realignment brought by the Cold War's end?"), the 1992 Cuban constitution explicitly affirmed all Cuban citizens' freedom to practice religion, thus clearing the way for religious believers to become members of the Cuban Communist Party. In an atmosphere of increased tolerance, organized religion experienced a dramatic boom, with congregations of varying stripes emerging from their quiet and even repressed past existences to reclaim a strong place in Cuban cultural life. Daily and especially Sunday Catholic masses filled. Methodists, Episcopalians, Baptists, Presbyterians, and Jehovah's Witnesses rediscovered their churches, encouraging new congregants to join their ranks. With outside support, training for new priests and ministers began, and as in the rest of Latin America, evangelical churches popped up, especially in Cuban cities. The Jewish community, which had shrunk from a high of 15,000 European war refugees to under 500 individuals by the 1980s, experienced a renewal as well with support from the Jewish communities of Mexico, the United States, and Canada especially. Among these varying groups, the Catholic Church maintained the most institutional weight. The Vatican stepped up an all-but-nonexistent dialogue with the Cuban government, which garnered the church enough leeway to create a space, as well as a resource for the needy, relatively independent of the Cuban state. Relationships between churches in communities in Cuba and the United States further helped provide the resources for rebuilding and expansion, all the while connecting Cubans to the United States in ways neither government could perfectly manage. Meanwhile, the syncretic practice of Santería, always a consistent part of daily life under the revolution, showed no signs of weakening, neither among traditional Afro-Cuban adherents nor among Cubans of all races who incorporated the popular lore of the faith into their lives to varying degrees. Even as Cuban citizens began to openly practice their more western Christian faiths and join or rejoin organized Christian and other religious institutions, the rituals, symbolism, and belief system of Santería remained common.

The Cuban state endeavored to manage this boom and contain its potential political consequences. The Communist Party's Central Committee opened an office of religious affairs, whose officials served as the party's liaisons with Cuba's religious leaders and their international counterparts, including in the United States. Most churches, meanwhile, emerged eager to protect the newly found space they had been granted rather than aggressively pushing boundaries. The hierarchy of the Catholic Church, for example, notably resisted suggestions from abroad that it could serve as a basis for overt political mobilization, as in Poland's transitions, while at the same time slowly creating a space for open expression. For example, visitors to the Basilica of El Cobre, the church outside of Santiago de Cuba dedicated to Cuba's patron saint, will find expressions of support for Fidel Castro alongside posters demanding freedom for political prisoners among the various offerings left at the shrine. Protestant Churches in some cases more explicitly aligned their theology with strongly liberationist approaches, creating a fusion with revolutionary principles, similar to the Cuban Catholic Church's more limited foray into this area during the 1970s. Today, in fact, some leaders of Protestant churches, practicing Catholics, and other religious believers are members of the National Assembly of People's Power and the Communist Party.

Still, the reemergence of religion did without a doubt challenge political boundaries. Indeed, Fidel Castro's dialogue with the Vatican was perhaps the most graphic demonstration of this fact. Havana's renewed spirit of open diplomacy with the Vatican sent a signal to Cuban believers and to the increasingly active Catholic dioceses throughout the country that the government and even Fidel Castro himself were tempering, if not entirely purging, their long-standing anticlerical tendencies. The high point of this new space for the church was the visit of Pope John Paul II to Cuba in January of 1998. From the moment Fidel Castro greeted the arriving pope at the airport in a business suit—an oddly deferential gesture for a man rarely seen not wearing his famed *verde olivo*—there was a clear sense that this visit was indeed historic. Over the course of four days of highly choreographed but memorable activities—including a dramatic papal mass in Havana's Revolution Square—the pope's visit raised expectations at home and abroad for further openings on the island. His central message, that the moment had come for "Cuba to open to the world, and the world to open to Cuba," captured the moment perfectly. In the aftermath of the papal visit, the Cuban state continued to regulate the activities of Catholic, Protestant, and other religious organizations. But today, Cuban citizens who attend mass and confession hold positions in the National Assembly, leading positions in the top tier of the Communist Party, and rank among the country's top professionals, scholars, and intellectuals. Religion is no longer a stigma or impediment of any kind.

Who was Elián González and what was his significance to Cuba and U.S.-Cuban relations?

On Thanksgiving weekend of 1999, a nearly 6-year-old boy named Elián González was found clinging to a piece of a destroyed raft adrift at sea off the coast of Fort Lauderdale, Florida. His mother and her boyfriend, with help from Miami relatives, had paid smugglers to bring them out of Cuba, but only Elián survived the trip. Because U.S. immigration policies allow Cubans who reach U.S. shores to remain in the United States, local immigration authorities contacted the boy's waiting relatives in Miami, who quickly took him to their modest home in Little Havana.

Upon hearing that his son had survived, Elián's father, with the support of Cuban authorities, demanded that the boy be returned to his custody. The United States first ignored this request. Then, citing immigration regulations, and in an atmosphere of growing media and Cuban American scrutiny, the Clinton administration waffled on returning the boy to Cuba. Together with Ricardo Alarcón, president of the National

Assembly and Cuba's point man for dealing with the United States, Fidel Castro made getting Elián back to his father a priority for which he would ultimately mobilize public opinion in Cuba, in the United States, and around the world on the boy's and Cuba's behalf. Cuban authorities viewed the controversy over Elián not only as an indicator of all that was sour in U.S. policy toward Cuba but also as an opportunity to goad the Cuban American community into potentially damaging missteps in its quest to keep the embargo in place. Yet Fidel wasn't the only one who saw Elián's story and his ultimate fate as a potent symbol. Indeed, suspicious that the Clinton administration was leaning toward a broader opening with Cuba toward the end of its second term, the Cuban American exile establishment, led by the Cuban American National Foundation (CANF), also sensed an opportunity to paint the Castro regime as a gulag to which no right-thinking parents would ever want their child returned, and to which no liberal democracy should extend the benefit of trade and recognition. On an emotional level, many Cuban Americans also tended to feel that if Elián's mother had sacrificed her life to bring her son to the United States, they should honor her wishes. Likewise in Cuba, many felt equally passionate about their belief that the boy should be reunited with his father. Thus began an eight-month odyssey lasting until the end of June the following year, involving adjudication and appeals in local, state, federal, and, finally, the Supreme Court.

The home of Elián's Miami relatives soon became a media circus, and Cuban American activists—from the well-known leaders of CANF to lesser known individuals who would go on to run Cuba policy for the Bush administration—certainly sought to mobilize attention to the case. Meanwhile, in addition to rallying domestic public opinion behind the controversy, the Cuban government took its case to U.S. public opinion outside of Miami, particularly in Washington, advocating for the fundamental rights of parents to be with their children. Castro didn't have to do much to demonize the Cuban American community for getting in the way of that basic right: The very notion that the boy should be separated from his father flew in the face of basic common sense and human instincts, although his mother clearly disagreed before she perished at sea. Although Al Gore endorsed an effort to keep Elián in the United States, rather quickly, U.S. public opinion and that of many otherwise conservative pundits and members of Congress turned against the Cuban American community and Elián's Miami relatives, while also questioning the merits of a policy environment that could generate such a spectacle and erect so many legal and political barriers to family ties.

By the spring of 2000, Elián's temporary home in Little Havana was surrounded around the clock by crowds who at all costs hoped to keep Elián out of reach from possible government action to return him to his father. Meanwhile, Elián's father Juan Miguel arrived in the United States to await reuniting with his son. In April of that year, both directly and through Catholic Church and third-country intermediaries, negotiations were ongoing between the United States and Cuba, as well as between the Justice Department and prominent members of the CANF board of directors. Yet before these talks yielded any results, U.S. authorities decided to take action. With Attorney General Janet Reno's authorization, federal agents stormed the Little Havana house in a surprise, predawn raid, seized the boy, and quickly ferreted him away to his father. After two months in Washington waiting out a courts appeal process and under 24-hour protection by the ATF, Elián and his father returned to Cuba as national heroes. The entire episode inflicted great damage, first and foremost to the boy and his family, while dealing a withering blow to those in the exile community who attempted to exploit his odyssey. Elián's father later translated his unexpected notoriety and political symbolism into a public career spending part of his time representing Matanzas province as an elected deputy in the National Assembly. Elián became a member of the Communist Youth at 14, in 2008. His Miami-based uncles and cousins have retreated to obscurity, while a local garage band, calling themselves "The Miami Relatives," became regulars on the New York indie rock scene.

How did the Elián González affair influence Cuba's domestic politics?

Ten years into the Special Period and with only marginal improvements in the travails of daily life, a new generation of Cuban young people was growing up with little direct appreciation for the revolution. A university or graduate education may have come at little or no cost at all, but there weren't enough appealing jobs waiting on the other end. The dollarized economy and the black market drew in many talents, but for many young Cubans and their professional parents, leaving the country—whether on the arm of European tourists or for family closer by in Miami—increasingly looked like the best, if often bitter, option. Moreover, in the 1990s, a sizeable number of Cuban young people fell through the cracks of the educational system, leaving behind their education at some point during or after high school and entering the ranks of a disillusioned, apathetic, and often angry cohort with little stake in Cuban socialism.

Mass public mobilizations in response to perceived or real American provocations have often served as opportunities for the Castro regime to drum up and revive popular support. The Elián González case was no exception. Virtually every public figure and institution in Cuba made getting Elián home the dominant issue of the day. Fidel also used the opportunity and context of nationalist fervor to launch what he called the "Battle of Ideas," an effort to mobilize constituents, especially Cuba's youth, at home around the virtues of the revolution's core ideological tenets. Emulating the 1960s literacy campaigns, the government started a social work program through which Cubans in their late teens and early 20s were sent around the country to begin putting a face on a government whose preoccupation with survival had left far too many Cubans in increasingly unlivable material conditions. Fidel also began to give a small group of ideologically committed Cubans in their 20s (known sarcastically as the "red brigades" or *talibanes* by many of their elders) responsibilities in overseeing government activities long under the control of more seasoned professionals.

Elián's return to Cuba was a huge domestic political and international victory for Cuba and for Castro. To this day, Elián remains a potent symbol for the Cuban regime, and his personal relationship with Fidel Castro in the aftermath of the Florida ordeal has become well known. Whether the Battle of Ideas has been as successful remains an open question. The social work programs and other associated initiatives to improve vocational and technical training have continued. But large pockets of Cuban youth remained disenchanted well into the new millennium.

Does Cuban art and music provide an arena and space for critical expression?

Yes. But it's not that simple. Music and art have always provided a way for people to voice opposition to or dissatisfaction with authority, the status quo, or societal ills. But by its very nature, much art allows artists to express themselves in code, leaving much of the artists' true intentions or "messages" open to interpretation. Especially in Cuba, where censorship has been present at varying levels of intensity over time, but where there are also clear redlines that one simply cannot cross, artists and cultural producers have learned to carefully manage their self-expression.

Still, Cuban authorities have not been afraid to permit and promote what they deem constructive critiques of Cuban life today. Especially during the Special Period, a period that sparked renewed questioning and a certain degree of open debate on many themes, artists were also able to overcome old boundaries. A good deal of the art that emerged during that 1990s—whether music, film, literature, or visual arts—combines harsh critiques of the revolution's failures with strong notes of nationalism and some acknowledgement of the revolution's successes as well.

The evolution of the *Nueva Trova* movement, a distinct product of the Cuban Revolution and the government's early efforts of cultural promotion, provides a good window into a number of these dilemmas. As alluded to on page 58 ("How did the regime deal with its adversaries in the exile community?"), after a period of initial ostracism, singers Pablo Milanés and Silvio Rodríguez emerged as preeminent figures in new movement of socially conscious Cuban folk song (with antecedents in Latin American leftist folk song of earlier years) deeply sympathetic to the idealism of the revolutionary project. Over time, as both have earned worldwide popularity, they have gained a significant degree of leverage with Cuban authorities and the space to be more open. As a result, Milanés in particular has often vocally criticized certain policies of the Cuban government, while always professing his support for the broader revolution. Today, new generations of Trova singers like Carlos Varela have pushed the boundaries even further, often penning songs with explicitly political content not lost on any informed Cuban listener.

U.S.-CUBA

How did the United States react to the end of the Soviet era in Cuba?

The first Bush presidency saw the Soviet withdrawal of money and advisors from Cuba as the potential beginning of the end of the Cuban Revolution. Nonetheless, there was little official or public cheering from Washington. Within the State Department, officials reportedly were placing bets on when Castro's regime would crumble, and during the annual May 20th speech commemorating Cuba's prerevolutionary independence day, President Bush did openly speak of the potential for regime change. Yet by and large, in foreign policy, the White House was preoccupied with the consequences of German reunification, the first Gulf War in Iraq, the breakup of the Soviet Union into over a dozen separate countries, and bailing out Moscow. Moreover, the first Bush administration did not put a premium on schadenfreude, at least in public. A long-standing strategic objective of U.S. foreign policy had been met; there was no need to look ugly in victory. With Central America on the path to peace and democracy, the White House took the rapidly diminishing Cuban threat as an opportunity to issue an executive order ending covert operations on the island.

Consistent with this approach, while running for a second term in 1992, the first president Bush initially sought to avoid endorsing a congressional initiative to tighten economic sanctions against Cuba, especially because the law was likely to tread on the commercial affairs of key U.S. allies. But by April of that year, Bush tempered his preference for keeping foreign policy separate from domestic politics, following his Democratic rival's lead. After meeting in Miami with Jorge Mas Canosa, the head of the Cuban American National Foundation, Bill Clinton took a bite of the domestic political Cuban apple. Proclaiming that the time had come to "put the hammer down on Fidel Castro," Clinton endorsed the Cuban Democracy Act, a piece of legislation conceived initially by Mas and sponsored by New Jersey Congressmen Robert Toricelli. Against his better judgment and to no political or electoral benefit of his soon to be one-term presidency, George H.W. Bush endorsed the bill and then signed it into law in October 1992, just before his defeat in the November elections.

What was the Cuban Democracy Act, who was behind it, and what did the law intend to accomplish?

Largely conceived by Jorge Mas Canosa, 1992's Cuba Democracy Act (CDA) came to be known as the Torricelli bill for its principal congressional sponsor, New Jersey Democrat Robert Torricelli. Although his district was not as heavily populated by Cuban Americans as other New Jersey districts, Torricelli became the standard bearer among members of Congress hoping to coerce Cuba into conceding defeat in the aftermath of the Cold War. With increased economic deprivation at home and growing pressure from the Cuban people, CDA supporters hoped the Castro regime would implode.

The law had two principal components: sanctions and a series of limited openings. On the sanctions side, the CDA reimposed the ban on trade with Cuba by subsidiaries of U.S. companies based in third countries, previously lifted in 1975. By 1991, such sales had reached $700 million. By putting an end to that practice, the CDA incurred the ire of American allies where subsidiary U.S. companies were based. Additionally, the CDA aimed to further cut Cuba off from trade with the West by prohibiting ships from docking in U.S. ports that had been in Cuban ports within the previous six months. Other provisions restricted Cuba's ability to use dollars for international transactions and in the international banking system. Finally, the law authorized the White House, through executive order, to impose restrictions on the amount of remittances that could be sent to the island.

To complement such punitive steps, the CDA, as its authors sometimes argued, also attempted to lay the groundwork for the Cuban people to begin seeing the United States not as their inherent enemy, but rather as a source of support in their struggle for freedom from tyranny. First, the CDA included provisions that allowed for telecommunications companies and the U.S. Postal Service to resume what until then had been nearly nonexistent phone and direct mail service with Cuba. Second, the CDA authorized the sale of medicine and medical products to the island, but required U.S. pharmaceutical companies to apply to the Treasury Department for export licenses for each sale. To ensure that the products were used directly by the Cuban people, "end use" verification by an independent monitor was required as well. In practice, this provision meant that should the Cuban government wish to spend its scarce dollars on U.S. medical products, it would have to affirmatively give the same country that sought to unseat the revolution the pleasure of its compliance with outside verification, a humiliation that went right to the heart of the country's sensitivities about sovereignty and independence. As a result of these complex and politicized regulations, actual sales seldom transpired. Indeed, Cuba would claim that the embargo was directly responsible for the death or illness of patients for whom Cuba was unable to purchase key equipment and medicines. Third, and more significantly, the CDA authorized the United States to provide assistance to individuals and organizations working for nonviolent change on the island through relevant NGOs and external partners, whereas previously assistance had been delivered covertly by the CIA or through third countries. The era of "overt" covert action ensued.

The CDA thus contained several provisions that, in theory if not always in practice, promoted communication with the Cuban people and created loopholes in the embargo for humanitarian and/or human rights purposes. CDA supporters regarded these as important elements of a "Track II strategy." In the Latin American context, however, where similarly named "Track II" programs had helped undermine Salvador Allende in Chile, Cuba regarded the CDA's supposed carrots as yet another example of American-led destabilization, aimed at softening the population's support for its government. As a result, Cuba interpreted the law's provisions—especially its authorization for open support to opposition groups on the island—as a clear violation of national sovereignty.

Congressman Torricelli boasted that the effects of the CDA would bring down the regime "in a matter of weeks." Clearly, such wild predictions did not come to fruition. The legislation would remain on the books, however, forcing the Clinton administration to mold its policies around the bill's principal tenets. Over time, the CDA proved to be more flexible than initially thought. Although the people-to-people provisions of the law were intended to connect Americans and Cubans without benefiting the Cuban regime, the CDA framed these measures under a broad rubric of lending "support" to the Cuban people. Clinton was thus left with a potent loophole through which he would later push further openings. Equally significant, the bill retained nearly full executive privilege over the embargo; if he saw fit, the president could still do away with most sanctions with the stroke of a pen.

How did the United States and Cuba resolve the 1994 refugee crisis?

Images of thousands of Cubans in dilapidated, jury-rigged rafts reflected poorly on both governments. While Cuba was seen as a country that many wished to flee, the United States seemed unable to control Fidel Castro or protect its own borders. Many lives had been lost and more were at stake each day of August 1994 as *balseros*, or "rafters," continued to leave the island. Hoping to avoid a Mariel-like crisis (and under increased pressure due to the simultaneous and mounting Haitian refugee crisis), the Clinton administration implemented a policy of temporary detention, under which Cubans intercepted at sea were brought to the Guantánamo naval base to await their fates. Yet the influx of detainees and the resulting overcrowding on the base highlighted the unsustainable nature of this temporary fix, pushing the Clinton administration to embrace immigration talks with Cuba.

Both countries had a stake in bringing the summer's events to an end and preventing future such episodes. Thus, by September 1994, secret talks produced a U.S.-Cuba Immigration Agreement, which was strengthened by additional accords the following year. To provide for the "safe, legal, and orderly" migration of Cuban citizens to the United States, the United States agreed to a floor of 20,000 visas for permanent migration to its shores each year. Both countries agreed to take steps to ensure the safety of exit and entry, which meant that Cuba would actively police its waters and no longer allow its citizens simply to jump in a boat and leave. For the United States, this meant that the U.S. Coast Guard would pick up those *balseros* found at sea and, after interviewing them on board or at the Guantánamo base, return to Cuba those without a legitimate claim to political refugee status. Coast Guard vessels thus began regularly entering Cuban ports to deliver *balseros* back to Cuba, a process that required a previously nonexistent degree of regular communication and cooperation between the two countries. Cuba likewise agreed to allow the United States to send its Havana-based diplomats to visit migrants returned to the island in order to make sure they were not suffering reprisals from local authorities. By allowing the United States to stick its nose so directly into Cuba's internal business, Castro helped the Clinton administration pacify critics of the agreement while simultaneously demonstrating how cooperation might advance the interests of both countries. The United States and Cuba also agreed to meet twice each year to monitor the agreement's implementation and effectiveness, meetings the Bush administration would later terminate in 2004.

The United States set up a lottery system to help fill the annual quota. Together these programs established a mechanism for Cuba's government to safely export much of its opposition. The agreement also provided an important financial lifeline, allowing Cuban wage earners the chance to join their families in the United States while sending remittances back to an increasingly cash-strapped economy at home. Rafters would, of course, not entirely disappear from the Florida Straits, and a growing human smuggling trade (of people of many nationalities) became a regular feature in these waters as well. Yet by 2006, nearly 300,000 Cubans had migrated to the United States under the provisions of the 1994/1995 agreements, reducing a potentially serious cause of bilateral conflict. In addition, like the Mariel generation of immigrants before them, Cuba's post-1994 émigrés were very different demographically from earlier émigrés, and would gradually help shift public opinion regarding U.S.-Cuba policy within Miami as well.

How did Cuban American activists and members of Congress react to these agreements?

Officials in the Clinton administration viewed the agreements as essential tools for protecting U.S. national security interests. By contrast, for top figures in the anti-Castro exile community and members of Congress sympathetic to their cause, the accords represented a betrayal. The idea that the U.S. Coast Guard would pick up Cubans at sea and bring them back to what they regarded as a gulag seemed flagrantly immoral. They also saw the accords as a violation of the 1966 Cuban Adjustment Act, a law that gave all Cubans reaching the United States the right to permanent legal status and a host of resettlement benefits. Yet even more to the point, because the agreements involved government-to-government cooperation, they compromised many exile leaders' beliefs in a strategy of complete isolation from the Castro government. In their view, the migration agreements conferred sovereign status on a regime considered illegitimate by the exile leadership. Jorge Mas Canosa, leader of the Cuban American National Foundation, led the attacks on the White House, with public protests as well as a coordinated media campaign. In addition, because he had not been consulted as the migration accords were being developed, Mas Canosa withdrew his offer to help raise and provide the millions of dollars needed to help settle the remaining 20,000 Cuban refugees in Guantánamo at the time. Clinton was justifiably anxious about the crisis on his hands. As governor of Arkansas, he had seen his first ultimately unsuccessful reelection bid badly damaged in 1980 when several hundred *marielitos* interned at Fort Chaffee by the Carter administration rioted and set fire to their jails in protest to their long detention. But more important, his successful courtship up to that point of a traditionally Republican source of campaign finance money and votes was now potentially at risk. In the end, those remaining emigrants who were not returned to Cuba were either resettled in third countries or brought to the United States, with the federal government footing the bill.

Was a broader U.S. opening toward Cuba in the cards?

Upon coming to office, the Clinton administration moved to signal its embrace of democratic movements, parties, and institutions in Latin America, distancing itself from the Cold War preference for stable authoritarian regimes. Yet when the Republicans swept the 1994 midterm elections (only months after the *balsero* crisis came to an end), none other than Jesse Helms, a hard-core anti-Communist crusader, became chair of the Senate Foreign Relations Committee, signaling that the Cold War was far from over.

On Cuba, the Clinton administration recognized both the limits of the policy framework then in place as well as the political constraints of the moment. With the Cuban Democracy Act designed to isolate the Cuban government and reach out to the Cuban people, the White House also sought to enlist U.S. allies' help in persuading Castro to begin a transition to democracy. At the same time, the administration publicly opened the door for a potential relaxation of the embargo, contingent on reform on the island. Secretary of State Warren Christopher called this approach one of "calibrated response." In other words, as Cuba took steps toward democracy and liberalizing the economy, the United States would respond by relaxing aspects of its sanctions against the island.

Yet even as Cuba adopted a number of measures that could have easily been described as economic reforms during this period, the administration did not respond with openings on its end. Many individuals within the U.S. government and Congress looked instead to the Eastern European experience, where the United States and other western countries had provided material assistance and political support to dissidents, civil society groups, and opposition leaders who over time built pressure upon their governments and ultimately succeeded in defeating communism. In that spirit, the administration emphasized human rights and civil society, awarding a $500,000 grant to Freedom House to advance those goals. USAID now supplies such grants to a range of U.S., Cuban American, and international NGOs that promote the government's policy objectives in Cuba. For Clinton officials, couching this approach in the trendy language of civil society support allowed Washington to open informal channels between Cubans and Americans while navigating the politics of the exile community. Yet the White House also pushed the boundaries. Seizing on the spirit of the CDA's mandate for actions that support the Cuban people, the government also slowly began issuing more licenses for travel to Cuba. American musicians, artists, writers, and filmmakers began traveling to Cuba with greater frequency, taking advantage of a little-known 1988 provision of embargo laws (the Berman Amendment) that allowed trade in informational materials. Slowly, cautiously, and ever-conscious of the domestic political implications, Clinton pushed the boundaries of travel and other regulations governing the bilateral relationship with the island.

Havana greeted Track II with derision, suspicion, and a splashy propaganda campaign highlighting the government's view of the policy's nefarious intent. Yet despite his hard-core anti-embargo rhetoric, Castro also understood the politics Clinton was navigating. Cuban authorities issued visas to visiting American scholars and permitted Cuban scholars and artists to visit the United States on extensive exchanges. Indeed, both governments came to regard, if obliquely, the Track II policies as a practical way to gain intelligence about one another's society. As a result, each was willing to tolerate the rhetoric the other used to frame the limited openings to their domestic constituents. United States newspapers opened bureaus in Havana for the first time since the early 1960s, and the two countries' professional, religious, cultural, and academic communities began to get to know one another.

What was Brothers to the Rescue, and why did Cuba shoot down two of its planes?

Beginning in the 1990s, Cuban exiles had taken to flying over the Florida Straits to find refugees lost at sea and radio their location to the U.S. Coast Guard. One organization, Brothers to the Rescue (BTTR, or *Hermanos Al Rescate*), led by Bay of Pigs veteran José Basulto, was even able to acquire, with the help of a recently elected Cuban American Congresswoman Ileana Ros-Lehtinen, old Cessna airplanes from the Pentagon's fire sales. BTTR representatives claim that their efforts over the years have reportedly helped to ensure the safety of some 4,000 rafters. Yet during the mid-1990s, instead of just looking out for refugees in the waters between the two countries, Basulto's flights took on a more explicitly political and provocative mission. With a fleet of several airplanes and a group of committed volunteer pilots, he started sending small planes into Cuban territorial waters, often dropping leaflets over Havana itself, exhorting the Cuban population to rise up against the government.

Not all of the Brothers to the Rescue flights flew over Cuban territorial waters, nor did they all fly over Havana. But enough did over the course of thousands of flights (with documentation to prove as much) that Cuba was on solid ground when it charged that Brothers to the Rescue's activities represented a clear provocation, an encroachment upon its sovereignty, and a clear violation of international law. Indeed, Cuba was closely aware of BTTR's activities, above all because at least one of the government's spies had infiltrated the organization and even participated in its missions. Through a number of back channels, including via then secretary of energy Bill Richardson, Fidel Castro sent messages to the White House warning of grave consequences unless the overflights stopped. In response, Clinton officials reportedly did order the Federal Aviation Administration to pull Basulto's license to fly. But, according to one former White House official (Richard Nuccio), because Basulto appealed the decision, he was able to retain his license as the appeal was being processed and continue his missions.

On February 24, 1996, with advance warning and intelligence from Cuba's agent within the organization, Cuban MiG fighter pilots shot down two Brothers to the Rescue Cessnas, killing the four men on board, three of whom were U.S. citizens born in Cuba and one of whom was a Cuban who had yet to become a naturalized U.S. citizen. Only one of the three BTTR planes flying that day, the one with Basulto on board, safely returned to Florida. Cuba claims that it was within its rights to shoot down those specific planes because they had entered Cuban airspace. Yet although Basulto's operation had violated Cuba's airspace in the past, the International Civil Aviation Authority, the adjudicating body where the United States and Cuba pled their cases, found the planes to have been outside of Cuban airspace at the time of the shoot-down. A subsequent UN investigation found that the two planes had knowingly violated Cuban airspace immediately prior to their shoot-down—something denied by Basulto. Even so, many also argue that because BTTR's planes were clearly unarmed, common aviation practice should have dictated that the Cuban pilots attempt to force the planes to land before shooting them down. As the UN investigation also concluded, both Cuba and the United States share the blame for the incident.

How did the United States respond?

The shoot-down provided the catalyst for Congress to move forward on a set of lingering, bipartisan moves to further tighten the embargo. Moreover, it occurred just as Bill Clinton was revving up his bid for a second term in office. With the GOP firmly in control on Capitol Hill and the Clinton team keenly aware of the importance of Cuban American campaign contributions and votes, the White House was loath to resist the strong legislative momentum and political pressure inspired by the shoot-down—even though it had at an earlier phase opposed the very same legislation. Co-sponsored by North Carolina Senator Jesse Helms and Indiana Congressman Dan Burton, the Cuban Liberty and Solidarity Act, known as the *Libertad* (freedom) Act, or simply Helms-Burton, was passed and signed into law within less than a month.

The new law included a smorgasbord of measures intended to squeeze Cuba from abroad and restructure Cuban society from within. Title III of the legislation created a right of action for Cuban Americans and others who lost property on the island during the 1960s to use U.S. courts to sue the Cuban government and foreign investors who "trafficked" in that property. In another effort to deter foreign investment, Title IV of Helms-Burton required that the executive branch deny entry visas to foreign executives and board members (as well as their families) whose companies "traffic," or invest, in confiscated properties. This prohibition applied to individual property owners as well. Behind many of these provisions was the active lobbying of the Bacardi distilled spirits company, founded in Cuba, but relocated abroad (currently, its headquarters are in Bermuda) after its property was nationalized in the early years of the revolution.

Helms-Burton also legislated a very specific and largely fantastical set of circumstances under which the U.S. government could eliminate its sanctions against Cuba. First and foremost, Fidel Castro and his brother Raul would have to be out of office, and a number of government institutions eliminated. Movement toward free elections, a free press, free labor unions, and the release of all political prisoners were also prerequisites for any substantial U.S. opening. To help this process along, Title II called for what would ultimately amount to hundreds of millions of dollars dedicated to democracy promotion. In lieu of the anti-Communist covert action programs of the old days, under the new overt paradigm, dollars openly administered by USAID through U.S. NGOs were intended to breathe life into a domestic opposition in Cuba and lay the groundwork for the transition the new law's champions felt was imminent.

In the final negotiations between the Clinton administration and Congress, the White House secured a waiver authority allowing the president to suspend implementation of Title III every six months. Clinton and his successors have exercised this authority like clockwork ever since. If Title III were ever enforced, the resulting claims for compensation from those who lost property would likely clog U.S. courts and expose the United States not only to widespread derision but also to counterlawsuits in courts abroad.

Yet even though the Clinton team was able to avoid such a logjam and save face with its allies, the president conceded a degree of executive authority that not even Jesse Helms had expected possible. Helms-Burton codified all existing provisions of the embargo. While the president would retain some authority to tinker with some restrictions on the margins, by and large the executive branch gave up its authority to lift or impose sanctions, turning over to Congress a substantial portion of its power to shape policy toward the island. Moreover, since Congress stipulated that sanctions could not be lifted without the Cuban government taking steps that would amount to committing political suicide, the United States had, in essence, given Fidel Castro himself the power to decide the pace of any potential change in U.S.-Cuban relations.

How did Cuba respond to Helms-Burton?

Helms-Burton allowed Castro to once again demonstrate that the United States was dead set on toppling the revolution. Ricardo Alarcón, president of the National Assembly, led a nationwide discussion about nearly every line of the law, going so far as to translate and print hundreds of thousands of copies so that Cubans could read it for themselves. Most ominous for many Cubans was not just the law's implicit suggestion that the United States and Cuban exiles sought to remake the island in their own design, but that Cuban exiles might even be able to use U.S. courts to seek to recover from their current residents the houses, apartments, and other residential property they had left behind decades earlier. If ever Castro needed justification for the government's siege mentality, or proof that he and the revolution were all that protected Cuban citizens from a return to the injustices of the Batista past, Helms-Burton was it.

In response, Cuba passed legislation of its own imposing stiff criminal penalties against the unauthorized sharing of information about the island's economy with foreigners. While the pace of foreign investment on the island slowed, it is unclear to what extent this was due to the law itself. Alternately, once Cuban officials saw that their enemies abroad were angling to pounce on any opening, Cuba's leaders may have elected to be more cautious about permitting the entrance of foreign capital.

After the dust settled from the shoot-down and Helms-Burton, how did Cuba policy take shape during Bill Clinton's second term?

Bill Clinton's endorsement of the Helms-Burton bill helped him secure 35% of the Cuban American vote in the 1996 presidential election, a margin almost 15% greater than in 1992. But by 1997, the White House was again looking for ways to craft a policy toward Cuba that gave Cubans a sense of hope and the United States a way to end the Cold War in Latin America. Put in less lofty terms, as much as the Clinton administration reviled Castro's breach of human rights and Cuba's lack of democracy, it recognized that, precisely because of the shoot-down, the two countries had real security interests that needed to be addressed together. Moreover, policy makers increasingly believed that sanctions and isolation were no way for the United States to be seen as a credible advocate of democratic reform. In addition, there was enough collective memory in Washington to know that throughout the Cold War and during the period of the end of communism, not only had the United States permitted travel and trade between East and West, but also these ties had been critical to activists on the ground pushing for change. Likewise, despite Clinton's quick and politically motivated move to embrace Helms-Burton, the shoot-down brought home the need to extract U.S. policy from the vise grip of hard-line Cuban exiles, whose provocations could have brought the United States and Cuba into direct military conflict.

A new strategy emerged. Embracing the Cuban Democracy Act's clause in favor of "support of the Cuban people," it used its limited executive authority to create 13 categories for licensed travel by Americans for what was somewhat awkwardly labeled nontourist "purposeful" people-to-people exchange. The administration also effectively lifted the ban on family travel by allowing once-per-year family visits. As a result, hundreds of U.S. NGOs obtained licenses to sponsor travel to Cuba and connect with their counterparts on the island in a variety of fields. Hollywood's film and New York's literary scene descended upon the island, with Arthur Miller, Steven Spielberg, Kevin Costner, Danny Glover, Henry Belafonte, and William Styron among many making well-publicized visits. The administration sponsored several of its own higher profile exchanges. For example, Cuba's national baseball team played a pair of exhibition games against the Baltimore Orioles, first in Havana, then in Baltimore. By the last year of Clinton's second term, well over 200,000 Americans had traveled to Cuba, half of whom were Cuban Americans. All of this travel demystified Cuba for Americans, put a face other than Fidel's on the Cuban population, and began to redraw the map of constituents within the United States with a stake and an interest in greater contact with the island. Couched officially as an effort to reach out to the Cuban people, Clinton officials also referred to the results of their Cuba policies as the "Buena Vista Social Club effect," named for the collection of Cuban music produced by Ry Cooder in 1996.

On the economic front, an amendment to permit cash agricultural sales to the island became part of a farm bill that Clinton signed into law in 2000. Half a dozen other legislative initiatives—from lifting the travel ban to lifting the embargo—moved through Congress but were stopped by the Cuban American congressional delegation, the GOP congressional leadership, and Florida and New Jersey Democrats eager to keep a lid on the embargo. Contrary to the party's political leadership at the time, many members of the Republican foreign policy establishment and business community did their part to help the White House push the door open further. With an eye on the 2000 election, however, the White House ruled out any bolder ventures, lest they damage Al Gore's chances at the presidency.

Internationally, the Clinton administration continued to press its case against Cuba at the United Nations Human Rights Commission in Geneva. At the same time, it attempted to broker settlements between foreign investors and Cuban Americans with claims on the island, while informally considering proposals that might have permitted direct negotiations with Cuba to settle uncompensated claims by U.S. companies that lost property in the 1960s. Likewise, Clinton endeavored to persuade Washington's skeptical allies in Canada, Europe, and Latin America that by pushing Cuba for democracy and human rights, they would help provide the necessary international context for the United States to continue a series of official and unofficial openings in the bilateral relationship. The papal visit in 1998 was significant in this regard as well, for it supplied the Clinton team with the kind of unimpeachable political cover necessary for the United States to further its carefully triangulated moves.

Even as the United States continued pressing the human rights and democracy agendas, Cuba responded in limited ways to American overtures. Cuba continued to accept the repatriation of Cuban refugees and allowed an American Coast Guard official stationed at the U.S. Interests Section in Havana to go out on counternarcotics missions with Cuba's border patrol boats. At Guantánamo, the commander of the U.S. base and his counterpart on the Cuban side, along with their respective teams, began meeting each month.

By the year 2000, it seemed that the United States and Cuba had found an approach to one another that permitted each to open the door without risking domestic political suicide. Cuba could rail against the embargo and imperialism and organize the entire world to vote against Washington at the United

Nations while reaping the benefits of remittances and visits from Cuban Americans, welcoming congressional delegations and American capitalists to huge trade shows, and sending its artists, musicians, and scholars on road shows around the United States, including to the Grammys and the Oscars. With economic sanctions still largely in place, the embargo allowed Cuba to determine for itself the pace it would integrate into the world economy, even as it began purchasing American agricultural products to feed its own population and growing numbers of foreign tourists. For its part, while continuing to emphasize human rights, the Clinton administration appeared to have hit on a strategy that ruptured the Cuban American hard-liners' monopoly over the policy debate, while building a new popular and bipartisan consensus across the country and in Congress favoring engagement and contact with Cuba. While neither country made a priority of normalizing relations with the other, a low-key approach to relaxing the long-standing enmity suited both.

How did the death of Jorge Mas Canosa affect the Cuban American community?

For nearly two decades until his death from cancer in 1997, Mas Canosa was the charismatic leader who gave the Cuban exile community its public face and its political strategy. In Miami, this meant that the Cuban American National Foundation had become without a doubt the most well-endowed and politically dominant exile organization. Mas Canosa and the CANF achieved this status through direct-mail fundraising that targeted the wealthiest among Cuba's old-money sugar families, Miami's newly moneyed entrepreneurial class, and *viejitas* (little old ladies) in Hialeah. Mas Canosa had a keen sense of the media's importance, controlling the public debate and keeping alternative voices muted through his ubiquitous presence in the Spanish-language media and a healthy dose of intimidation. In Washington, though he often lobbied Congress with other

CANF executives or board members, only Jorge Mas Canosa combined charm and pressure tactics in a package that could move Republicans and Democrats to see things his way. His checkbook and extensive Rolodex also allowed him to create a PAC that aggressively helped keep members of Congress (particularly new members) loyal to the anti-Castro cause.

After Mas Canosa's death, his son Jorge Mas Santos took over leadership of the CANF. With the Catholic Church playing a role, a debate surfaced about whether some of the long-standing orthodoxies of the organization were the best way to ensure the regime's collapse. Despite successfully lobbying for the Cuban Democracy Act and Helms-Burton, individuals within the group began to realize that the longer the Castro regime lasted without its Soviet patron, the more CANF's strategy risked irrelevance. The pope's visit to Cuba in 1998 provided the opportunity for reform-minded CANF members, including Mas Santos, to steer the organization away from his father's rigid isolationist approach by supporting family ties and dissidents on the island. After Mas Canosa, new Cuban American voices and organizations gained some political space in Miami and in Washington. By slowly adapting to a new reality of family ties and more forcefully promoting the potential of a viable opposition on the ground within Cuba, the CANF was able to retain a shot at relevance under a new generation's leadership. But a more existential threat to exile unity and to the CANF was looming in the form of a nearly 6-year-old boy named Elián, soon to arrive on Florida's shores.

How did the Elián González episode affect the end of the Clinton presidency, the 2000 presidential election, and the Cuban American community?

The Elián González episode, followed by the contested 2000 election, dashed any expectation that the end of Clinton's presidency would bring dramatic moves by the White House toward Cuba. If the Cuban American community was outraged by Janet Reno's dark-of-the-night raid to seize Elián and reunite him with his father, Al Gore saw his political future on the line. Leaving no pandering stone unturned, the vice president had already called for the boy to be kept in the United States against his father's wishes, going so far as to invoke his authority as president of the U.S. Senate and sponsor a resolution calling for Elián to be made a U.S. citizen. But when the administration he served decided otherwise, Gore knew he would be hard pressed to sustain Clinton's impressive gains in Cuban American votes in 1996. And he didn't: Gore lost Florida to Bush by 537 votes, but he lost Cuban American votes by a much wider margin, winning just under 20% to Bush's 80%, a more than 15% decline relative to the Democrats' win in 1996. Nothing dramatized the political backlash of the Elián affair as much as the spectacle of Cuban Americans participating among the crowd of demonstrators in December 2000 who succeeded in forcing, literally, an end to the Miami-Dade recount, and ultimately to Al Gore's shot at the presidency.

In 1998, Pope John Paul II's visit to Havana had provided a rare opportunity for Cuban Americans to connect to their families on the island and to their country of birth outside of the ideological and censorious environment of South Florida, making contact across the straits less taboo. By contrast, the 2000 Elián saga in some sense redrew the line between Miami and Havana. Yet although their votes damaged Gore and the Democrats, Cuban Americans ultimately did themselves no favor by aggressively exploiting the Elián affair. As betrayed as they felt by the Clinton administration's handling of Elián's reuniting with his father, Cuban Americans also recognized that the scandal had tarnished their national reputation. In the resulting quest to place blame and assign responsibility, Cuban Americans confronted just how much they had changed. Mas Canosa was dead, ties between families on and off the island would persist, and a younger generation less single-minded and passionate about overthrowing Castro had emerged. As a result, the community soon turned on itself. The CANF board of directors split, and the most conservative hard-liners went on to found the Cuban Liberty Council, an organization that opposes virtually all family or humanitarian ties to the island. Meanwhile, a group of Cuban American businessmen founded the Cuba Study Group (CSG) in order to promote certain forms of conditional engagement with the island. The CSG would also help spearhead the efforts of Consenso Cubano, a new umbrella group that brought together moderate to conservative-minded exile organizations with representatives of some dissident groups. Overall, however, political unity (one of Fidel's signal historical achievements) eluded Miami's Cuban American establishment.

By 2002, strong majorities in the community continued to support the embargo itself. Yet new majorities were also acknowledging the failure of current policies and supporting family travel and other humanitarian measures for reaching the Cuban people. By the 2004 presidential election, and with very little Spanish-language media advertising or direct campaigning among Cuban Americans, Democratic candidate John Kerry's position supporting family travel and people-to-people ties helped the Democrats recover somewhat from their 2000 lashing in South Florida (although they still lost the Cuban American vote) and the state as a whole.

How did the September 11, 2001, attacks affect U.S.-Cuban relations?

Shortly after taking office, the George W. Bush administration appointed a host of conservative Latin America hands to key positions in the government. Some had worked for Jesse Helms in the Senate during the heyday of Central America's civil wars and as foot soldiers crafting the Helms-Burton legislation. Others of Cuban origin had lobbied for the bill and carried Reagan's torch in Latin America during the 1980s. Together, they were intent on plugging a leaky embargo even though public opinion (whether nationally, in the business community, or among Cuban Americans) was clearly supportive of the Clinton-era openings. Moreover, the president himself (whose brother, Governor Jeb Bush of Florida, had developed deep political and business ties with Cuban exile leaders) had campaigned on a promise to bring down Fidel. Nonetheless, prior to September 11, 2001, the new government paid scarce attention to Cuba. In Latin America it focused instead on a Summit of the Americas in Canada; migration talks with the new president of Mexico, Vicente Fox; and an emerging irritant in South America, Hugo Chávez of Venezuela.

For its part, the Cuban government felt a certain degree of confidence from its extensive ties to American business, political, and cultural circles developed in preceding years—not just among Democrats but Republicans as well (particularly among representatives of agricultural states that benefited from growing food exports to the Cuban market). The Cuban government was under no illusion about the hard-line proclivities of the Bush administration's Latin America hands. Yet with the GOP's emphasis on business and its taste for law and order, Castro probed signs that it might still be possible to establish a quiet modus vivendi with Bush while continuing momentum in the U.S. Congress for further economic openings. In the aftermath of 9/11, however, such possibilities would quickly fade.

On the day of the attacks, when the United States shut down its airspace, the Cuban government privately offered to open its airfields for American planes to land there and offered medical teams to assist with the disaster and recovery. Both offers were ignored. That night, Fidel Castro went live on Cuban television with a speech that, while reminding viewers of Cuba's own experience with political violence, categorically and unequivocally condemned the attacks and terrorism. Moreover, Fidel personally expressed Cuba's and his own solidarity with the people of the United States.

For Bush administration hard-liners, such gestures rang hollow. Instead, they came to believe that the attacks created an opportunity to accelerate plans to up-end the Clinton-era openings. After all, with Cuba still on the State Department's list of state sponsors of terrorism—a designation that rang with new potential significance—the political climate seemed to favor a sharpening of the U.S. approach to Cuba. The president's January 2002 State of the Union address threatened tough action against an "axis of evil," and although Bush did not single out Cuba, his warning against the proliferation of weapons of mass destruction by such states created an opening. In a matter of months, and at the same time it was preparing its rationale for the invasion of Iraq, the administration started building a case that Cuba was developing biological weapons capabilities (with what was called "dual-use" biotechnology) and had the potential to export its know-how to other rogue nations such as Libya, Syria, and Iran. Hard-liner John Bolton, then a State Department official, claimed that Cuba's potential threat to U.S. national security had been "underplayed." In the inflamed post-9/11 war-on-terror zeitgeist that engulfed Washington, allegations of possessing weapons of mass destruction, which were advanced at the same time as the pretext for military action 9,000 miles away in Iraq, spelled extreme risk for a country long a U.S. enemy and just 90 miles away.

In Cuba's case, however, cooler minds in the intelligence community and in the U.S. Congress prevailed. Strong pushback against the allegations strengthened the hands of more rational actors in the administration, while Cuba's invitation for Jimmy Carter to visit its Biotechnology Institute helped dampen the plausibility of the charges. Though Bush administration hard-liners were forced to back down and instead focus on the far less glamorous work of rolling back the Clinton-era openings, they exacted personal and professional revenge against those intelligence professionals who had the integrity to substantiate a less politicized assessment of Cuba's dual-use capacity.

Why is Cuba still on the State Department's list of state sponsors of terrorism?

The Reagan administration first added Cuba to this list for its support of the FMLN guerrilla in El Salvador in 1982. By 1992, the State Department reported that Cuba had stopped training and funding leftist rebel groups and was actively involved in pressing groups in Colombia, El Salvador, and Guatemala to pursue peace accords and renounce armed struggle. Throughout the 1990s, the State Department continued to believe that Cuba had ceased its support for armed revolution abroad, and a 1997 review conducted by the entire U.S. intelligence community concluded that Cuba no longer constituted a threat to American national security. After the September 11, 2001, attacks, Cuba signed and ratified all 12 United Nations resolutions against terrorism. Nonetheless, the new Bush administration's first "Patterns of Global Terrorism" report (produced by the State Department) in 2001 stated that Cuba still supported terror as a tactic of revolution, citing as evidence both Cuba's broad rejection of the U.S.-led "war on terror" as well as the presence of Basque separatists, Colombian rebels, and U.S. fugitives (Puerto Rican separatists and Black Panthers) living in Cuba.

Such accusations lacked context. Castro gave members of the Basque group ETA a place to retire, essentially as a favor to then Spanish prime minister Felipe González. Likewise, at Colombia's request, Havana has been the principal location for peace talks between successive Colombian governments and the smaller ELN rebel group for years, just as Mexico, without landing on the terrorist list, served as a third-country location for talks with the FARC. Finally, Cuba has offered to negotiate the return of some U.S. criminals living in Cuba in exchange for the return of Cuban-born citizens currently living in the United States who have committed violent acts against Cuba, such as Orlando Bosch and Luis Posada Carriles.

Despite publicly charged rhetoric throughout the Bush administration, American military officials credit Cuba with consistently providing cooperation in counterterrorism (and counternarcotics as well) during this period.

Who are the "Cuban Five"?

The "Cuban Five," known in Cuba as the *Cinco Heroes,* are counterintelligence agents and spies, sent by the Castro government to infiltrate several Miami-based exile groups in the 1990s. Based on their work, the Cuban government passed information to the Clinton administration's State Department and directly to an FBI team that visited Havana to investigate the alleged plans of those groups under surveillance to commit terrorist attacks against Cuba. In the fall of 1998, the FBI subsequently arrested the five Cuban informants, charging them with a variety of crimes, from falsifying documents to conspiracy to commit espionage. Between the arrest and the beginning of their trial, the five spent almost three years in jail, including 17 months in solitary confinement. In June 2001, all were found guilty. In December of that year, three were given life sentences; the other two, shorter terms between 15 and 19 years.

Until the Cuban Five were sentenced, Cuban officials did not move aggressively to bring sustained public and international attention to the case. Coinciding with the launch of the Bush administration's "war on terror," their sentencing gave Cuba an appropriate context and trigger to do so. Havana argued that the five agents had been carrying out a patriotic duty to defend their homeland against attack in a country with a long history of tolerating and at times supporting exile extremists and terrorists. In this way, the Cuban government impugned the Bush administration's commitment to fighting terror as disingenuous and selective—yet another example of hypocrisy from the empire. United States prosecutors had argued that the five had intended to gather intelligence against the U.S. government itself. But attorneys representing the five strongly contested this notion, arguing that none of the accused, including one individual who had been employed as a janitor at the United States Southern Command, had any intention of inflicting damage upon the United States or the American people.

As the saga of the five was unfolding, Ana Belén Montes, a then Defense Intelligence Agency analyst, was arrested in September 2001 and pled guilty to charges of espionage on behalf of Cuba in October 2002. The Cuban government raised no protest over the arrest. By contrast, the Cuban Five had infiltrated not the U.S. government, but exile groups like Commandos F4, Alpha 66, and Brothers to the Rescue. Unlike the first two groups, which openly market themselves as armed anti-Cuba paramilitary groups on their websites, Brothers to the Rescue carved out a reputation within and beyond the Cuban American community for ostensibly humanitarian activities. Nonetheless, because of BTTR's close links to hard-liners in the U.S. Congress and because of its intentionally provocative incursions into Cuban airspace, the Cuban government regarded whatever humanitarian impulse that might have guided BTTR's members as a flimsy cover for what the regime saw as a direct threat to Cuban national security. For Cuban authorities, the work of the five was thus viewed as a step necessary for national self-defense in the absence of greater U.S. efforts to crack down on the groups in question.

If the Elián González affair had handed Fidel a highly sympathetic, indeed photogenic opportunity for domestic and international political mobilization, bringing attention to the case of the Cuban Five proved more challenging. Still, the faces of the *Cinco Heroes* were plastered on public spaces all over Cuba (and remain so today). In cities across Europe and Latin America, as well as in Washington D.C., New York, and San Francisco, the government helped to make their case a cause

célèbre among Cuba solidarity groups as well. Most important, as the constitutional and foreign policy dimensions of the
Bush administration's "war on terror" became increasingly
vulnerable to charges of illegality and hypocrisy, the case of
the Cuban Five suggested that the United States cannot stand
for fighting terrorists while denying the right of other governments to do the same.

Was Castro a target of assassination attempts during this period, and what efforts were made to prosecute their authors?

In 1990, following intensive lobbying from the Florida congressional delegation, the first President Bush pardoned long-time
anti-Castro terrorist Orlando Bosch, one of the two principal
intellectual architects of the 1976 explosion of the Cubana
Airline passenger flight that killed all 73 people on board. In
2005, his co-conspirator, Luis Posada Carriles, crossed into
Texas from Mexico, and after a period of one month in detention, was released. Both now live in the Miami area.

In the 15 years between when Bosch and Posada each emerged
from the anti-Castro underground, violent efforts against Cuba
continued. Some thwarted assassination attempts and violent
acts were associated with Posada, others with long-time terrorist
groups such as Alpha 66 and Commando L. In 1998, for example,
Posada told the *New York Times* that he had organized a spate of
1997 hotel bombings in Havana, one of which killed an Italian
tourist, with financial support from Cuban American National
Foundation leaders and its chairman, Jorge Mas Canosa. Mas
Canosa and the other CANF executives denied the charges.

The last known assassination attempt against Fidel Castro
took place in November 2000 on the eve of a speech Castro
planned to deliver before a group of university students while
in Panama for the 10th Ibero-American Summit. Working off
information from Cuba's security forces, Panamanian officials
arrested four exiles, among them Posada, found with weapons,
explosives, a map of Fidel's route to the forum, and an agenda of

the summit's meetings. After three and a half years in Panamanian prisons, all of them were suddenly pardoned by President Mireya Moscoso, who left office under a cloud of corruption charges. It was a year later when Posada, a naturalized Venezuelan citizen, snuck across the Mexican border using a false U.S. passport.

Particularly since Posada's reappearance on American soil in 2005, Venezuela has aggressively sought his extradition from the United States. In part, this activism relates to Hugo Chávez's own ties to Castro. Yet beyond this obvious ideological link, Venezuela also has much at stake in this case. In the early 1970s, Posada had become a naturalized Venezuelan citizen and risen to serve as chief of operations for Venezuelan intelligence. It was while running a private security agency in Caracas that he planned the 1976 Cubana bombing. He was prosecuted in Venezuela for this crime, but escaped from custody twice. The Bush administration largely ignored Venezuela's extradition request, arguing that Caracas failed to present enough evidence. More likely, given the amount of declassified documentation available on the case, Bush officials bowed to pressure from Posada supporters who claim he would be tortured if returned to Chávez's Venezuela. Yet neither has the United States endeavored to hold Posada accountable for his crimes. Although the Patriot Act permits the United States to indefinitely detain "excludable aliens" who are authors of terrorist attacks, Posada now lives, and is occasionally and publicly celebrated, in Miami, though generally by an aging group of his peers rather than by the majority of Cuban Americans. Posada may eventually be extradited to Panama, where the Supreme Court has ruled that former president Moscoso's pardon was unconstitutional.

What were the main features of U.S. policy toward Cuba under George W. Bush and how did Cuba respond?

As the United States entered the new millennium, Elián fatigue, embargo fatigue, and widespread annoyance with the domestic politics of the Cuba issue had helped create a bipartisan consensus in favor of dramatic policy change. No one necessarily thought this would be easy. Prior to 9/11 and the subsequent accusations about Cuba's weapons of mass destruction capabilities, Bush's nominee for secretary of state, Colin Powell, was forced to retract comments in his confirmation hearing that mildly acknowledged Cuba's successes in health care and education—not an encouraging sign. Still, the momentum for policy change continued into the next year, when the GOP-controlled House of Representatives voted to end trade and travel restrictions. By then, however, the Bush White House had made clear its intention of vetoing any such legislation.

Nonetheless, for most of 2002, Havana gingerly probed for evidence that it was possible to reach a modus vivendi with Washington. Raul Castro offered to return detainees from the war in Afghanistan to Guantánamo in the event they tried to escape. At the request of the Colombian government, it sent a Colombian drug trafficker to the United States. Even in the wake of early 2002's specious accusations regarding Cuba's supposed potential to develop and proliferate technology for bioweapons, the Cuban government still permitted President Carter's historic visit in May and allowed the Varela Project petition to be submitted without significant incident. This gesture would mark the high point of their generosity, however.

Beginning in early 2003, the Bush administration set out to largely undo the people-to-people openings launched by the Clinton administration. Acquiring or renewing a license for NGO-sponsored or educational travel became more difficult. New requirements obliged American groups wishing to travel to Cuba to demonstrate how their travel would benefit religious, human rights, dissident, or other opposition groups on the island. Soon, almost all of the legal travel categories created under the rubric of "supporting the Cuban people" had been eliminated.

Yet it was the run-up to the war in Iraq and the new mantra of preemptive security that really shook Havana's expectations of the Bush White House. One dimension of the Castro government's efforts to cultivate positive vibes in Washington had been its relative tolerance of a variety of dissident groups (many of which had been infiltrated), from small scale to higher profile. Congressional delegations visiting Havana could return to their districts and to Washington having met with such individuals, lending their visits, which often explored possible commercial ties with the regime, an air of human rights credibility. But the benefits of allowing such oxygen evaporated once Washington started to advance its regime change agenda with military power, albeit in Iraq. Havana reasoned that allowing the groups to continue to function could also give an in-road to an enemy whose designs may well turn belligerent. Thus, in the eyes of Cuban officials, the national security prerogatives of cracking down on domestic opposition activists were well worth the near-universal international backlash Cuba was likely to (and did) incur. It is no surprise that the "black spring" arrests of 75 dissidents occurred in March 2003, the day before Bush formally declared war on Iraq.

Several months later, President Bush launched the Commission for Assistance to a Free Cuba (CAFC), a new interagency initiative chaired by a series of cabinet officials. The commission's recommendations offered few surprises: Keep sanctions in place, step up efforts to penetrate the government's "information blockade," interrupt any moves by a successor regime to replace Fidel Castro, but offer assistance to a transitional government willing to hold elections, release political prisoners, and adopt the marks of freedom stipulated by Helms-Burton. In the scenarios envisioned by the commission's first 500-page report, an American "transition coordinator" (a position created soon after at the State Department) would judge when conditions in post-Castro Cuba would make it eligible for aid and other accoutrements that accompany a U.S. seal of approval.

One policy change to emerge from the commission's work was the president's move, notably in 2004, an election year, to massively scale back Cuban American family travel and remittances. Since 1999, Cuban Americans had been permitted to travel annually to the island to visit any member of their extended family. The new regulations cut these visits to once every three years, and only to see immediate family. New restrictions on remittances reduced the legal quantity that could be sent and also stipulated that only immediate family would be eligible to receive such transfers. Previously, they could be sent to "any household."

Measuring the impact of these changes with any certainty is nearly impossible. In 2006, the CAFC could only claim that the new policies had reduced remittances "significantly." Yet while Cuban families certainly felt the pinch, there was no appreciable effect on the Cuban regime's capacity to stay in power or repress its citizens. As relatives found alternative and sometimes illicit ways to get money to their loved ones (sometimes through illicit travel), it is likely that remittance flows experienced some recovery. Travel numbers have not bounced back, however. In the same period, Washington denied virtually all requests by Cuban professionals to travel to the United States unless applicants could claim they had been victims of political persecution by the regime. With the exception of a host of institutional exchanges, such as those conducted by Harvard University, most professional collaboration in science and the humanities dried up. In 2004, the United States also called a halt to the twice-annual migration talks because the meetings allegedly gave the appearance that the United States conferred legitimacy upon the Cuban government. Cuba's annual allotment of 20,000 migration visas continued, but human smuggling in the Gulf of Mexico did as well.

In response to these measures, Cuba reduced its public relations campaigns around lifting the embargo, convinced that they were not, for the moment, worth the effort. Guantánamo once again became a tool to mobilize domestic nationalism. Initially, Cuba's security establishment had hoped to show off its national security bona fides by tolerating the base's conversion into a detention center for suspected terrorists. Yet as allegations of torture surfaced and the legality of the detentions came into question, Guantánamo became, as it did for many of America's global critics, a symbol of American imperial hubris, one which in the Cuban case also allowed Havana to highlight the island's own history of grievances over American violations of its sovereignty. At the same time, fully cognizant of George W. Bush's bellicosity, the Cuban government appeared to cautiously avoid dramatic provocations of the sort that could lead to a repeat of past migration crises or the 1996 shoot-down.

Among the last public gestures of goodwill under the George W. Bush administration was Fidel Castro's offer to send hundreds of medical professionals and disaster relief workers to New Orleans in the aftermath of Hurricane Katrina. But Washington wrote off the offer as a publicity stunt. The embarrassing prospect that Fidel's teams of doctors and nurses might have something to contribute to New Orleans residents outweighed any calculus that could actually deliver help to Katrina's victims.

CUBA IN THE WORLD

How did Cuba adapt its foreign policy to the end of the Cold War?

With the dissolution of the Soviet bloc, political, material, and ideological resources for supporting revolution abroad dried up, forcing Cuba to develop new strategies for projecting itself as a global player. In a sign of the times, after nearly four years of negotiations, nine Cuban generals joined counterparts from the Soviet Union, South Africa, and the United States at the United Nations in late 1991 to celebrate an agreement calling for the withdrawal of remaining Cuban troops from Angola, the independence of Namibia, and the end of apartheid in South Africa. By 1992, there was no money and little strategic capacity for Cuba to pursue military activities outside of its own borders. Instead, still reeling from the Ochoa affair (see page 73, "Who was General Arnaldo Ochoa and why as he executed?"), Cuba's chastened and more modest military services turned their attention to defending the homeland and administering major portions of the island's economy.

The break with Moscow had not been easy. On one hand, Cubans made no secret of the relief they felt upon being freed from the ideological constraints of their Soviet benefactors, whom they largely disrespected. But on the other, Moscow had left Cuba saddled with an enormous amount of debt and a plummeting economy. Meanwhile, reformist, anti-Communist governments in Prague, Warsaw, and Budapest—newly independent from the iron curtain—railed against Havana's insolence and revolutionary defiance, conspiring with the United States to promote a tropical velvet revolution. Continuing a trend begun in the 1980s, Cuba's foreign service cultivated trade and diplomatic ties regardless of ideology, improving relations with Mexico, western Europe, Canada, the English-speaking Caribbean, and many Latin American countries as well. In Asia, Cuba worked to improve its on-again off-again relationship with China, while also forging ties with Japan and an increasingly capitalist-minded Vietnam.

Public diplomacy became gradually more important as well. Cuban artists and scholars began performing, studying, traveling, and living internationally. Doctors and nurses became part of an aggressive strategy of highly effective medical diplomacy combining charitable impulses (disaster-relief operations in Indonesia, Turkey, Iran, and Pakistan, among others) with revenue-earning foreign medical missions.

How did relations with Europe and Canada help Cuba survive after the Soviet collapse?

American allies in Canada and Europe were noticeably peeved when the U.S. Congress twice took aim at their trade and investment ties with Cuba in the 1990s. So was the Cuban government. But Havana also adapted to renewed efforts at

U.S. isolation to suit Cuban interests. The extraterritorial reach of U.S. laws not only helped Cuba highlight its victimization by the United States at various international forums, bilaterally, and with the American public but also increased the determination with which other countries sought to distance themselves from the U.S. approach. Over the course of the 1990s, Canada became one of Cuba's largest investors and trading partners, principally in energy, mining, telecommunications, and tourism. Though a solid diplomatic ally of the United States, Canada represented to Cuba a kinder, gentler version of Anglo-America with none of Washington's heavy baggage. At times, Canada even played a useful balancing role between the White House and Havana. Yet in the instances when Canadian heads of state fancied themselves as brokers of grand bargains, poised perhaps to extract human rights and democracy concessions from Castro in exchange for a relaxation of U.S. sanctions, Cuban diplomacy, directed always by Fidel himself, set Canada straight. Cuba might well have appreciated Canada's independence from the United States and its investments on the island, but the embargo was never painful enough to force Fidel to accede to third-country initiatives that might require him to make internal changes for which any foreign power, however benign in its intentions, could take credit.

Across the Atlantic, Cuba faced the dual challenge of dealing with the common foreign policies of the European Union and also building bilateral relations with each of the EU's member states. As with Canada, Europe came to be an important source of trade and investment for the island. Also like Canada, throughout the 1990s, the EU pursued dialogue with Havana around themes of human rights and democracy. For its part, Cuba was at times amenable to discussion and interested in the financial assistance an associated cooperation agreement could yield. Spain was a particularly important partner in boosting this renewed spirit of engagement. Over the course of a decade of openings, the former colonial power gradually became Cuba's largest foreign investor, mirroring its overtures throughout Latin American during the 1990s, dubbed the *reconquista*, or "reconquest," by some. Hopefuls in both countries looked to the post-Franco-pacted transition to democracy in the late 1970s as a possible model for Cuba to follow. But as with Canada, Cuba was never willing to entertain the kinds of political reforms imagined by numerous European interlocutors and required by the EU for formal cooperation and assistance packages. With the election of José María Aznar as Spain's primary minister in 1996, and the subsequent Spanish assumption of the EU's rotating presidency in 2000, Europe's posture toward Cuba gradually evolved. By 2003, when Cuba arrested and jailed over 75 human rights activists and dissidents, the prospects for a human rights dialogue to add any real value collapsed, and the EU imposed diplomatic sanctions to limit high-level contacts and support Cuban opposition groups. Yet after the terrorist bombings of Madrid's metro system in 2004 (widely thought to be the result of Aznar's involvement in the Iraq war, despite the prime minister's initial attempt to pin the blame on Basque radicals), the Socialist Party swiftly returned to power in an election scheduled just days after the attacks. Aided by the growing antipathy in Europe for any policy associated with the presidency of George W. Bush, incoming Prime Minister José Luís Rodríguez Zapatero would soon launch Spain and Cuba, and Cuba and the EU, on a path to diplomatic recovery.

How did Cuba use its long-cultivated clout at the United Nations?

Like most Latin American countries, Cuba regards its active membership in multilateral institutions as part of a strategy to help deflect encroachments upon its sovereignty by American power. Although the United States has successfully kept Cuba out of international forums like the OAS, the World Bank, and the IMF, Cuba has been able to remain quite active in organizations across the globe, first and foremost the United Nations. In fact, one could argue that Cuba's multilateral diplomacy has actually been strengthened as a result of U.S. isolationist tactics. There are also intrinsic reasons motivating Cuba's activism multilaterally. As a founding member of the WTO and of the UN, Cuban diplomats take pride in carrying on a tradition that preceded the revolution. Whether to promote its social agenda, organize a global coalition against the U.S. embargo, or attempt to refute accusations of human rights abuse, multilateral institutions are a critical component of Cuba's diplomatic resources. Cuba has been among the leading countries of the developing world to argue for diluting the veto power of the UN Security Council's five permanent members and allowing more representative participation from Latin America, Asia, and Africa. Although not always successful in deflecting U.S. criticisms of its human rights record, for many years, Cuba went toe to toe with the United States at the Geneva-based UN Commission on Human Rights until its abolition and replacement by a new Human Rights Council (in which the United States declined to participate) in 2006. And, beginning in 1992, for 17 straight years Cuba has secured widespread and increasing support for its resolutions at the UN General Assembly condemning the U.S. embargo. In 2008, for example, the resolution was approved by a lopsided vote of 185 to 3.

How did Cuba relate to Latin America in a newly democratic environment?

After the Cold War came to an end, Castro viewed the emerging liberal democratic capitalist order in Latin America as a threat to social justice and a potential recipe for the political marginalization of the left. But he also knew Cuba stood no chance of altering this state of affairs. In Nicaragua, it was painful for Castro to watch the Sandinistas lose an election he had advised against even allowing. Still, by the early 1990s, Cuba stopped supporting leftist guerrillas in Central America and had even begun playing a constructive role in brokering peace throughout the region. As the decade progressed, Castro watched as social activists and left-wing politicians with long-standing ties to his country embraced the new rules of the game, assuming leadership positions as elected officials, heads of national organizations, or business leaders—all within a framework of multiparty, and essentially capitalist democracy. Yet rather than criticize former comrades for compromising their earlier revolutionary aspirations, Cuba's leadership emphasized the importance of respecting political "diversity" (including Cuba's own one-party system) as a signal feature of democracy in Latin America. The end of Soviet support reinforced the need for such pragmatism.

In Brazil, for example, Cuba and Fidel had long cultivated ties to the Brazilian Workers Party (PT). Headed for decades by Luiz Inacio Lula da Silva, the PT was originally organized around the principles of democratic centralism, but had made a strategic decision in the early 1980s to participate in democratic politics. Over two decades, as the party came to run towns, cities, states, and eventually the entire country, its leaders continued to view Fidel and Cuba as spiritual comrades and steadfast allies, even as they lost interest in the practical applicability of the Cuban model. As a result, when Lula was elected as president first in 2002 and then reelected in 2006, Cuba found itself with a loyal friend holding the presidency of the eighth largest economy in the world.

In Chile, the 2006 election of Michelle Bachelet produced another sympathetic ally. Like many of her compatriots, Bachelet's family had suffered dearly under the repression of the Pinochet dictatorship. After the murder of her father and her own imprisonment, she and her mother would flee to exile in Australia, East Germany, and the United States before returning to Chile in 1979. As president, she also expressed gratitude to Cuba for welcoming so many exiles of the fallen Allende regime, some of whom were leftists close to Havana ideologically, while others were Social Democrats who bristled at Cuba's authoritarian bent but in some cases owed their lives to the country's magnanimity. Early into her term, she announced her intention, unrealized at this writing, to visit Cuba during her presidency.

A similar story repeated itself in Bolivia (2005), Ecuador (2006), Nicaragua (2006), El Salvador (2009), and earlier (1998) in Venezuela, where newly elected heads of state or their cabinet members had often studied in Havana as teenagers and young adults or traveled there later in life as part of the Latin American Left's conference-trotting cohort of revolutionaries, professionals, and social activists. By 2009, Cuba had restored diplomatic ties with every country in the hemisphere but the United States.

Mexico, however, presented a greater challenge. For 70 years, Mexico's one-party state had never broken ties with Cuba, defending the principle of self-determination even at the peak of the OAS's efforts to isolate the island in the 1960s. With the inauguration in 2000 of Vicente Fox, a former Coca-Cola executive and head of a conservative-leaning opposition political party, Mexico took a different tack as it embarked upon its own political transition. Fox brought a new foreign policy to Mexico, one that sought to closely tether the country to the United States for domestic political, economic, and strategic reasons. Fox also sought to distance Mexico from the repressive domestic policies of the long-dominant Partido Revolucionario Institutional (PRI). Thus, together with foreign minister Jorge Castañeda, its principal architect, Fox's foreign policy set about casting the country as a champion of human rights and democracy, not only at home but also abroad. In that context, relations with Cuba would have to change. Mexico soon dropped its habitual opposition to the yearly American resolution against Cuba at the UN Commission on Human Rights while also cultivating ties with Cuban exiles and dissidents on the island. In 2002, an embarrassing incident almost brought Cuban-Mexican relations to the point of rupture. In the lead-up to the UN Development Aid Summit in Monterrey that year, Fox suggested over the phone that Fidel attend but simply "eat and then get going," before President Bush was to arrive, so that Fox could avoid an awkward diplomatic moment. The episode came to light publicly when Castro subsequently played on Cuban television a recording of his phone conversation with Fox. A deeply angered Mexican Left quickly denounced Fox's abandonment of Mexico's historic stance of nonintervention. Castro's gesture also put the rest of the region on notice that his shift from promoting revolution to forging official diplomatic, trade, and commercial ties required reciprocity. Any country seeking to meddle in Cuba's internal affairs risked the prospect that Cuba might exploit its extensive and long-standing social and political networks throughout the region to do the same.

What did Cuba have to do with the election of Left/Populist governments in the region, especially in the Andes?

Between November 2005 and the end of 2006, Latin Americans went to the national polls in 12 countries. Left and center-left leaders were elected or reelected in 8 of the 12—Brazil, Chile, Bolivia, Ecuador, Nicaragua, Honduras, Venezuela, and Uruguay—and came within striking distance of victory in Peru and Mexico. Beyond the national level, a spate of municipal, provincial, and gubernatorial elections put left-leaning political parties in office and in national legislatures in many countries as well. Together, these impressive electoral outcomes (and close losses) signaled an increasingly empowered electorate's demands for public policies to address vast inequality, poverty, social exclusion, and rampant crime.

With Venezuela's Hugo Chávez absorbing the lion's share of Latin America's public oxygen on the regional and, at times, global stage, and with Cuba and Venezuela's deepening ties, much discussion focused on to what extent either country had anything to do with this apparent re-emergence of the Left in Latin America. Venezuela was accused in a number of cases of interfering in elections or supporting the campaigns of leaders it deemed favorable. Cuba had few resources for such schemes. But had the island played a roll? Indirectly, yes.

As described above, by the late 1980s to early 1990s, the Latin American Left had by and large renounced armed struggle and actively participated in democratic political processes. Ceasing its support for armed movements, Cuba pragmatically encouraged this process. Today, no contemporary Latin American leftist political party, with the possible exception of some factions in Venezuela, seeks to emulate the Cuban model. Ideology has become vastly less important than pragmatically solving the region's enormous economic, social, ethnic, and security problems. Nonetheless, Cuba's long-standing critique of "savage capitalism," American power, and the failure of regional elites to invest in their own people came to be shared not only by the democratic Left but also by political parties, leading intellectuals, scholars, and increasingly elites themselves, across the ideological spectrum. Moreover, during the 1990s, when the mantra of neoliberalism called for a dramatic scaling back of the state as Latin America confronted the consequences of debt crises and import substitution industrialization, Cuba served as an important symbolic anchor in a broader debate about the role of the state in providing social welfare and sustainable development. Governance in Cuba could hardly be characterized in most cases as efficient or well managed. Still, in Latin America today, with the Left resurgent, Cuba can be credited with having contributed to a new regional consensus: That is, through well-funded and fiscally competent institutions, a government's primary role is to deliver the building blocks of opportunity, dignity, and social rights to populations long excluded from the region's wealth and resources. By the end of his presidency, even George W. Bush indirectly conceded this point by attempting to frame U.S. policy toward the region as helping Latin Americans achieve social justice, appropriating language once the preserve of Cuba and the region's Left. Still, unlike Cuba, the Democratic Left in Latin America (again with the partial exception of Venezuela) continued to believe that social justice could not be divorced from basic individual and democratic rights. Thus, while Cuba's international message continues to resonate, its domestic model is largely seen as an anachronistic holdover from a prior era.

What is the scope of Cuba's relationship with Venezuela and Hugo Chávez?

In the years since Hugo Chávez was first elected president in 1998, Venezuela and Cuba have grown increasingly close. Chávez and Fidel Castro's public displays of affection demonstrated a deepening alliance, and the two share similar critiques of American power, often collaborating to build new alternative regional organizations that embody their distinctive world views. Of course, Venezuela has also provided Cuba with substantial sums of discounted oil—approximately 100,000 barrels per day—a critical source of support for Cuba's struggling economy. Yet many outside observers have wrongly assumed that Chávez has positioned Venezuela to exercise substantial influence over Cuba internally. If anything, the opposite is the case. Despite its apparent economic leverage via the oil subsidy, Venezuela is not a domestic political player in Cuba. By contrast, Fidel and a host of close advisors have been crucial in helping Chávez consolidate executive power and build new institutions at home. It is Cuban doctors and personnel who have largely staffed Venezuela's most important social initiative: the *misiones*, or social, medical, and educational teams deployed to poor neighborhoods throughout Venezuela. Likewise, Cuban advisors have helped Chávez in his attempt to unify an array of leftist parties under one "Bolivarian" political umbrella.

In 2000, Cuba and Venezuela signed the oil-for-doctors arrangement that to this day forms the substantive core of their bilateral ties. But in political terms, and loosely tracking the estrangement between the United States and Venezuela, the Caracas-Havana link has evolved in two stages, 1998–2004 and 2004 to the present, with a critical turning point in 2002 when a coup attempt briefly removed Chávez from office. During his initial years in power, Chávez held out some hope that he could articulate a critique of Venezuela's political elites as well as their allies in the United States without jeopardizing long-standing and largely healthy bilateral diplomatic and commercial ties with Washington. Early in his tenure, however, Bill Clinton refused to invite the new head of state to the White House, and Chávez stopped the DEA's overflights to monitor drug trafficking. Both moves set the United States and Venezuela on a path toward estrangement. Once George W. Bush came to office, hard-liners in his administration picked upon a theme that emerged by the end of Clinton's tenure: Chávez was moving Venezuela disconcertingly toward the "Cuban model." Turned off by Chávez's provocative rhetoric and leery of his government's proposals for agrarian reform and a host of other structural, economic, political, and judicial changes aimed at wresting power from traditional elites, the Bush administration offered tea and sympathy, and some financial assistance, to a host of opposition groups in Venezuela and pouring into Washington at the time. When in April 2002 Chávez was briefly ousted in a coup, the White House and the U.S. embassy in Caracas issued statements indicating that they looked forward to working with the new government. The president of the congressionally funded International Republican Institute even praised the coup attempt. Leaders throughout Latin America were justifiably appalled at Washington's seeming approval of a fundamentally undemocratic act. Indeed, just months earlier in September 2001, Colin Powell had stood with Latin Americans to sign the OAS's Inter-American Democratic Charter, which explicitly banned coups from the region's political playbook. From that point on, U.S.-led "democracy promotion" would ring hollow in the region; Cuba and Venezuela's own approach to "participatory democracy," meanwhile, gained some breathing room.

With significant experience confronting Cuba's own domestic opposition as well as Washington's destabilization efforts, Fidel closely counseled Chávez throughout the weekend-long coup, even preparing to receive him in Havana in the event that he was unable to return to power. Short of a clear way back to the presidency, Fidel advised Chávez to ensure his safety, lest he meet Salvador Allende's fate and allow his ousters to fill a power vacuum (in 1973, Allende committed suicide when troops led by coup leader August Pinochet began bombing the presidential palace). Several days later, however, the coup leaders backed down under international pressure, and Chávez returned to Miraflores, the presidential palace in Caracas.

In the aftermath of the coup, the Cuba-Venezuela partnership deepened significantly despite the fact that a number of important differences continued to separate the two countries. Perhaps most fundamentally on the political front, unlike Castro, Chávez had been elected and reelected as Venezuela's head of state in multiparty elections deemed by credible international observers to have been, by and large, free and fair. Facing increasing opposition at home, he again prevailed in a 2004 national referendum that had the effect of strengthening his government's hand domestically. But to translate these various electoral successes into the kind of political staying power Chávez desired, he needed help. Cuba was a natural partner. With significant experience abolishing old institutions and creating new ones to advance a revolutionary political project and consolidate power, Cuba provided advice and advisors to do the same in Venezuela, along with up to 20,000 doctors serving in the country at the high point of bilateral cooperation, always in exchange for discounted oil. High oil prices and ideological sympathies made this relationship mutually beneficial. On the global stage, Chávez relished the role of provocateur, absorbing many of the American slings and arrows Fidel had so expertly managed in years past. Chávez deeply admired Fidel's revolutionary example, and Fidel seemed to enjoy the stagecraft of anointing Chávez as his seeming successor in the hemisphere. Yet Chávez was no Fidel, and Venezuela was no Cuba. Despite his bluster and rhetoric, Chávez continued to rely on democratic elections to legitimate his power. Dissent and free expression remained strong, and a weak but organized opposition gained strength, especially as Chávez's radicalization alienated many even among his long-time supporters in the military and in the country's "Bolivarian" political establishment. Under such constraints, Havana knew full well that it could not rely indefinitely on largesse from Caracas nor depend exclusively on only one outside patron. As a result, many in Cuba took Chávez's firm embrace and ideological affinity as politically expedient, happy to pursue a range of cooperation agreements knowing full well that while interests remain permanent, alliances never are.

What were the main features of Cuba's integration into the world economy after the Cold War?

With a population of just over 11 million, Cuba's GDP (roughly $45 billion in 2007) falls closest to neighbors like the Dominican Republic or Ecuador. GDP per capita is comparable to that of Guatemala or Honduras. But unlike any of these countries, Cuba has attempted to shield most of its population from the dynamism and pressures of globalization, remaining committed to spreading its wealth (or lack thereof) more equally than in the outside capitalist world. While largely weaning itself off of sugar, Cuba has channeled foreign capital to tourism, mining (mostly of nickel), biotechnology, oil exploration, telecommunications, and, more recently, infrastructure development in energy, housing, and transportation. Foreign exchange earnings are generated primarily from tourism, nickel, medical services, tobacco and related products, citrus, and fishing. Remittances offer an important influx of foreign exchange as well. Overall foreign direct investment has reached only $6 billion since 1991, with $3 billion actually disbursed. In the Dominican Republic, by contrast, a country with a smaller population, FDI during the same rough period has exceeded $10 billion. Contracts for offshore exploration and drilling have been signed with state and private companies from Spain, Norway, China, Canada, Venezuela, and Brazil, among others. Although agriculture has been somewhat decentralized and private farmers' markets are now ubiquitous, Cuba still imports over 80% of the food consumed by Cubans and foreign tourists, with a sizeable percentage from the United States since 2001.

From the mid-1990s into the new millennium, it looked as though the economic crisis would oblige Cuba to gradually open its economy to a wide variety of joint ventures, with state enterprises gaining a degree of financial independence from the central government. Cuba also considered opening sectors outside of traditional export-oriented or strategic industries to foreign capital, such as beach-front and residential property in upscale Havana suburbs. But particularly from 2004, and as discussed more thoroughly on page 134 ("What kind of foreign investment began in Cuba, what consequences did this investment bring to the island, and how did authorities respond?"), Cuba began to benefit from a more favorable global environment (minerals and other commodity prices began rising) as well as a bigger cushion from Venezuela. As a result of this stronger position, the government actually reversed some of the measures that had given state enterprises a degree of autonomy in managing their external affairs. In addition, the Ministry of Foreign Trade resumed greater control of all imports and exports.

Cuba certainly welcomed the outsized role that Venezuela played during this period, but the government has also slowly built a diversified though modest trade and investment portfolio, thus endeavoring to break with its past dependence on a single crop, commodity, or country. Going forward, trade with and capital from Venezuela, Canada, Spain, Brazil, China, Russia, and, over time, perhaps the United States will grow in importance to Cuba's global integration.

How did Cuba react to the war in Iraq?

During the first Gulf War, Cuba held a rotating seat on the UN Security Council and, while denouncing Iraq's land grab in

Kuwait, had been one of only two countries to oppose resolutions authorizing U.S. military action. Not surprisingly, the
second time around, with George W. Bush lacking the kind of
broad international support that his father had gathered previously, Cuba was again a vocal opponent of U.S. war plans. As
a result, while most countries quickly closed their embassies in
Baghdad, Cuba's diplomats defiantly kept their doors open in
a stand of solidarity with several other countries critical of U.S.
unilateralism (though not necessarily supportive of Saddam
Hussein's regime).

Like many nations and publics around the world, Cuba
believed the United States' preemptive invasion of Iraq lacked
international legitimacy. As evidence mounted regarding
the manipulation of prewar intelligence, civilian casual-
ties, the destruction of Iraqi historical sites and infrastructure, and the torture of detainees, Cuba joined the chorus of
international actors whose opposition to the U.S. invasion and
subsequent occupation became even more resolute. But unlike
many western opponents of the war, Cuba also saw in the Iraqi
experience—and in the doctrine of preemptive attack that had
framed the invasion—its own possible fate at the hands of the
United States. In this way, and as explored in more detail on
page 187 ("What were the main features of U.S. policy toward
Cuba under George W. Bush and how did Cuba respond?"),
the outbreak of the war in Iraq reinforced a closed national
security mindset at home, contributing to the motivation for
the March 2003 crackdown on dissidents. Moreover, U.S. policies of "de-Baathification" in Iraq (or the wholesale purging
from public office of virtually all Iraqis employed in Saddam
Hussein's Baath party institutions) seemed to strongly mirror
the Bush administration's own recommendations that Cuba rid
itself of nearly all vestiges of the revolutionary era, outlined in
detailed fashion by the Commission for Assistance to a Free
Cuba. Thus, in addition to serving as a general warning about
the implications of unchecked American power, the Iraq war
helped the Cuban regime highlight to its own population the

risks of opening the door too quickly to reform policies that would leave Cuba vulnerable to an American-designed transition plan. Abroad, the war in Iraq helped Cuba to further establish its bona fides on the international stage as it associated itself with a broadly shared critique of the United States—whether at the UN, at the Ibero-American Summits, or within the Non-Aligned Movement—that transcended politics, ideology, and geography. With the prisons at Guantánamo a daily reminder of the human consequences of one country rewriting the international rules of war, Cuba was able to deflect attention from its own prisons and political prisoners onto those jailed by a foreign power on its own territory.

AFTER FIDEL, UNDER RAUL

DOMESTIC

*How did the Cuban government deal with Fidel
Castro's illness in 2006?*

On July 31, 2006, Fidel Castro's staff secretary appeared on
national television to read a statement in which the aging
revolutionary leader announced that he was turning over
provisional power in order to undergo surgery (for what
most now believe was an acute attack of diverticulitis). In the
months before the announcement, no public sign of illness had
surfaced. Just five days earlier, Fidel had given two speeches
(one at dawn in Bayamo that lasted two and a half hours and a
slightly shorter one several hours later in the town of Holguin)
to celebrate the 53rd anniversary of his attack on the Moncada
army barracks, the event that launched the 26th of July Movement. The week before he had joined Hugo Chávez in Cordoba,
Argentina, for a week-long MERCOSUR summit, also visiting
Alta Gracia, Che Guevara's birthplace. Indeed, Fidel's only
serious health concern in recent years (as far as the public is
aware) had been the knee and arm injuries he suffered after
a fall a few years earlier. On that occasion, Castro underwent
knee surgery without general anesthesia; an epidural permitted
him to stay conscious and remain in charge of the country. His
illness during the summer of 2006, however, was much more

serious and would eventually require several surgical interventions. As a result, Fidel elected to turn over provisional power to his brother Raul and to half a dozen members of his inner circle.

As his condition worsened and complications emerged in subsequent months, it became clear that Cuba was undergoing more than a temporary change in political leadership. The country had largely recovered from the external shock of the Soviet collapse and survived relentless though ineffectual efforts by the United States to end the revolutionary experiment, including, by Havana's count, several hundred attempts to assassinate Fidel Castro. Yet throughout the government and its scholarly community, it was no secret that some revolutionary regeneration was overdue, lest the social and ideological values of the founders crumble under the weight of the general population's frustration with scarcity and deprivation. A number of high-level officials made public their awareness that corruption in government agencies, youth disaffection, and continuing economic hardship could cause the revolution, as Fidel put it, "to destroy itself." But beyond some uncharacteristically frank press exposés about corruption in state enterprises and some very quiet discussion in a handful of select venues, by the middle of 2006 there was still little public evidence of tangible plans for policies to redress the domestic malaise. Public exhortations to embrace revolutionary ideals seemed increasingly out of touch with the public mood.

What happened in the immediate aftermath of the announcement of Fidel's illness?

Technically, Fidel's decree transferring power was provisional, suggesting that he would return to power once his health improved. But Castro later acknowledged that at the time, he believed he had quite possibly taken his last trip abroad and given his final speech. Raul fully assumed his brother's duties as first secretary of the Cuban Communist Party, head of the

Politburo, president of the Council of State, and commander and chief of the armed forces—all while continuing as minister of defense. Responsibility for managing what Fidel described as the "strategic" sectors of health, education, energy, foreign affairs, and finance was transferred to a half-dozen national figures, a mix of younger and older cadre, some who fought in the Sierra Maestra, others who had cut their political and managerial teeth largely in the post-Soviet era. Aware that Fidel Castro's sidelining from power could create a pretext for violent action against the island, whether at the hands of his enemies in Miami or Washington, Cuban defense and domestic security authorities put massive numbers of police and soldiers on alert.

The Cuban public's reaction to the announcement was one of palpable concern, anticipation, and, notably, calm. For many, Fidel's tenure in power had come to be viewed as both the continuing flame behind what remained of the Cuban Revolution's initial zeal, as well as the Achilles heel of the Revolution's sustainability. Cubans tend to have personal and complex relationships with Fidel Castro, often combining feelings of veneration, respect, or love with frustration or even hate. Thus, even for many of those long disaffected with the revolutionary process, and certainly among his still extensive fan base, Fidel's physical wellbeing was a matter of personal concern and national consequence, but not a pretext for political agitation or unrest. The kind of civil upheaval that many abroad had expected and planned for with Fidel out of the picture simply did not transpire. There was no Ceausescu moment.

In September of 2006, Cuba assumed the chair of the Non-Aligned Movement for the first time since its tenure between 1979 and 1983. Heads of state from around the world descended on Havana amid speculation of a possible appearance by Fidel. Before his illness, the chance to return to a leading role among a host of states that shared his critique of American power and globalization could have been the perfect golden parachute as Fidel entered his 80s. Yet Fidel's health was still too precarious.

By December of 2006, when Cubans and a host of Fidel's friends from around the world gathered for a postponed 80th birthday celebration and ceremony honoring the Cuban Armed Forces, again Fidel defied anticipation he would make at least a pro forma appearance, remaining hospitalized and unable to digest whole foods. Periodically, Cuban state media released photos and video images of a bedridden Fidel with Hugo Chávez, who became a frequent visitor (beginning in August 2006, just several weeks after the initial transfer of power), or one of the few to be publicly acknowledged. As Cuba celebrated the 49th anniversary of the revolution, Cubans and the outside world had accepted the possibility that Fidel's transfer of provisional power might turn out to be more than temporary.

Who is Raul Castro and why was he chosen to succeed Fidel?

It would be easy, but mistaken, to conclude that dynastic politics alone made Raul Castro the only choice to assume Cuba's presidency, for Raul is much more than simply Fidel's younger brother. He is and has been a key official in the Cuban Revolution, responsible for building Cuba's revolutionary state from the ground up since his days commanding troops of the Rebel Army in the Sierra Cristal. In addition to his long-standing history of leadership, Raul also possesses an expansive institutional base from which to operate.

Raul Castro's political trajectory has involved several phases, and his reputation as a leader has likewise evolved over time, in occasionally contradictory ways. In the Sierra and during the early years of the revolution, he became known for his rigor, discipline, and loyalty, as well as for a taste for draconian measures to keep those around him in line. After the revolution triumphed, he played a central role in building the institutions of state—both the repressive and defensive mechanisms necessary to consolidate and keep power internally as well as the military and intelligence capabilities geared toward defending the nation against external threats. From his early days leading

Cuba's military forces, Raul prioritized and, for the first time in Cuban history, succeeded in maintaining the state's monopoly over the use of force, earning a reputation of brutality along the way. Defectors and critics as well as intelligence analysts in the CIA, meanwhile, have for years floated rumors of alcohol abuse and other personal foibles. Raul played a critical role in helping Cuba adjust to the end of the Cold War. After Cuban troops withdrew from southern Africa, he oversaw the transformation of the Cuban military into an institution largely devoted to national defense and the stewardship of large swaths of the state-dominated economy. During and after popular Cuban General Arnaldo Ochoa's fall from grace in 1989 (described on page 73, "Who was General Arnaldo Ochoa and why was he executed?"), Raul played a major role in purging the country's security forces and consolidating the Ministry of Interior under the purview of the Ministry of Defense, which he led.

Raul is credited with inserting a voice of pragmatism into the Cuban leadership's debates about economic issues during the 1990s, pushing Fidel to accept reforms that allowed Cubans to feed themselves more easily and employ themselves in limited trades and services. But during the same period, he also demonstrated an acute and abiding ideological impulse. At the 1995 congress of the Cuban Communist Party, Raul made the public case that a number of scholars in party-sanctioned think tanks who had advocated economic reforms had grown dangerously close to outside powers, specifically the United States. Calling them "fifth columnists," his assault (conducted in collaboration with the current first vice president of the country) resulted in a wholesale purge of some of the most talented and creative thinkers in the country.

Today, Raul Castro seems to believe that his own legacy to Cuba will be less closely tied to the institution building or brutality of the 1960s if he is able to successfully reinvigorate the revolution's long-term staying power. Known now as a family man who keeps regular work hours, gives concise speeches, and holds those around him to high but more human standards than his brother Fidel, Raul demonstrated a very different leadership style immediately following the transfer of power, with far less emphasis on mass mobilization and voluntarism and more of a focus on productivity and efficiency (two qualities he and all Cubans now openly observe are sorely needed). Even those who had suffered the effects of the purge in the 1990s saw him as the right person to manage the post-Fidel era. That he possesses the complete trust of his brother does not mean the two agree on all fronts.

How did Cuba's provisional leadership respond as the reality of Fidel's absence took hold?

Without the protection of Fidel's legendary personal charisma, Raul Castro and the governing leadership moved quickly to signal their awareness that Cuban society was in need of some oxygen. Raul openly recognized that Cubans had grown bone weary of material deprivation and the absence of personal freedoms. This did not mean that the successor regime was ready for multiparty elections monitored by the OAS and Jimmy Carter. Nor did it mean inviting the IMF to Havana to orchestrate shock therapy to liberalize the state economy. Moreover, authorities remained unwilling to move beyond the low-intensity repression that had come to be so effective in maintaining domestic stability. Yet Raul's early acknowledgement of significant problems did pave the way for an extensive national discussion within the framework of the revolution about what kinds of changes Cubans want for their country. More specifically, Raul began removing the lid Fidel had kept on discussions of markets, property, and productivity. In the pages of the notoriously timid and, until recently, vapid state-run press, as well as in schools, workplaces, and meetings convened throughout the country, Raul Castro effectively opened the national suggestion box, cajoling the country to vent, argue, disagree, and constructively offer ideas for reforms—again within the context of socialism. In a climate that many observers noted was the most free of fear and the most democratic in Cuban revolutionary memory, Cubans responded. In one notable incident that received global press attention, a leaked video to the BBC showed several university students asking a number of provocative questions to National Assembly President Ricardo Alarcón at a government-sponsored forum regarding the injustice of the dual currency system, restrictions on travel abroad, and lack of contact between common citizens and their representatives in the Cuban legislature. Likewise, the national press, especially the daily *Juventud Rebelde*, published a series of investigative pieces on the state sector of the economy, exposing the corruption, inefficiency, and often sheer absurdity that plagued government social programs and state-run enterprises.

Fidel's presence just off stage helped contain expectations of dramatic or abrupt changes. Yet all in all, these public discussions served as an enormous pulse-taking exercise for the regime while giving the Cuban population a sense that their future might actually improve after Fidel. They also provided the backdrop for a series of institutional events, including municipal, provincial, and national elections for People's Power representatives at the end of 2007, as well as a number of professional "congresses" of writers, artists, and journalists. Importantly, the government announced that it would hold the long-postponed sixth congress of the Cuban Communist Party in late 2009, likely to be a key event where significant reforms may be undertaken, as they have been at past party congresses. At the same time consensus building and personnel changes within the revolution's leadership, and some experimentation with deregulation in the agricultural sector, helped Raul consolidate political support for further reform.

How was Raul Castro elected president of Cuba?

According to Cuba's 1992 constitution, every five years in Cuba elections are held for the 609 seats in the National Assembly of People's Power. National Assembly members then go on to elect members of the Council of State, which consists of 31 members, including one president, one first vice president, and five vice presidents. The president of the Council of State is also the president of the republic and the commander in chief of the armed forces. The Council of State then appoints the cabinet, known as the Council of Ministers. There is considerable overlap in the membership of the two bodies, as well as between the membership of the Council of State and the Politburo of the Cuban Communist Party.

At the end of 2007, Cubans voted in one-party, multiple candidate slates for the local and provincial People's Power representatives. In January 2008, the whole country voted for the National Assembly's membership. Following these elections, Fidel Castro issued a statement on February 19, announcing he would no longer "aspire to nor accept...the position of President of the Council of State and Commander-in-chief." Under these circumstances, Raul Castro, who had served as first vice president, was elected president by members of the National Assembly on February 24, 2008.

Since becoming president, what has Raul done and how have Cubans reacted?

In an inaugural speech of less than 40 minutes, Raul broadly outlined the agenda for his first and perhaps only five-year term. The speech made clear that in the 18 months following Fidel's illness, public expressions of grievances had been paralleled by a behind-the-scenes policy discussion of considerable range and potential consequence. With Fidel's health improved and stable, and with his legacy and views still very much part of Cuban public discourse, the first thing Raul made clear was that Fidel had been and would continue to be consulted on major decisions of state, both domestic and foreign. A resolution to this effect was approved unanimously by the National Assembly. Raul then went on to deliver a number of important messages. First, he indicated that in subsequent weeks and months a number of modest and moderately paced measures would be rolled out. Some would address a bloated and inefficient administrative bureaucracy; some would crack down on corruption in state enterprises. Others would help improve the lives of Cuban people. Second, he emphasized the importance of measures to enhance the productive and efficient use of resources, a clear indication that with the reduction in the size of the state would come the introduction of more market mechanisms. In particular, the speech highlighted agriculture as an area of special focus. Third, though Raul made clear that the United States was still very much in the business of seeking to derail the revolution, he also notably stressed that Cuba's problems were largely homegrown and could only be solved by Cubans themselves.

As expected, a number of limited but significant reforms followed, focusing initially on consumer demands. Access to the Internet for now remains heavily controlled or off-limits entirely, but the government has liberalized the sale of computers (prices remain prohibitive for most). Already, however, the government understands that its ability to control Internet access is limited; with bootleg connections Cubans are increasingly plugging into YouTube, Facebook, and MySpace, and even entering the blogosphere. There seems to be an ongoing debate within the government about the risks and rewards of further opening access to the Web, as Cuba's exposure to all things global and technological is recognized as inevitable. Cell phones, though present in Cuba for well over a decade, are also now available to anyone who can afford them (previously their use had been restricted to authorized individuals), and remarkably high numbers have been sold. In addition, Raul tackled one of Cubans' most common complaints by eliminating prohibitions on citizens' access to hotels, specialized beaches, and other tourist facilities. Surprisingly, though prices for a one-night stay are several times the average monthly wage, summer bookings by local customers at Cuba's beach resorts soared. Even for those who cannot afford such indulgences, by removing restrictions Raul eliminated what the Cuban population regarded as an unjust denial of their basic rights.

Though some in the Bush administration dismissed these changes as simply "cosmetic," other reforms are far less susceptible to this charge. Long a man clear on the political as well as nutritional importance of food on the Cuban table, Raul lifted the ban on farmers buying their own supplies and equipment and initiated a process through which more unused state lands are being turned over and leased to independent farmers and cooperatives (a trend that first began to a limited degree in the 1990s as state-owned agricultural enterprises lost efficiency). As of February 2009, Cuban sources reported that more than 45,000 farmers had received such land grants. Deregulation of the production, distribution, and sale of milk saved the state millions, Raul reported. In order to boost food supply, additional agricultural sectors were expected to see similar measures. In what may be a small boost to private property, the state sped up the process through which some occupants are being granted title to their residential properties (freely selling these properties still remain prohibited, though practiced on the black market). Raul also reportedly probed the possibility of eliminating the *tarjeta blanca,* the onerous and widely reviled permission slip long required for all Cubans to leave the country and travel abroad (though some restrictions would likely remain for doctors, recent university graduates, and security officials). Also in the area of personal freedoms, and as a prelude to improving diplomatic ties with the European Union, Raul Castro oversaw Cuba's signing of two important international human rights agreements, although the extent or pace of the government's intended implementation of their provisions remains in question. In addition, Castro commuted the death sentences of all but a small handful of prisoners who had been sentenced to capital punishment, though he did not indicate that the death penalty would be eliminated from the penal code. With each modest measure, hope for greater reforms increased, but expectations, and the potential cost of not meeting them, did as well.

Another policy move actively discussed but yet to be implemented is the elimination of Cuba's current dual currency (peso and CUC, or convertible peso) system in favor of conversion to a single convertible currency (for the origins of Cuba's dual currency system, please see page 131, "What were the regime's economic reforms and why were they so limited?" and page 134, "What kind of foreign investment began in Cuba, what consequences did this investment bring to the island, and how did authorities respond?"). Today, state-sector employees paid in traditional Cuban pesos earn salaries far less valuable than foreign-sector workers, informal-sector hustlers, and recipients of remittances who are able to convert their hard currency income into more valuable CUCs. CUCs, in turn, provide access to products and services simply not affordable for those whose income depends on traditional Cuban pesos. This fundamental inequality has been one of Cuban citizens' strongest grievances. For now, currency reform appears to be on hold, likely because it requires the accumulation of foreign reserves that Cuba does not currently possess. In the meantime, by legalizing hard currency tips and bonuses made by foreign businesses, cleaning up corruption, cracking down on the black market, and streamlining state enterprises, the state intends to absorb a share of revenue from the substantial underground economy and to move more Cuban employment from the informal to the formal sector.

Still, to make any push toward formalization sustainable and raise the kinds of hard currency necessary to make currency conversion possible, job creation is urgently needed. Job creation will in turn require more foreign investment beyond the traditional sectors of tourism and commodity extraction. Indeed, some new foreign investment has materialized from major regional players such as Brazil, notably for agricultural, industrial, infrastructure, and energy projects. A freer labor market will also be necessary, as the government seems to recognize. Sounding more like Margaret Thatcher than Karl Marx, Raul cautioned that "socialism means social justice and equality, but equality of rights, of opportunities, not of income...equality is not egalitarianism." Egalitarianism, he added, could be "a form of exploitation of the good workers by those who are less productive and lazy." With that, Cuba's Socialist government announced it would eliminate the cap on salaries and wages paid in state enterprises, indicating a measure of tolerance for inequality as a trade-off for productivity and fairness. Moreover, in the future, Raul hinted, Cubans may no longer be able to count on such extensive subsidies for a host of programs and products and should in fact expect to be taxed (a concept foreign to most Cubans) as the state gives citizens greater space to earn incomes independent of state enterprises. Indeed, pressure is building for an expansion of the 1990s reforms legalizing limited individual enterprise. Cuba recently announced it will issue new taxi licenses for the first time in many years, and the construction industry has also benefited from policies aimed at decentralization, perhaps paving the way for greater employment of the island's thousands of licensed and unlicensed independent skilled tradesmen—an urgent priority given the need for massive rebuilding of housing and other buildings destroyed by hurricanes Gustav, Ike, and Paloma.

Such market-based measures may be increasingly necessary as Cuba faces looming demographic challenges. According to Raul Castro, with a rapidly aging population, in the year 2025, there will be 770,000 fewer citizens in the workforce than today. Moreover, beginning in the year 2020, there will be more citizens leaving the workforce than entering it. Financial strains on the government's social security and benefits systems will thus only increase, leading the government to take the preliminary step of increasing the retirement age for men from 60 to 65. The public revelation of such sobering statistics during the summer of 2008, coupled with global highs in the prices of imported food and oil at the time, seemed to dampen some of the initial optimism at the start of Raul's presidency. Still, despite the economically and socially costly intrusion of hurricanes Gustav, Ike, and Paloma, other reforms and active debates continue, with Cuban economists purged by Raul Castro and Cuba's First Vice President José Ramon Machado Ventura in the 1990s once again circulating proposals for far-reaching changes. Moreover, economic authorities are keenly eyeing the potential for Cuba to become a major oil producer (with government estimates of 20 billion barrels in offshore reserves).

How has public discourse and debate evolved under the presidency of Raul Castro?

Consistent with his policies as provisional head of state, Raul Castro emphasized at his inauguration the importance of disagreement and dissent as key ingredients to obtaining policy outcomes that are seen as legitimate by the majority and beneficial to the public's welfare. Dissent outside of the constraints and framework of state socialism, however, would still be largely proscribed, as the following direct quote indirectly suggests: "There is no reason to fear discrepancies in a society such as ours, where its very nature precludes the existence of antagonistic contradictions, since the social classes that make it up are not antagonistic themselves. The best solutions can come from a profound exchange of differing opinions, if such an exchange is guided by sensible purposes and the views are uttered with responsibility."

Despite this caveat, the degree of public debate has, by all comparisons to the recent past, been remarkable. Shortly after assuming the presidency, Raul and the other Council of State members gave their blessing to the most forthcoming and wide-ranging series of publicly broadcast discussions about culture and society in decades: the April 2008 Congress of the Union of Cuban Writers and Artists (UNEAC). UNEAC brings together Cuba's most prominent and lesser-known artists, writers, musicians, dancers, filmmakers, and poets. Against the backdrop of the recent reappearance of individuals associated with the cultural repression of the early 1970s on state television, participants in the 2008 congress frankly and forcefully discussed the need for greater openness, freedom of expression, self-criticism, and reflection, so long as all debate is constructive and respectful of the Socialist framework. Significantly, key national leaders were in attendance as well, including Raul Castro, Carlos Lage, and Abel Prieto (minister of culture). In the aftermath of the congress, artists continue to make their voices heard, with prominent cultural figures like writer Leonardo Padura and musician Pablo Milanés voicing, both at home and in the international press, very strong critiques of government policies and the need for change while still upholding their faith in the revolution itself.

Yet as if to reinforce Fidel's own admonition made decades earlier at a similar forum—"within the revolution everything, outside of it nothing"—the regime continues to issue warnings, make arrests, and deny space to Cuban activists and artists seeking to express their dissent outside of formally sanctioned state channels, specifically those associated with or financed directly or indirectly by the USAID programs designed to promote democracy in Cuba. Indeed, more recently, such programs seem to have incorporated a new focus on mobilizing Cuban youth. Thus, in a series of incidents, Cuban police harassed young adults wearing bracelets printed with the word *cambio* (change), reportedly distributed in Cuba by the U.S. Interests Section and international NGOs. Later, state security stormed a church in Santiago de Cuba to arrest several young dissidents who had been advocating for university autonomy. The church protested and authorities apologized for the incident. More recently, Havana police briefly detained a quirky and irreverent punk musician, Gorki Aguila, front man of the band Porno Para Ricardo, for his frontally aggressive antiregime lyrics. On one hand, the episode demonstrated the state's orthodox association between free speech and counterrevolution. Yet when artists in Cuba and the young man's fans (abroad and at home) complained, authorities also demonstrated a certain flexibility, releasing him with only a small fine.

Repression has also continued against independent activists who in some cases promote causes that the state already supports. One example concerns the topic of gay rights. Under the leadership of Raul's daughter, Mariela Castro, head of the National Center for Sex Education (CENESEX), Cuba has undertaken a wholesale public education campaign against homophobia, heralding the importance of recognizing the decidedly liberal, even "neoliberal" concept of "diversity." But plans for Cuba's first ever Gay Pride Parade in 2008, a major step in and of itself, were interrupted because the march was organized by gay rights groups not sanctioned by the state. As the state permits freer expression concerning some sensitive social issues, its crackdowns continue, even where public expressions are perhaps critical of the state in some respects (particularly its past legacy of homophobia) but ultimately consistent with evolving definitions of necessary and permissible debate.

Another important critical phenomenon since Raul's assumption of power has been the rise of an independent Cuban blogosphere based on the island and cultivated through illegal Internet connections, USB flash drives, and furtive entrances into hotel Internet cafés. Yoani Sánchez, a trained philologist who left the island in 2002 for Switzerland only to return for family reasons in 2004, has received the most international attention for her pithy writings assessing the daily hardships and realities of life in Cuba on her blog "Generation Y" (a reference to the many Cubans of her generation who were given nontraditional names beginning with that letter). Sánchez is critical of the Cuban government in many respects and writes about the need for a more open society with greater political freedoms. She seems to identify with some dissident voices, while also keeping her distance. She defines herself as a "citizen" describing her daily life, and she writes from a fundamentally humanistic rather than ideological or political perspective, earning her a global following. Her writings earned her the prestigious Ortega y Gasset prize (Spain) for digital journalism in 2008, but she was denied permission to leave the country to receive the award. *Time* magazine named her one of the world's 100 most influential people, a stretch, to be sure. In response to such publicity, censors have endeavored to block access to Generation Y within Internet cafés and more broadly across the island. A number of government-supported blogs expressing various perspectives about life in Cuba have emerged as well, a tacit recognition of the importance of this new medium. From the government's perspective, Sánchez's work points to the risks and rewards of allowing broader access to the Web. With greater Internet availability across the population, many more insightful bloggers critical of the government may emerge. On the other hand, a growing chorus of critical voices is less likely to draw the kind of exclusive international attention and personal scrutiny that Sánchez's case has generated.

Will there be any political reform?

It is hard to imagine the kind of rapid political reform in Cuba that took place in the former Soviet bloc countries or in the democratic transitions in South America—at least, any time soon. There is no indication of any kind that the Communist Party and its leadership will give up power, nor that it feels pressured or compelled to do so. The pace and stability of the succession so far indicates as much. Raul has said repeatedly that the only replacement for Fidel Castro is the party itself. In other words, Cuban officials will only be able to sustain and regenerate the revolution in Fidel's absence through more accountable institutions, not individuals. How they interpret the concept of accountability, however, will surely differ from liberal notions of multiparty electoral politics. We have already seen that within the framework of the Communist Party, the Cuban government has engaged itself and the population in a serious debate about exactly how to make the revolution last. It may well be that in the planning for the sixth party congress scheduled for the fall of 2009, Raul and others promote a far more open form of discourse and permit a much greater range of ideas to be publicly discussed and reported. But however distinct from Fidel's approach, which was ever vigilant against revealing to outsiders the extent of internal debate, whatever emerges in Cuba in the short term is unlikely to look like multiparty political democracy in the liberal Western world. In the longer term, the major challenge the Cuban regime has set for itself is to convert the Communist Party into an instrument seen as the legitimate institutional umbrella for capturing, containing, and reflecting a range of views and debates while setting policies that reflect broad participation and buy-in from the Cuban public at large.

Can Cuba's successor government open up economically without promoting unmanageable political strife?

A constellation of forces—internal and external—appears to favor a stable succession in the short to midterm, one that will permit Raul, the party, the cabinet, and the military to gradually introduce economic reforms without political upheaval. To be sure, considerable state resources remain devoted to low-intensity repression, and the hurricanes, which may have cost the government up to 10% of its GDP, have presented an unprecedented economic and social challenge. But in his own way, Raul is undertaking real politics in an attempt to stably guide the country beyond the orthodoxy of the Fidel era. At home, he has begun to reinforce the legitimacy of the state by telling people what to expect—whether good or bad—and acting accordingly. Indeed, because expectations were so low for so long, especially among Cuban youth, measures designed to modestly enhance personal freedom (to travel and to consume, for example) can deliver concrete improvements to the Cuban population while increasing hope for greater change—an important psychological side effect. Of course, for those Cubans hit hardest by the hurricanes, material deprivation and exposure to the elements may well overtake the initial boost of hope provided by Raul's early moves. Regardless, what can be said for certain is that the government fully understands the need to undertake reforms that help Cubans fulfill their deeply felt demands for greater economic and professional opportunities, but hopes to do so without dramatically undermining the authority, stability, and position of the state as a central arbiter in Cuban political and economic affairs. Though less exposed to the global financial crisis than other more open economies, Cuba too will face a credit squeeze and experience the effects of the global shortfall in investment capital.

In the nearly 19 months between the announcement of Fidel's illness and his formal renunciation of power, Raul's authority and credibility allowed him to build consensus support for the measures he has subsequently implemented as president. Going forward, if Raul can demonstrate that productivity, market-based incentives, decentralization, and a wider frame of permissible dissent are not recipes for political suicide or renewed American domination, the government is more likely to back further liberalization, primarily in economic areas. It is a tricky balancing act, to be sure, one that requires carefully managing the Cuban people's often countervailing demands and expectations for change. On the one hand, the Cuban population is clamoring for the state to get out of its way. Many would love nothing more than to be able to bring their black market businesses into the open. On the other hand, after half a century of getting almost everything for free from cradle to grave, there remains a deeply ingrained expectation among Cubans (one embodied in the constitution, in fact) that they are entitled to an array of state benefits.

The balance only becomes more difficult with an eye toward the longer term, as Raul clearly recognizes. Any program of economic liberalization would not be undertaken in a way that fundamentally threatens the state's ability to provide critical social services like health, education, and pensions—key legacies and tangible sources of the regime's legitimacy. Yet, as described above, Cuba's working-age population is now declining quickly in comparison to its growing cohort of retirees. Raul seems to recognize that unless the government can generate more productive economic activity and tax it, both involving political risk and benefits, demographics alone could jeopardize the sustainability of the revolution's key social programs and most significant domestic legacies. The external environment presents Cuba with a complex set of waters to navigate in carrying out plans for a slowly paced series of reforms. On the one hand, the global credit crisis; the decline in the world price of one of Cuba's key commodity exports, nickel; and the global food and fuel crises have all dramatically increased or, with the financial crisis, otherwise complicated the cost of putting food on the table. On the other hand, a diverse though modest trade and investment portfolio, aided substantially by Venezuela's subsidized oil and, until recently, high global commodity prices, has helped the island emerge from the Special Period of extreme material deprivation. Now that Hugo Chávez has gained the constitutional authority to stand for reelection indefinitely, even with oil prices at well less than half their 2008 highs, Venezuela's alliance with Cuba is likely to provide a source of stable material support for the foreseeable future. Brazil is positioning itself for a very active role in Cuba as well. Not only can greater involvement help the Lula government enhance its regional geopolitical status, but also Brazil's leaders, old friends of Fidel's, appear intent on seeing a soft landing on the island; in their view, greater economic engagement can further the trend toward liberalization. As an aspiring regional energy powerhouse, Brazil also has a keen interest in Cuba's oil and ethanol potential. Led by Spain, the European Union has also renewed its dialogue, and offered millions in hurricane relief, to signal its support for a stable succession in Cuba, even as it places the issues of human rights and democracy squarely on the table.

Even before the hurricanes hit, high food and oil prices were making themselves felt on the island's balance sheet, and the Cuban government had acknowledged that these difficulties would make certain "adjustments and restrictions inevitable." Yet the more difficult external environment that characterized the end of Raul's first year in office could cause the government to accelerate the kinds of reforms that will unleash the entrepreneurial energies of the population and take some of the burden to finance everything off the state. One key dimension of the external environment for 2009 will be whether the Obama administration, by executive order, or the U.S. Congress, undertakes a relaxation of travel and trade sanctions against the island.

Finally, Fidel, at this writing, is still alive. That fact alone tempers expectations of dramatic change, just as the cautious and conservative nature of Cuban society favors the go-slow approach that has unfolded since his illness.

What is Fidel's role since he stepped down from the presidency?

Even while coping with an extremely debilitating illness, Fidel was able to orchestrate his own withdrawal from public life and, according to many close confidants, weigh in on a number of decisions that brought Cuba to the moment of his resignation in early 2008. On occasion, images and brief reports of a physically diminished Fidel receiving foreign visitors—Hugo Chávez, Luiz Inacio da Silva, Cristina Fernández de Kirchner, and Michelle Bachelet, for example—make it into Cuba's press and circulate abroad. Hardly one to go quietly, he has taken up the pen, issuing "reflections" published in the state press, on Cuban government Web sites, and in leading European dailies on subjects ranging from climate change, biofuels, and the global food crisis to the role of U.S. Southern Command, the 2008 U.S. presidential election, the election of President

Barack Obama (which Castro described as the fulfillment of the American dream), North and South Korea, his friendship with Gabriel García Márquez, Guantánamo, and Cuban history. Occasionally, he has weighed in—critically—about measures undertaken by his brother. Raul has even quipped that the two disagree not on fundamentals, but rather over degree and emphasis, likening their differences to those between the Democratic and Republican parties in the United States. Whether or not Fidel is actually writing these hundreds of essays himself or with help—a topic of constant speculation—is less important than their significance. Fidel Castro continues to have a huge base of popular support and respect in Cuba, and the essays allow him to continue shaping his legacy. Moreover, his presence as great sage in chief compels the new government to modulate its moves within a policy framework that will not excessively offend Fidel's sensibilities, nor those of the individuals in the Council of State who remain his close ideological and political comrades. Notably, he has not appeared in public, other than through images broadcast on Cuban television, for over two years. To be sure, many in Cuba and among his fiercest critics abroad speculate that Castro could well be pulling many a string on the island, and it is hard to know exactly what he does and does not do and say in private. But his conscious choice to stay out of the limelight, save a couple of hundred words a week in the press, has laid the groundwork for Cuba and the world to look clearly toward life after Fidel.

U.S.-CUBA

How did the United States react to the news of Fidel turning over provisional power?

Just weeks before the announcement, the Bush administration had released the second report of the President's Commission for Assistance to a Free Cuba, chaired by Secretary of State Condoleezza Rice and Secretary of Commerce Carlos Gutiérrez (the rest of its membership—principally other government officials—remained unknown to the public for reasons more of cattiness than substance). As with its first report issued in 2004, the commission's second 430-page assessment assumed that once Fidel and Raul were out of the picture, the Cuban people would automatically seek to move toward a top-to-bottom political transition. Accordingly, the United States would first focus on advancing that transition (through a significant expansion in funds dedicated to democracy promotion efforts) and second, with a transitional government in place, adopt a host of policies to "assist" that new government. The report also made explicit that U.S. policy should endeavor to ensure that the Castro regime's "intrinsically unstable...succession strategy does not succeed."

After the Cold War, the American intelligence community and State Department commissioned countless studies and simulations to spin out various scenarios for a post-Fidel Cuba. But the lion's share of these scenarios started from the assumption of his death or, at a minimum, his complete absence from the island's political stage. Even though a handful of free thinkers in the U.S. government pushed their colleagues to see the regime as more than a flimsy house of cards, doing so within the self-censoring and analytically constricted environment that colored most discussions of Cuba in Washington would have required acknowledging some degree of institutionalization and legitimacy. Of course, after a half century of cloudy political judgment and visceral anti-communism, this prospect was not only virtually unthinkable but also a possible professional risk. Thus, when news of Fidel's illness broke, officials reiterated the common wisdom: Like a helicopter with a broken rotor, Cuban communism without *el comandante* at the helm would inevitably crash. With no concrete information about the nature of his illness and few analytical tools to anticipate how the regime could last without him, the Bush administration was left utterly flat-footed in subsequent weeks and months. Other than placing the Coast Guard on alert for a possible refugee crisis, there was little evidence to suggest

Washington did anything other than keep U.S. policies in place and wait. Decades of attempting to isolate Havana had left Washington with few direct sources of information; its Interests Section on the island, with among the largest staffs of any U.S. diplomatic mission in Latin America, was largely cut off from contact other than with foreign embassies in town or the dissidents it supported.

Initially, there was one bright spot in the U.S. reaction, and it came from George Bush and Condoleezza Rice immediately following the announcement of Fidel's illness and temporary transfer of power. Both clearly stated something that to most Cubans and Cuban Americans was obvious, but to some in Miami was not: The future leader of a democratic Cuba was in Cuba; change must come from within. This nod to reality, coming from a government that for nearly 50 years had tacitly and at times overtly supported the notion that Cuban exiles might have a political role in their island's future, was a significant acknowledgement in and of itself. But it was also likely directed specifically at Cuban American Republican members of Congress, especially Fidel Castro's nephew by marriage, Lincoln Díaz Balart, whom some still believe has ambitions to hold political office in Cuba one day. Nonetheless, several months later, the president took a notable step backward from this note of realism in a highly publicized speech at the State Department intended to help the United States regain moral authority on the Cuba issue lest the succession consolidate further. Though once again focusing on internal actors as the source of Cuba's future leadership, and despite making a nod to the importance of reconciliation ("If Cuba is to enter a new era, it must find a way to reconcile and forgive those who have been part of the system but who do not have blood on their hands"), Bush described U.S. policy toward the island as favoring "freedom" over "stability." Consistent with his 2004 inaugural speech heralding America's support for freedom and democracy, Bush used these words to stress his endorsement of peaceful campaigns for fundamental change rather than accepting the stable succession and the status quo under Fidel's brother. Yet such scarcely veiled bellicose language also carried the implication that violence might be an acceptable price to pay for freedom (the same logic used in Iraq), thus reinforcing Havana's suspicions of Washington's "democracy promotion" motives.

In the U.S. Congress, reactions ranged from a loud drumbeat of delight from hard-liners most committed to unseating Fidel to a far more sober recognition in both parties that by clinging to current policy the United States risked being completely side-lined from having an impact on developments within Cuba. Proposals dormant since 2002 for relaxing or entirely ending sanctions circulated once again. Public opinion in the United States had long favored new policy toward the island: Gallup polls found that 65% of Americans were ready for a different approach. Among the foreign policy cognoscenti, embargo fatigue had set in nearly a decade earlier with the pope's visit and then the Elián fiasco. Fidel's illness was widely seen as an opportunity to bury the hatchet and to make the case that a policy based on domestic politics simply did not suit American national interests.

Has Raul Castro taken a different approach to the United States than his brother Fidel?

In substance, no, but stylistically, yes. Within weeks of taking provisional power, Raul made clear in an interview Cuba's disposition to talk to the United States regarding a host of bilateral issues with the understanding that his country would make no political concessions in the process. He has reiterated the offer on several occasions since, stressing themes of mutual respect and mutual interest, while also indicating that perhaps such talks might become more viable under Obama. In a sense, this is nothing new. Cuban officials such as Fidel Castro, Ricardo Alarcón, Felipe Pérez Roque, and a host of other spokespeople have made similar statements since Cuba began winding down its support for revolution in Central America. What distinguished Raul's comments was their tone: Not only did they lack his brother's stridency, but they also dropped the suggestion that the United States has something Cuba absolutely needs. Repairing relations with the United States (to gain access to the U.S. market, to move away from a fundamentally unnatural dynamic between families, and to reduce economic and security costs incurred by U.S. hostility) was more of a priority for Cuba in the earlier part of this century. By 2002, Cuba all but ended actively lobbying for the end of economic sanctions even as its spokespeople continued publicly and privately to assail virtually all features of U.S. policy toward the island. Under Raul, the prospect of dialogue with Washington has emerged as but one of many foreign policy issues Cuba is managing. Rapprochement is not by any means the government's first priority. Havana's posture toward the prospect of talks seems to be one of caution. Should the Obama administration do little or nothing to change the tone and begin to change policy toward the island, and allow the U.S. Interests Section in Havana to continue its distribution of cash to dissidents under the rubric of "democracy promotion," Cuba's continued rejection of Washington's support for dissident activities on the island may crowd out all other issues that are ripe for positive movement on the bilateral agenda. Still, in what can only be regarded as an extremely serious step toward laying the groundwork for dialogue, Raul designated Cuba's most senior career foreign service official, Jorge Bolaños (an individual who served as Cuba's ambassador in London, Brasilia, and Mexico City and who is also deputy foreign minister and a highly decorated revolutionary), as his representative in Washington.

Over the years, and regardless of the political winds blowing in Miami, Washington, or Havana, Fidel Castro was known for cultivating close personal relationships with hundreds of Americans from every race, profession, and ideological background. He also eagerly entertained visiting American congressional, NGO, and business delegations from practically every state of the union, as well as artists, writers, and performers. By contrast, Raul has left the lion's share of such activities to other senior officials. The message? When the time, conditions, and agenda are propitious, Cuba will welcome talks with the United States; until then, domestic issues are Raul's priority. Cuban foreign policy will be largely managed by those designated to do so. Of course, as long as he is around and capable, Fidel Castro will continue to have a say as well.

Once a stable succession was evident, how did the U.S. government adjust its view of Cuba?

The longer it became clear that a stable succession was indeed unfolding on the island, the more U.S. efforts to advocate regime change were exposed as complete failures. At the end of the day, none of the instruments of policy—whether economic sanctions, human rights condemnations, pleas to U.S. allies, funds to build an opposition movement, or broadcasts by Radio or TV Martí, all of which fed the domestic political demand for aggressive anti-Castro policies—had made much of a dent within Fidel's or Raul's Cuba.

The stability of Cuba's succession, coupled with the ascendance of reality-based professionals within Bush's Latin America team, generated a notable if uncomfortable willingness on the part of the administration to acknowledge and slightly adjust to the obvious: The Cuban regime had not imploded. Raul's initial reforms came to be regarded as acts taken out of self-preservation and, among the less politicized in Washington, measures intended to demonstrate the government's accountability to its population. Indeed, statements from top intelligence officials did acknowledge that Raul's government possessed some awareness of and connection to its own constituents' needs, beyond an eagerness to repress them. There was also a consciousness, even sensitivity, within the U.S. government that its partners in the hemisphere (especially Mexico,

Brazil, and Canada) and the European Union wanted to see a soft landing in Cuba and regarded U.S. policy as an obstacle to this goal. Moreover, some Bush administration officials tacitly recognized that greater involvement from any of these countries in Cuban affairs could counterbalance Venezuela's influence on the island. Thus, upon Raul's formal ascension to the presidency, Secretary of State Condoleezza Rice's statement was notably devoid of the kind of hardened ideological language long associated with U.S. policy toward Cuba. Subsequently, when Brazil stepped up its financial and economic role in Cuba, some Bush officials even described these steps as positive, a departure from the administration's past tendency to criticize allies who dared defy the United States. In the case of the European Union, although some true believers lobbied for Brussels to keep diplomatic sanctions in place, others took care to not stand in Europe's way. These mixed signals clearly reflected signs of disagreement within the administration about the U.S. approach to Cuba. They also signaled a broader recognition that it did not behoove U.S. interests to antagonize key allies on what ultimately is an issue of little strategic importance. Indeed, in light of the United States' plummeting reputation globally and the necessity of collaborating with a variety of partners in Afghanistan and elsewhere, aggressively pushing other governments to toe the U.S. line would have created an unnecessary diplomatic thorn, likely without yielding any positive results.

Beyond these subtle changes in tone and language, changes in policy were nominal at best. The administration dismissed Raul Castro's early reforms as "cosmetic" and continued to insist that Cuba quickly adopt a "path" toward democratic elections—something the nationalistic Cuban government rejects as code for regime change. Likewise, officials continued their activism on behalf of political prisoners, awarding the Presidential Medal of Freedom in absentia to prisoner of conscience Oscar Biscet, and even organized a global Cuba solidarity day in an effort to raise awareness about the plight of dissidents and democratic activists. Not surprisingly, Cuban authorities responded with their own highly staged press conference reporting new allegations of dissident collaboration with officials of the U.S. Interests Section in Havana.

As the 2008 presidential election season kicked in, the prospect of major White House policy changes faded. Likewise, USAID officials contended with the challenge of trying to spend nearly $50 million for "democracy promotion" in Cuba, knowing full well that the majority of their funds would wind up feeding an anti-Castro cottage industry in Miami and Washington, rather than in the hands of activists on the island (whose activities were often infiltrated by Cuban security in any case). Still, amid growing suspicion of corruption, graft, and waste in these programs, the administration rolled out some small changes. Shortly after Raul's government announced that Cubans would be able to purchase cell phones and phone cards freely, the administration announced it would allow Americans to donate cell phones to family members on the island. Licenses for sports teams and other American groups to travel to Cuba picked up pace. In Congress, a long dormant bill to allow family travel passed the first of many legislative hurdles, while the hurricane damage prompted bipartisan legislation calling for the end to restrictions on family travel, humanitarian aid, and remittances, as well as, significantly, a Senate measure to suspend the embargo for 180 days to permit Cuba to purchase reconstruction materials. For its part, the Bush administration offered $5 million in aid, which Cuba rejected, arguing that Washington could do more to help by lifting the embargo—even on a temporary basis— instead. Moreover, Cuban officials questioned whether the offer was genuine in light of one senior administration official's comments suggesting that the hurricane damage could provide a lever to unseat the regime.

On balance, Fidel and Raul Castro did the Bush administration and the presidential candidates of both parties a favor by carrying out a stable succession in the middle of an election season. George W. Bush left the White House without achieving his promise of bringing down the revolution. Yet peeling back the layers of rhetoric, in the wake of Fidel's illness, both countries recognized they had a stake in avoiding the humanitarian and security nightmare of a refugee crisis or the provocation of political violence long foreseen, even desired, by extremists in Washington and Miami. Indeed, with Fidel no longer the public face of the revolution, no longer mobilizing mass protests against this or that American infraction against Cuba's sovereignty, it became considerably easier for many in the United States (including former senior officials in both parties, from Madeline Albright, Brent Scowcroft, and George Shultz to a host of retired military officers) to publicly call for a new chapter in the U.S.-Cuba relationship, including an end to the ban on travel and trade. Momentum continued under Obama.

How has the Cuban American community reacted to Fidel's illness and Raul's assumption of the presidency?

Long before Fidel's illness, Cuban Americans had ceased to speak with one voice. When news of Fidel's transfer of power broke, Little Havana's Calle Ocho was the scene of spontaneous (but ultimately brief and muted) celebration, and Miami's radio programs filled with exhortations heralding the end of an era. With the announcement, community leaders broadly acknowledged that the island had reached a clear turning point, creating an opportunity, some hoped, to forge consensus behind commonly shared objectives for Cuba's future. But unity, one of Fidel's long-term strategic objectives on the island, has remained elusive in the diaspora. Indeed, by the time Fidel formally renounced the presidency a year and a half later, there were no street celebrations, no public expressions of exile angst—a clear recognition that the hopes so many had pinned on the departure of Cuba's imposing leader had not materialized. Rather than present a united front, various exile actors continue to debate the merits of competing approaches, priorities, and visions. As a result, some members of the community fear that Cuba's political evolution, at this moment of profound change, will bypass Miami altogether.

Divisions have been most palpable, however, in the wake of a series of inquiries into the efficacy of USAID democracy promotion programs for Cuba. A 2006 report of the General Accountability Office (GAO) showed that much of the funds disbursed to Cuban American NGOs finance overhead costs in Miami and frivolous spending on chocolates, sweaters, and Game Boys rather than providing concrete benefits to Cuban civil society activists. Several dissidents have said as much, demanding improvements in the programs and also criticizing, with increasing frequency, restrictions on travel and remittances. Accusations within and between organizations have sowed even greater divisions. Against the backdrop of a Raul Castro government, such infighting persistently frustrates those in the community who had hoped Fidel's departure from power would unify Cuban American activist groups around a common agenda.

The hurricanes further dramatized the community's differences while also creating an avenue for unity. For example, religious leaders in Miami, led by the Catholic Church, raised $400,000 (as of October 2008) for a Cuba hurricane relief fund, dedicated primarily to the efforts of Caritas Cubana, one of few U.S. NGOs authorized to provide relief aid. But the crisis also exposed anew divisions over U.S. policy, with some groups calling for a temporary suspension of restrictions on family travel and remittances and even the embargo itself, while some opposed any and all measures that would benefit the regime.

The intensity of such divisions only underscores the significant evolution under way in the Cuban American community, both as demographics change and individuals young and old are forced to come to terms with the fact that Cuba after Fidel— the individual so long the focus of a community's enmity— might not by default transition to their vision of a democratic future. Polls since the year 2000 show a steady and growing recognition among Cuban Americans that current U.S. policy is ineffective. By 2007, a majority in the community favored the elimination of all travel restrictions, not only on Cuban American family travel but also all Americans. Strong majorities likewise recognize that the embargo has been a failure, although majorities still believe it should be kept in place. Shifting opinions reflect demographic changes as well. First-generation Cuban Americans long associated with the policy hard-liners in Miami and Washington are receding from the political stage, if for no other reason than age. Second- and third-generation Cuban Americans, meanwhile, have ceased to be single-issue voters; especially under the Bush administration, many among this predominantly Republican voter base have grown disillusioned with a range of domestic and foreign policy blunders of the era. They are also far more likely to be among the passengers on some 30 weekly charter flights between Miami and Havana to visit and support family members on the island. The end result may not be a clear consensus in favor of dramatic policy overhaul, but as the community undergoes a period of extensive reflection and diversification, the political climate in Miami today is the most contentious and open it has been in recent memory.

Together, the backdrop of Fidel's illness, evolving Cuban American opinion, and an influx of immigrants to South Florida from other Latin American countries (even Calle Ocho today is Cuban in name, but increasingly Mexican in population) have contributed to the development of a new political landscape in South Florida, one which for the first time in many years challenged, though unsuccessfully, the GOP's lock on the three congressional seats representing traditionally Cuban American constituencies.

In a variety of ways, and occasionally at cross purposes, members of the Cuban American community will continue positioning themselves to stay relevant, to play a role in the future of a country they consider their own. For some, this sense of propriety comes with a sense of entitlement, anger, and a desire for revenge. But for most in the Cuban diaspora at this stage, whether in the United States, Spain, or sprinkled throughout Latin America, the cultural and historical predilection of believing that all Cubans have a stake in the island's future is simply a natural part of being Cuban. Indeed, the Cuban diaspora may well play an important role in the island's future, as a logical source of investment and know-how. The Cuban government, however, will naturally resist this prospect as long as it is accompanied by demands for political change, whether by the community or by their representatives in Congress or the White House.

How did Cuba play in the 2008 presidential primaries and general election?

American public opinion broadly favors a complete overhaul of U.S. policy toward Cuba—including ending the embargo and normalizing diplomatic ties. Likewise, cooperating with Cuba at a minimum on national security issues would bring clear benefits to U.S. national interests. Yet neither fact overrides the political importance of Florida to winning the White House. The state of Florida has 27 electoral votes. Cuban Americans comprise just over 7% of the total voting population there, but contribute millions of dollars to congressional and presidential campaign coffers. Thus, for many years, appealing, often pandering, to the Cuban American electorate has been an accepted part of the conventional wisdom guiding American electoral politics.

Although Florida can still determine an election, in 2008 two new developments changed circumstances somewhat. First, the new government in Cuba forced a broader discussion in Washington and even in Miami about what kind of policy might give the United States some influence on the island. Second, evolving demographics and public opinion in South Florida generated conditions for a serious Democratic challenge to the GOP's South Florida congressional representatives, whose districts are no longer populated mainly by single-issue Cuban American voters.

During the primary season, Republicans, with the exception of Ron Paul (a libertarian from Texas), endorsed more of the half-century same-old. In the 2000 election, John McCain, who with John Kerry had led the U.S. rapprochement process with Communist Vietnam, had voiced support for a change in policy toward Cuba along similar lines. But for the 2008 election, with Florida top on his mind, he amassed a host of hard-line Latin America advisors and gained the endorsement of Republican Cuban American Congressmen Mario and Lincoln Diaz-Balart and Congresswoman Ileana Ros-Lehtinen from South Florida. United States Senator Mel Martinez, as well as Florida's highly popular Governor Charlie Christ, signed on to his campaign as well. Democrats, on the other hand, seeking to distinguish themselves from George W. Bush's foreign policy across the board, conducted more of a debate on Cuba. Hillary Clinton, whose political viability in Florida was stronger than that of any other Democratic contender, supported increased family travel. But with Cuban American Senator Bob Menendez her campaign's cochair, Clinton held tight to the status quo of no policy change without evidence of real democracy.

Barack Obama, on the other hand, came to the race with a history of bolder policy prescriptions. Before announcing his candidacy for president, the first-term senator from Illinois had voted against funding for Radio and TV Martí in the Senate and, in 2004, called for an end to the embargo, declaring U.S. policy toward Cuba a total failure. In a 2007 primary debate broadcast on YouTube, Senator Obama was asked: "Would you be willing to meet separately, without precondition, during the first year of your administration, in Washington or anywhere else, with the leaders of Iran, Syria, Venezuela, Cuba, and North Korea, in order to bridge the gap that divides our countries?" He replied, "I would." Those two words eventually helped define the Obama campaign's approach to diplomacy (though he would later qualify them by highlighting the need for exten- sive preparation before any talks), prompting accusations of naïveté from Hillary Clinton and from Republican candidates while distinguishing Obama from Bush and forcing a debate in the United States about the national security and foreign policy merits of speaking to, without necessarily endorsing, one's enemies.

Like candidates and presidents before him, Obama chose the May 20 independence day festivities and a gathering of the Cuban American National Foundation to make his Cuba policy pitch. But unlike his predecessors, the presumptive nominee departed from the conventional Miami wisdom, outlining a hybrid position to polite, even generous applause. In a speech devoted to Latin America as well as Cuba, Obama described the two principle features of his approach to the island: (1) while keeping the embargo in place for "leverage" with Cuba, he would seek to open a dialogue with Raul Castro, which would include issues of democracy and human rights; and (2) he would eliminate all restrictions on family travel and remittances, an important gesture for support among more moderate Cuban American voters. The organization's new sense of pragmatism and flexibility, its desire to remain politically relevant, and some of its board members' active support of South Florida's Democratic congressional challengers, were all clearly on display that day, a remarkable change from just 10 years ago.

On November 4, 2008, President Barack Obama won the state of Florida without the votes of Cuban American hardliners. Because of massive voter registration drives across the state, registered Hispanic Democrats outnumbered Hispanic Republicans by 513,000 to 445,000. Obama won 57% of the Florida Hispanic vote, up from 44% for John Kerry in 2004. In Miami-Dade County, 55% of Cuban Americans under 29 years old voted for Obama, while 84% of Cuban Americans over 65 years old voted for McCain, following the national trend. And although only 35% of the total Cuban American voting population (a 10% increase over John Kerry's 2004 showing,) voted for Obama, it was the non–Cuban Hispanic vote and other votes across Florida, especially in the African American community, that increased his margin enough to carry the state. These gains were less a result of the needle Obama threaded on American policy toward Cuba than on the strength of his overall platform and campaign. His triangulated position on Cuba perhaps prevented those Cuban American voters inclined to vote for him in any case from voting against him, but John McCain still carried most Cuban American votes. In the Miami congressional elections, where three Democrats supporting only family travel mounted competitive challenges for the three Cuban American Republican seats in South Florida, all three still lost to the incumbents by wide margins. Their races were less about Cuba than about the real issues working Americans face. Although the three Cuban American Republican hard-liners have been safely reelected, they are now in the opposition. And because Obama's Florida victory was the result of a constellation of non–Cuban American votes, his Cuba policy need no longer defer to the Cuban American political and policy status quo of the last 50 years.

What might be expected from the Obama White House in its policy toward Cuba?

In the foreign policy realm, the new president will be preoccupied predominantly with Iraq, Iran, Afghanistan, Pakistan, and a host of issues, such as skyrocketing energy and food prices and climate change, all in the context of a global financial crisis and domestic recession. Latin America will likely fall somewhere toward the middle to the bottom of the priority list, with the exception of Mexico (because of its drug, security, and border challenges), Colombia (because the United States has a made huge investment in improving security there), and Brazil (which has become a major regional and global player on economic and climate change issues and as a source of food and energy). Stability under Raul, along with the potential political costs of major policy change, may actually limit the time any president is likely to devote to Cuba. But with the symbolism of Guantánamo (which Obama addressed on his first day in office by pledging to close the detention camps there), the opportunity presented by Fidel's retreat from the scene, and the modest, ongoing steps Raul is taking to improve the material lives and personal freedoms of the Cuban people, the stars may align for Washington under a new administration to definitively bury the hatchet with Havana. This will not happen overnight, but a process could begin to unfold in 2009.

With a stronger Democratic majority in Congress and a Democrat in the White House, moves to loosen travel and economic sanctions and to talk to Havana may pick up steam, both in Congress and the executive branch. From the executive branch, the president might, as he campaigned, issue regulations allowing unlimited Cuban American travel and remittances. Yet such a measure might be challenged on the grounds that it is unconstitutional to deny one group a right that has been granted another. In that case, the White House might also issue regulations restoring the Clinton-era people-to-people "purposeful" options for more than just Cuban American travel to Cuba under license. By taking some or all of these steps, an Obama White House would signal to the U.S. Congress that, unlike its predecessor, it will not veto legislation passed to loosen or lift the embargo. A number of initiatives—whether to end the travel ban, end the embargo, or even perhaps repeal Helms-Burton—could pick up substantial Democratic and Republican support and may well make it to the White House for the president's signature.

At the same time, consistent with Raul Castro's and Barack Obama's explicit statements in 2007 and 2008, direct bilateral talks could start. A full agenda could occupy teams from both countries, even eventually, the two men themselves. Discussions might cover a host of security issues Havana and Washington have a stake in dealing with together, such as migration, human smuggling, and drug trafficking. With the United States already pledging to close its prisons at Guantánamo and Cuba's repeated demands for the United States to leave altogether, discussions about the base's future might involve converting it into a regional research and development center on climate change, energy and food security, or public health. Additionally, as Cuba, in partnership with a number of foreign oil companies, begins deep-water exploration for potentially significant reserves in the Gulf of Mexico, talks might address prospects for environmentally sustainable resource management. There are a number of other thornier issues, such as the uncompensated claims by U.S. companies whose properties were nationalized by the revolution and, as Cuba will likely demand, compensation for the economic damage to the island inflicted by the U.S. embargo. Cuba will likely press the United States to extradite Luis Posada Carriles to Panama or to Venezuela and to release the "Cuban Five," its spies currently serving sentences, some up to life, in U.S. federal jails. The United States may, in turn, press Cuba to return American fugitives to the United States. The merits of Cuba's presence on the U.S. State Department's list of state sponsors of terror is sure to come up as well. Matters of Cuba's internal affairs, whether political prisoners, human rights, or the absence of political democracy, will surely be raised by the United States. Yet as long as the United States continues to promote the objective of democracy by clandestinely funneling aid and other supplies to dissidents while at the same time keeping in place its economic sanctions, it is unlikely that Raul Castro or anyone authorized to negotiate on Cuba's behalf will allow the United States to put Cuba's domestic issues on the bilateral agenda. Still, Cuban negotiators are flexible enough to see that if they really want to create political space for a new American president to substantially change U.S. policy without characterizing internal changes as concessions to imperialism, the regime may ultimately take steps that can be characterized as, and may actually be, genuine openings that advance a more democratic and open society on the island.

CUBA IN THE WORLD

Did the succession arouse any changes in Cuba's foreign relations?

Not dramatically. As in previous periods, Cuba continues to pursue a global foreign policy meant to promote the country's national interest. Fidel Castro has always served as Cuba's top foreign policy strategist and followed global events assiduously—reading piles of cables from around the world every day and allegedly becoming a devoted surfer of the Web. But well before his illness, he had distributed the foreign policy portfolio among a number of confidants and protégés who travel the world to attend international events, represent Cuba at inaugurations, renegotiate debt, develop cooperation agreements, open embassies, and explore business deals.

Under Raul Castro, this pattern has largely continued, albeit with several changes in style, substance, and personnel. Although Raul seems not to spend as much time as Fidel receiving foreign dignitaries or traveling abroad, the scope and pace of Cuban diplomacy under his and now deposed Foreign Minister Felipe Pérez Roque's leadership has intensified, with presidential visits, cooperation agreements, ministerial dialogues, and summit participation. In late 2008 and early 2009, Raul Castro visited Brazil, Venezuela, China, Russia, and Algeria. Brazil's president Luis Inacio Lula da Silva, Russian President Dmitry Medvedev, and Chinese President Hu Jintao all visited Havana in 2008, while Chilean President Michelle Bachelet and Argentine President Cristina Fernández de Kirchner both paid visits in early 2009. Spanish Prime Minister José Luis Zapatero has announced his intention to visit Cuba in 2009, and a visit from Mexico's President Felipe Calderón is likely as well. In a break with a near-two-decade pattern of exclusion, Latin America's Rio Group, composed of 22 Latin American states as well as CARICOM, or the Caribbean Community, made Cuba a member, part of a pattern of increased Cuban participation in regional summits and institutions, including new entities convened by Brazil. Indeed, Raul

Castro received a rousing welcome from Latin American heads of state at the first Summit of Latin America and the Caribbean on Integration and Development hosted by the Lula government in the northern Brazilian state of Bahia. More important, although planned well in advance, just days after Raul formally took office as Cuba's president, Cuba signed two covenants under the purview of the Universal Declaration of Human Rights: the Covenant on Civil and Political Rights and the Covenant on Economic, Social, and Cultural Rights. Cuba had long refused to sign these documents, claiming that the United States would cynically exploit the occasion to unfairly attack Cuba at the UN Commission on Human Rights. Yet once the commission was dissolved and replaced by a Human Rights Council populated by Cuba's allies (and where the United States declined participation), Cuba likely judged it could now ascribe to the agreements without risking U.S. interference (or, as critics of the Human Rights Council would argue with some reason, without risking an extensive degree of scrutiny). But Cuba was not only responding to the United States or to the geopolitics of the Human Rights Council. Since Raul's tenure as provisional president, Cuba has moved closer to Brazil, one of the hemisphere's most important democracies. The island has also renewed its dialogue with the European Union, where friendly countries, led by Spain under the Socialist Prime Minister José Luis Zapatero, are gingerly moving to create the space for Cuba to pry open its closed society without losing face to the Americans. Cuba has indicated that it will interpret the agreements in its own way and on its own time. No one expects immediate or dramatic reforms in the arena of political rights, and during the February 2009 review of Cuba's human rights record by the UN Human Rights Council, Havana's representatives continued to vigorously reject Western calls for the release of political prisoners (while maintaining the support of the majority of the Council's members). Nonetheless, for the first time in 50 years, Cuba has signed an agreement that in theory guarantees its citizens the rights to self-determination, freedom of expression, peaceful assembly, freedom of religion, privacy, freedom to leave their country, equal protection, fair wages, social security, education, and health. While it is by no means certain how quickly or to what extent Cuban authorities intend to implement the spirit of these provisions, Cuba's decision to sign the two covenants signals an awareness among the island's foreign policy establishment that Havana must begin accommodating its traditionally rigid defense of national sovereignty to a world in which the nature of a country's society, especially as Cuba deepens its ties to democracies, is increasingly relevant to its foreign relations. Perhaps as a sign of this reckoning, in a major departure from the past, Cuba invited the UN's special investigator on torture to visit the island.

Cuba has also moved to sustain ties with the Vatican and with Pope Benedict. The week Raul took power, Vatican Secretary of State Cardinal Tarcisio Bertone visited Havana with a large delegation to celebrate the 10th anniversary of Pope John Paul II's historic visit to the island. A statue of the late pontiff traveled throughout the island, and most of Cuba's senior leadership joined Cardinal Bertone for a televised evening mass at the Cathedral of Havana in the heart of Old Havana. Over the course of the visit, Bertone spoke out against the U.S. embargo and discussed a variety of issues with Cuban authorities, including religious freedom and the fate of political prisoners. Despite the revolution's early anticlericalism, the church today is in the process of constructing a new seminary in Havana, and Catholic social service programs have been given greater freedom to operate alongside those of the state, reinforcing a trend toward more space for the Catholic Church in Cuban public life.

What are the principal features of Cuba's ties with Latin America today?

Cuba maintains active and extensive relations with a diverse array of Latin American countries, encompassing significant trade, investment, scholarly, and cultural links. As in the past, Cuba continues to provide significant humanitarian assistance to the region, especially in the aftermath of natural disasters and for basic public health needs and education. Cuba's revolutionary model may no longer be seen by many in the hemisphere as a practical example to follow as it once was. Still, as a result of Cuba's extensive efforts cultivating ties through public diplomacy and foreign aid, today Cuba finds itself with many friends in Latin America at every level of society, from social activists to the highest officials in government and business—and not just on the Left.

In Central America, Cuba maintains proper diplomatic ties with every government, including Costa Rica and El Salvador. Havana also continues close relations with the Left political parties it once supported when they were conducting armed insurgencies, but takes great pains not to be perceived as interfering in their domestic affairs. In Nicaragua, where Daniel Ortega was reelected in 2006, Cuba has discovered a much-changed old friend, while in Panama, Havana has rebuilt ties after a long period of dormancy. While simultaneously maintaining close ties to Washington, the Panamanian government could request the extradition of Luis Posada Carriles, the Cuban exile terrorist, after the country's Supreme Court found that Posada's pardon in 2004 by then-president Mireya Moscoso was unconstitutional.

After Fidel's fallout with Vicente Fox and the near-total rupture in relations, Cuba's ties with Mexico have undergone a significant turnaround. Indeed, Raul Castro and current Mexican President Felipe Calderón have gone to considerable lengths to put the nastiness behind them. In addition to reviving trade and diplomatic ties across the board, the two countries negotiated a migration agreement to deal with the sharp surge in Cuban migrants being smuggled illegally through Mexico en route to the United States.

Together, Cuba, Venezuela, and Bolivia, more recently joined by Nicaragua and the island of Dominica, have formed the

Bolivarian Alternative for the Americas (ALBA), an attempt to create an alternative trade bloc of sorts to the free trade agreements the United States has negotiated with a number of Latin American countries. Yet despite ambitious plans for cooperation in energy cooperation, education, development financing, and telecommunications, currently the agreement is not much more than barter and rhetoric, with Venezuela footing the bill. In the Andean region, Cuba has proper ties with Peru's Alan García, who has left behind his Populist presidency of the 1980s and now leads a center-right government in Lima. In Bolivia, indigenous President Evo Morales's ties with Fidel and Cuba go back nearly two decades. Not surprisingly, Cuba has provided significant public health aid, educational support, and other technical assistance to his government. In the case of Colombia, where Fidel as a student in 1948 first experienced Latin America's violent politics, Cuba maintains cordial and professional relations with the government of Alvaro Uribe, despite clear ideological differences. In part as an outgrowth of Castro's abiding and close personal friendship with Colombian Nobel laureate Gabriel García Márquez, Havana continues to host peace talks between the government and the ELN rebels (a guerilla movement inspired, at least initially, by Cuba's own) while pushing privately and publicly for the FARC (a more powerful leftist insurgency) to get out of the business of drugs, kidnapping, and terrorism.

In the Southern Cone, the governments of Chile, Argentina, Uruguay, Paraguay, and Brazil are each led by individuals or political parties with deep ties to Cuba and, in some cases, to Fidel Castro personally. Most notably, and as referenced at various points earlier in this section, under Luiz Inacio Lula da Silva, Brazil significantly expanded its engagement with Cuba at the same time that it developed what Brazilian diplomats describe as its best relationship ever with the United States under George W. Bush. Fidel and Lula have known one another for over two decades (Fidel helped Lula and a handful of his comrades from the Worker's Party [PT] as Brazil was beginning its transition from years of military rule and repression to democracy). In 2008, Lula made one of the few publicly announced visits with Fidel since the illness, offering Havana $1 billion in credits to finance food purchases, housing, oil and mineral exploration, and a number of other ventures. A few months later, Brazil's foreign minister arrived in Havana with a planeload of businesspeople and announced his country's desire to become Cuba's number one commercial partner, moving beyond current trade in food, agricultural machinery, transportation equipment, tobacco, biotechnology, and pharmaceuticals. Cuba and Brazil signed 10 bilateral cooperation agreements in science, technology, development, and social programs. As they open offices around the country, Brazilian companies are likely to soon step up investments in petroleum exploration, mining, infrastructure, and agriculture. Significantly, and despite Fidel Castro's public critiques of the ethanol industry as a threat to food security (made public after Brazil and the United States signed an alternative energy cooperation deal), Lula and Raul Castro may be moving to revive Cuba's sugar industry with an eye toward eventual ethanol production. Moreover, given recent oil discoveries of as much as 1 billion barrels off its coast, Brazil may become a potential source of imported oil for Cuba in the long term, helping to relieve some measure of the island's dependence on Venezuela.

Brazil's multidimensional approach to Cuba balances that of Venezuela. In late 2007, Hugo Chávez lost a referendum on measures extending executive authority. But in early 2009, he won passage of a referendum amending the constitution to allow him to be reelected in 2013 when his current term ends. Although oil prices had by then declined to their 2004 levels, and Venezuelans braced themselves for some domestic spending cuts, there is no evidence that Cuba's ties to Venezuela are in jeopardy. On the contrary, Cuba's ties to Venezuela have boomed since 2006, with some 300 cooperation projects and 30 joint venture operations currently on the books, including a $5 billion petrochemical complex currently under construction in Cienfuegos near the refurbished oil refinery (also brought online with Venezuela's help), as well as ample assistance for hurricane relief and reconstruction.

Until nearly the end of the 1990s, most Latin American governments were inclined to publicly endorse, if not always privately embrace, the United States' emphasis on the need to promote democracy and human rights in Cuba. Indeed, with many Latin American countries struggling throughout that decade to overcome the legacies of human rights abuse at the hands of a repressive state and by state-sponsored death squads (some of which still operate in the region), there was and still is a measure of hope among some in the region that Cuba can one day become a more open and democratic society as well. Yet by and large, Latin Americans do not see the Cuban case as directly parallel to the military dictatorships they themselves endured. Moreover, they are loath to support a democratization campaign guided by an interventionist ethos whose principle cheerleader is the United States. Indeed, the United States can hardly claim to have been a consistent champion of democracy or human rights in the hemisphere, having tolerated for most of the 20th century the suppression of both in the name of national security. Today, Latin America's democratic consolidation has advanced to a point where the United States can no longer say or do much to fundamentally shape the region's political landscape. The loss of American hegemony in Latin America, let alone the Bush administration's disastrous experiments with democracy promotion by force in the Middle East, have clearly signaled that there are limits to imposing one brand or another of democracy on a neighboring country. And whatever the island's faults, Cuba's symbolic and tangible commitment to social justice (even within a framework of low-intensity repression) remains a potent reminder of Cuban exceptionalism that resonates with public opinion in the region as a whole. As a result, whether or not they share deep historic ties to Fidel's revolution, and regardless of the extent to which they admire Cuba's closed domestic political model

(most do not), Latin American governments today generally
see gradual reform under Raul as the path most likely to bring
about a more plural, open society on the island but also maintain the stability necessary to keep the United States at arm's
length. And they have begun to call directly—in private and
public—for Washington to find a new, sanctions-free modus
vivendi with Havana.

How has Cuba expanded its ties with Russia, China, and Iran?

As part of its efforts to diversify its diplomatic and trade portfolio, Cuba has increased cooperation with Russia, China, and
Iran in recent years. Under Vladimir Putin, diplomacy between
Moscow and Havana has yielded debt forgiveness, modest
trade ties, financing for Cuba to purchase Russian commercial airplanes, weekly Havana-Moscow flights, some common
positions against the United States, hurricane assistance by
the planeload, a modest level of family and cultural ties that
continue from the Soviet era, and high-level, high-profile
diplomatic visits. For China, Cuba is a small piece of a much
larger Latin American strategy of investment, commodity,
energy, and natural resource accumulation. China has become
Cuba's second largest trading partner, exporting electronics,
buses, trains, light manufactured goods, and now tourists as
well. Joint ventures in nickel extraction, onshore oil exploration, and biotechnology are under way. Renovations of China's
embassy in Havana's Vedado neighborhood are expanding the
complex to occupy an entire city block. Historical ties bind the
two countries as well: Chinese laborers settled in Cuba beginning in 1847, working predominantly on sugar plantations,
and today 1% of Cubans on the island have Chinese family
roots. Ties between Cuba and Iran picked up following a visit
to Havana by Iranian President Mohammad Khatami in 2000
and a visit by Fidel to Tehran the next year. Cooperation in
science and biotech expanded, prompting the Bush administration to unsuccessfully argue that Cuba had the intention

of exporting bioweapons to a rogue regime. Joint ventures and cooperation have expanded, with Cuba selling vaccines, medical services, and medical training to Iran, while Iran in exchange has provided Cuba with a modest line of credit for trade. The two countries have found common cause in their fight against American imperialism and aggression at the UN and most recently in 2006, when President Mahmoud Ahmadinejad attended the Non-Aligned Movement's summit in Havana.

What is the status of Cuba's deep-water oil exploration and what foreign governments and companies are involved?

Since the end of the Cold War, Cuba has made some modest investments in its domestic petroleum industry and today produces and refines approximately 60,000 to 80,000 barrels of crude oil per day. A handful of foreign oil companies entered into joint ventures with Cuba in the 1990s but yielded no dramatic black gold booms. Geological findings indicating the potential for vast deep-water petroleum stores sparked a new wave of interest in offshore exploration and drilling beginning in 2002. The U.S. Geological Survey estimates reserves of up to 9 billion barrels of petroleum, while Cuba's state oil company, CUPET, announced its conservative estimate at approximately 20 billion barrels in reserves. In 2005, bidding for exclusive rights to 22 separate exploration blocks in the Gulf of Mexico north and northwest of Cuba and in the Caribbean Sea to the south yielded a number of contracts with private and state-run energy companies from countries such as Canada, Spain, Norway, India, Malaysia, Venezuela, Brazil, and Vietnam. For now, China's exploration and refining ventures are on land, not offshore. American law currently prohibits U.S. companies from the deals, but the potential for drilling within miles of the Florida coast has put some in that state on alert while also piquing the interest of others (in the Texas energy industry, for example) eager to get in on the action in the future. Should current exploration produce a major find, given the energy crisis in the United States and globally, the attractiveness and convenience of Cuban oil could well produce a rapid push to open U.S. investment in Cuban petroleum.

Has the European Union moved closer to Cuba since Fidel stepped aside?

In 2003, the European Union imposed diplomatic sanctions on Cuba after the arrests in Havana of 75 dissidents, human rights activists, and independent journalists. Until that time, EU member countries had made a practice of inviting such activists to their embassies and visiting them in their homes. Moreover, several member countries, often in concert with the United States or U.S.-based NGOs, had also helped provide resources and promotional support to nascent opposition movements. The arrests were intended to signal, primarily to the United States, but also to the EU, that Cuba would not tolerate outsiders paying for what it considered the illegitimate activities of counterrevolutionaries. For the majority of the international community, such a rationale was either rejected out of hand or viewed as an entirely insufficient justification for the arrests. The United States already had sanctions in place, of course, and its principal response to the arrests was condemnation, although the incident perhaps also provided a further impetus and rationale for the increasingly hard-line policies from the Bush administration. The EU, which since 1996 maintained a "common position" toward Cuba that favored "constructive engagement" with Havana as a way to encourage increased freedoms and an eventual transition to pluralist democracy in Cuba, voted for diplomatic, not economic, sanctions, which banned high-level Cuban officials from visiting EU countries. The Cuban government also simultaneously froze relations with some EU countries that had been more active in their contacts with the dissident community.

In many ways, the EU's sanctions had a mostly symbolic effect, and were in fact "suspended" (though not technically eliminated) in 2005. By 2008, Cuba had released over 20 of the 75 arrested and jailed five years earlier, and the European diplomats had ratcheted down contacts with dissident and opposition groups, leaving the EU poised to essentially return to the approach of its previous common position favoring engagement. With Raul Castro taking a number of preliminary but important steps toward reform, most EU members concurred with Spain, which argued that contact and dialogue were the only hope for promoting a democratic future on the island. The holdouts were primarily Poland and the Czech Republic, two countries that had not only received substantial U.S. support for their own democratic transitions but also become key American allies in the campaign to build a viable opposition in Cuba. As a result of their pressure, in voting to lift the 2003 sanctions, the EU imposed a set of reservations or modest conditions rather than simply reverting to the old common position. In short, members stipulated that the decision to definitively remove sanctions would be reviewed after one year in light of whether Cuba had complied with two demands: access for all citizens to the Internet and permission for visiting EU diplomats to meet with both Cuban officials and dissidents. Nonetheless, regardless of Cuba's degree of compliance, continuing rapprochement seems fairly certain. Although the succession under Raul has included a continued pattern of crackdowns on dissident activity, it has proven overwhelmingly stable, leading Europeans to the same conclusion that most Latin Americans have reached—namely, that Cuba's path is Cuba's alone: Countries can either attempt to be present and engage, and in that context discuss human rights and democracy with Cuba, or confine themselves to the sidelines. With trade, investment, culture, and tourism tying many parts of the continent to the island, European diplomats have opted for the former, cognizant of the regime's redlines against outside meddling but also of its inability to go it entirely alone. With these dynamics in mind, the European Union has launched a new high-level dialogue on social, civil, and political rights and resumed development assistance—all with an eye toward the full normalization of relations and the creation of a new framework to govern political, economic, and trade cooperation.

How extensive is Cuba's cultural projection—music, art, film, literature—on the global stage?

Whether in film, literature, or contemporary art, Cuban culture continues to grow in its influence around the globe. Arguably, Cuban music is the most easily recognized cultural product from the island today, in all of its diversity and distinctive character. Beyond the lasting appeal of more traditional salsa, rumba, and *son*, paragons of the *Nueva Trova* movement such as Silvio Rodríguez and Pablo Milanés continue to pack concert halls across Europe and the Americas, while more recently Cuban rap and reggaetón stars have gained popularity—the product of Cuba's intensified encounters with western culture during the Special Period and beyond. Cuba is also well known for popularizing the style of *timba*, a subset of salsa, pioneered by such groups as Los Van Van and Irakere and continued today by groups like Charanga Habanera. Cuban film, meanwhile, has carved out a distinctive niche on the world market, with the work of notable directors like Fernando Pérez making the rounds on international film festival circuits.

Much of Cuba's artistic production—music, plastic arts, and film—has undergone a notable depoliticization in recent times, as artists and the state-run cultural agencies that support them continue to accommodate the demands of the international market and international media partners. In this way, even artists explicitly linked to revolutionary political values in the past—such as the founders of *Nueva Trova*—have broadened their messaging, appealing more to humanistic or secular themes than Socialist ones. Yet it would be false to say that politics has disappeared completely from Cuban art. Cuban rap continues to voice a significant degree of Afro-Cuban and youth disenchantment with material deprivation and revolutionary politics, although those artists who have gained most international prominence are largely nonpolitical in nature. Likewise, younger generations of *Nueva Trova* singers popular internationally have taken up the critical spirit of their predecessors to criticize Cuba's contemporary maladies. More broadly, the state continues to play an important mediating role in the arts, providing the platform, resources, and basic ideological framework through which many musicians and other artists pursue international success. Independent cultural spaces and products do receive occasional foreign attention, and it is in these spaces where political messages are often most clearly critical of the government. Yet the government also recognizes that there is a public diplomacy advantage to permitting a certain level of critical expression among those artists promoted by the state who gain international renown. Indeed, many Cuban artists have learned to speak on multiple levels in their work, including narratives that legitimate several dimensions of the revolutionary ethos alongside potent critiques of Cuban political, economic, and cultural life.

A CHANGING CUBA UNDER RAUL CASTRO'S PRESIDENCY

What are the principal elements on the landscape of
Raul Castro's presidency?

President Raul Castro took office in 2008. By his own account, he will serve as president of Cuba for a total of two five-year terms, ending in 2018 when he will be 87 years old. Under newly established term limits, however, he may serve as secretary general of the Cuban Communist Party until as late as 2021. If so, upon retirement Raul will have presided over a 15-year process of succession and transformation, beginning the moment in 2006 when life-threatening illness first compelled Fidel to step aside.

In some ways, Raul has set out to rebuild the fundamental relationship between the state and the individual, dramatically increasing expectations of the latter and reducing the obligations of the former. Reforms that at a glance may look economic in nature are in fact deeply political, even as Cuba remains a one-party state. Impatient and clearly conscious that time is working against him, Raul berates and cajoles the party faithful and the Cuban public to get to work. His mantras? That equality of opportunity does not mean equality of circumstances, and that productivity, efficiency, private ownership, and even profit are not anathema to socialism. He has attempted to disaggregate the party from government and governance while imposing the rule of law over a bureaucratic, personalistic political culture. He has established systems for accountability at the ministerial level, cut budgets and superfluous ministries, and begun to give greater tax and budget authority to local governments. The old joke that Cuba is a country where "no one works but everyone is paid" no longer gets a laugh, because by 2014 nearly half of all Cubans of working age are expected to be off the state's payroll, working in the private sector. Raul has overseen a slow expansion of private markets and ownership in agriculture and real estate. Likewise, a growing, but many would say excessively micromanaged number of occupations (largely in the service sector), have become eligible for private employment and business. With the iconic ration card, salary caps, and other subsidies slated to be phased out over the next few years, and with the government moving to widen a progressive income tax, the new Cuba molting from within the old will be one of considerably more autonomy and uncertainty for the individual, all within the context of a substantially transformed society. Building political support for such changes has meant taking the time to construct a consensus within the party for the very openings Fidel once warned would give the United States the opportunity it long craved to sew disunity and potentially destroy the revolution.

Making the Cuban economy productive without a massive privatization of its strategic sectors stands as Raul's top challenge. To do so, he needs to not only change what he refers to as the "mentality" of the Cuban people but also institute several structural, institutional, and personnel reforms to make Cuba attractive to foreign investment without giving away the store. The obstacles are substantial. For one thing, Cuba's labor force is shrinking and its population is aging. Elderly Cubans live longer because of the country's fraying but still cradle-to-grave health care system, but the birthrate is too low to replace either the coming waves of retirees or the continued out-migration of younger Cubans seeking better opportunities abroad. Although wages should rise as the government trims the number of employees on public rolls, for the moment salaries in the state sector remain woefully insufficient for daily expenses, bolstering the black market and reliance on foreign remittances. (Indeed, whatever their overreliance on the state for big-ticket items like subsidized food, jobs, and health care, since the 1990s many Cubans have had to supplement state incomes or fend for themselves in the informal economy to get by.) Furthermore, excessive investments in higher education and underinvestment in vocational and technical training have left the Cuban workforce depleted in a variety of fields. Meanwhile, weeding out corruption, unifying the wacky and highly unpopular dual currency system, and creating a credit and wholesale market for new small businesses are all reforms thus far slow in coming. Management capacity is limited. Tourism, mining, telecommunications, transportation, and energy enterprises have been the subjects of substantial corruption investigations, leading to indictments of Cuban nationals and foreigners. Together with paying its foreign debt, these moves may represent essential housecleaning prior to a vitally necessary opening to foreign investment, an attempt to extirpate the bureaucratic and political beneficiaries of the status quo ante, or both.

How, then, are these developments perceived by everyday Cubans themselves? Reforms certainly have moved quickly by comparison to Fidel's era. Depending on whom you talk to, the prospect of private sector expansion and continued state layoffs elicits enthusiasm, anxiety, or both, especially among state workers who may lose their jobs. Authorities insist the process will proceed gradually, and this has provided some reassurance. Nonetheless, in some areas, the government's piecemeal, methodical, cautious approach to policy change "not in a hurry, but without delay" (to use Raul's words) has caused considerable frustration. After Raul and other officials alluded to the liberalization of travel and immigration policy on numerous occasions, in 2013 a new law took effect eliminating the fees and permission slip required by the government for Cubans to leave the island (known as the "tarjeta blanca"), a major step in human rights with significant political and economic consequences. Although high-level officials have, on occasion, railed against the state media's failures to engage in more analytical journalism, and while more expansive debates in academic circles and some investigative reporting by the state media are more prevalent than under Fidel, one can hardly say that an independent press is alive and well in Cuba. This is a shame, because an independent press would only facilitate the greater government transparency and accountability that Raul argues are necessary to save and reinvent Cuban socialism. More recently, a steep hike in import taxes has left many Cubans on island and off bewildered and angry. While intended to cut down on the illicit traffic of so-called *mulas* (members of the Cuban diaspora who, for a fee, routinely run remittances, clothing, and all manner of goods and supplies to the island), the measure is also likely to have strong consequences for Cuba's small business sector, short of any government initiative to expand state-generated wholesale markets at home. As it is, members of the Cuban diaspora, through the *mulas*, play a crucial if informal role in the rather brittle supply chain on which many struggling small businesses have depended to get off the ground.

The international context for this rather substantial reform agenda is far from benign. The global financial crisis raised energy and food prices while at the same time hurting Cuba's tourist industry. The U.S. embargo, which Cubans call the "blockade," remains solidly in place; while sales through the agricultural loophole proceed, and while Cuban-Americans are legally pumping remittances into the island as never before, the Obama administration has actually more aggressively enforced sanctions on third-country and third-party financial and commercial transactions than did its predecessor. In this kind of environment, cutting the budget deficit, repaying debt, and attempting to eke out a 3% growth rate in 2012 show a level of ambition that complements the cautious pace of change.

Raul has had some success diversifying the country's trade and diplomatic portfolio. Challenging Venezuela's primacy as a trade partner, Brazil has extended a $600 million line of credit for food and agricultural machinery imports and is beginning to invest heavily in infrastructure, health care, tourism, and the restructured sugar industry. One of its signature investments, the $900 million renovation of the port of Mariel, will give Brazil an anchor in the Gulf of Mexico just miles from the United States and position Cuba to benefit from the boom in Caribbean maritime traffic projected to result from the expanded Panama Canal.

Raul's successor will almost certainly come from the rising ranks of problem-solving doers, next-generation party leaders and locally elected officials often from the provinces who have been promoted under his presidency to national positions. If he serves out two full terms as president, the Cuba he hands over will look substantially different from the one he set out to remake when Fidel stepped aside. Social democracy, market socialism, state capitalism—whatever the labels, combination of features, consequences, strengths, or weaknesses—Cuba's political and economic system will be a hybrid engineered by Cubans on their own terms.

What is the role of the Catholic Church in Cuba during Raul Castro's presidency?

Since the 1990s, the Catholic Church has become the largest non-state social service provider in Cuba, sponsoring national aid programs, community-based soup kitchens, medical dispensaries, *casas de ancianos* (like retirement homes), and other initiatives supporting Cuba's most vulnerable populations. But aside from its social and pastoral work, the institution has asserted a significant degree of autonomy with respect to political, social, and economic matters on the island. Catholic-sponsored publications like *Espacio Laical* and *Palabra Nueva* are elevating new voices within the island's somewhat fragile public sphere— from agnostic intellectuals and socialists, to Christians and other believers, to members of the Cuban diaspora. Through their pointedly political and decidedly constructive commentary on a wide range of topics, these authors provide an important alternative to the state-controlled media.

In March 2012, Pope Benedict XVI visited Cuba, marking the second papal visit to the island coordinated by Cardinal Jaime Ortega, archbishop of Havana. Prior to the visit, Raul Castro announced that Cuba would pardon 2,900 prisoners as a "humanitarian gesture" to Catholic officials and relatives who had asked for their release. This significant step followed Raul Castro's decision to abolish the death penalty earlier in his term, a policy change in alignment with Catholic doctrine. Shortly after the visit, Raul Castro satisfied a request from the Catholic Church, declaring Good Friday a legal national holiday.

These changes are symbolic of a further shift in how the Castro government perceives the Catholic Church. No longer deemed an adversary, the institution is seen as a partner of sorts, largely supporting the very reforms the government wants to move forward. The church's role in mediating a solution for the release of political prisoners was unprecedented. Indeed, the church's increasing influence is clearly on display in a variety of settings. Construction of a new seminary in Guanabacoa was recently completed, and in 2011, the church opened the country's first-ever MBA program, structured to teach Cubans how to start, run, and market a business. After years of government-imposed limits, the church in 2011 organized an island-wide procession of the Virgen de la Caridad del Cobre, Cuba's Patron Saint.

To be sure, the church has an interest in guarding this hard-won institutional space carefully. Yet, lest the Cuban Catholic Church be seen as a mere lapdog for state interests (an accusation frequently, and unfairly, levied against it by its detractors in the Cuban exile community), voices within the church and the Catholic media also frequently hold the government's feet to the fire, demanding that promised reforms proceed apace (or more quickly) while also spreading awareness about their limitations and potentially difficult consequences. In addition, the church promotes a nationalist message of building a more inclusive Cuba for the benefit of all Cubans, not just Catholics. On the one hand, this is broadly compatible with Raul Castro's message of "updating" the revolution. But the church's rhetoric is hardly inscribed strictly with the Revolution's traditional ideological parameters. While sharing the state's concern for Cuban sovereignty and its critique of U.S. policy, voices connected to the church speak not simply of a revised "revolution" but a newly founded "Casa Cuba" (or Cuban "home") in which the foundations of not just economic but also political citizenship on the island undergo substantial redefinition.

The Catholic Church under Cardinal Ortega's leadership has also served as an agent of family and personal conciliation with the Cuban-American community and more broadly with the Cuban diaspora, whose considerable charitable contributions help support a number of the church's new institutions. Ortega's message of moderation, national unity, and conciliation; his advocacy of gradual change; and his willingness to see the Raul Castro government as a legitimate agent in the broader transformations that Cuba needs have all inflamed the traditional hard-liners in the Cuban-American community. While Cardinal Ortega has refrained from using the church as a center for anti-regime opposition, choosing instead to play a mediating role, American tax dollars (from U.S government funding provided to Radio and TV Marti as well as U.S. Agency for International Development [USAID] regime change programs) have helped finance attacks against Cardinal Ortega's leadership of the Cuban Catholic Church.

What is the status of gay rights in Cuba?

Cuba has made considerable progress on lesbian, gay, bisexual, and transgender (LGBT) rights since the turn of the century. This shift follows a time, not so long ago, when gays, lesbians, transgenders, and other sexual minorities faced widespread, institutionalized ostracism: in the mid-1960s, for example many LGBT or presumed LGBT individuals were sent to labor camps for "reeducation." In 2008, by contrast, the Cuban government began covering gender reassignment surgery under the country's universal healthcare system. Transgender Cubans can now legally change their gender identity on official identification documents. The year 2012 also marked the fifth anniversary of Cuba's now annual march against homophobia, centered in the capital Havana, with supporting activities in Santiago, Cienfuegos, and other provincial cities. As in all societies around the world, forms of prejudice and discrimination against Cuba's LGBT community persist. Government-affiliated and independent activists continue documenting occasional police harassment of LGBT individuals.

The leading figure promoting the rights of gays and sexual minorities in Cuba is Mariela Castro Espín, the daughter of Raul Castro and the director of Cuba's National Center for Sex Education (CENESEX). In the interest of fostering inclusiveness and wider social participation, she launched a nationwide educational campaign against homophobia and has championed efforts to provide greater government protection to LGBT individuals. Some of the clear results of these efforts are cited earlier. During a recent Cuban Communist Party Conference in January 2012, moreover, government and party leaders for the first time debated a provision to prohibit discrimination on the basis of sexual orientation and sexual identity. Objectives under discussion include updating Cuba's family code to legalize same-sex civil unions.

Skeptics criticize CENESEX's dominant influence (under the auspices of the Ministry of Health) over gay rights activism to the exclusion of smaller independent civil society groups more critical of, and thus seen with suspicion by, the Cuban state. Still, when Cuba's delegation at the United States voted in late 2010 to remove language referring to sexual orientation from a somewhat routine resolution condemning diverse motives for extrajudicial state executions, state and non-state actors on the island coincided in critiquing the Ministry of Foreign Relations' equivocal position. In 2011, Cuba for the first time supported a resolution at the UN Human Rights Council condemning violence and discrimination against individuals because of their sexual orientation.

What's the story with the release of political prisoners?

The number of political prisoners and regime opponents jailed in Cuba has fluctuated greatly for decades. Jimmy Carter and Jesse Jackson each negotiated large-scale releases. Notably, Pope John Paul II's 1998 visit to the island prompted a release of political prisoners as well. The number then increased again during the 2003 government crackdown.

In 2009, Cuban foreign policy under Raul Castro moved pointedly toward a diplomatic rapprochement with the European Union, chaired during the second half of that year by Spain's Socialist Party government under Prime Minister José Luis Zapatero. Together, the Cuban, Spanish, and EU members undertook a dialogue with an eye to eliminating the "common position," partial economic sanctions, and standing prohibitions on full-blown aid and cooperation agreements with the island. The near permanent presence of political prisoners in Cuba, however, had become a political albatross for Castro, representing both a significant challenge to Havana's Europe strategy as well as a substantial obstacle to writing a new chapter in U.S.-Cuba relations with the Obama White House. Quietly, and with Madrid's assistance, Cuba had begun to release small groups of political prisoners who accepted exile to Spain.

But the process hit a considerable landmine in February 2010 when a man named Orlando Zapata Tamayo died on a hunger strike. Zapata Tamayo undertook his hunger strike to demand better conditions in Cuban prisons. The legitimacy of these demands, Zapata Tamayo's background, and the reasons for his imprisonment in the first place—not to mention the circumstances of his death—all provoked wide debate and controversy. Though Zapata's prison term dated to a 2003 arrest concurrent with the detentions of better-known dissident activists at the time, he also possessed a considerable rap sheet for violent and petty crimes prior to that date. Cuban authorities, moreover, insist that his links to opposition groups on the island and their supporters abroad began only after his imprisonment. Sympathizers contest that account. Needless to say, his death prompted confrontations between opposition activists—especially the dissident group Las Damas de Blanco (Ladies in White), who saw Zapata as a hero and martyr— and government supporters, who argued he was a common criminal manipulated by foreign interests bankrolling the dissident movement to begin with. Reports of the confrontations described incidents of intimidation, harassment, and violence; photos of pro-government demonstrators pulling the hair of the Ladies in White spread across the international media. These actions, along with Zapata Tamayo's death, garnered international condemnation, threatening the prospect of normalizing relations with Spain and other European countries, as well as the regime's efforts to create conditions internally that would support domestic economic reforms.

At this juncture, Cardinal Jaime Ortega, head of Cuba's Catholic Church, emerged as an unlikely interlocutor. After Ortega condemned the so-called Acts of Repudiation against the Ladies in White and publicly called for dialogue, Raul Castro communicated to the cardinal a request that the church serve as mediator. Together with the input of the Spanish government, Castro, the Catholic Church, and dissident groups brokered a deal for the release of 52 political prisoners and their departure to Spain together with their families. Remaining prisoners from the 75 sentenced in 2003 who expressed a desire to remain in Cuba were also eventually released and permitted to stay on the island.

The number of political prisoners in Cuba is now at its lowest recorded level. All 75 of the political prisoners detained and sentenced in the 2003 "black spring" have been released.

Moreover, in late 2011 Raul Castro announced the release of 2,900 additional prisoners, including some convicted of political crimes. In total, an estimated 166 political prisoners were released in 2011. That said, there have been increased reports of politically motivated, short-term "catch and release" detentions.

How did the Obama administration's policy toward Cuba distinguish itself from its predecessors?

Shortly after taking office, President Obama raised expectations in Cuba, Latin America, and the United States by explicitly referencing the "failed" U.S.-Cuba policies of the past and hinting that his administration sought a "new chapter" in the bilateral relationship. But more urgent international and domestic priorities and the perception that domestic political repercussions could tilt the risk-reward pendulum soon overtook any White House taste for change.

For example, the Florida and New Jersey congressional delegations in both parties—including major power players like Debbie Wasserman Shultz, chair of the Democratic National Committee—maintain a strict allegiance to their Cuban-American members and reliance on their campaign finances. These members uniformly oppose any change in the hard-line status quo. Thus, despite bipartisan support for trade and travel openings, special interest congressional pressure, along with the administration's erroneous readings of internal politics in Cuba and a mistaken assumption that Raul Castro's top foreign policy priority is to get the embargo lifted, caused the Obama White House to resist spending its political capital on the Hill.

Misplaced electoral jitters provide another source of friction. At the outset of his first term, and in part to signal to Latin America Washington's broader responsiveness to the region's long-standing demands for U.S.-Cuba policy change, Obama moved quickly to eliminate restrictions on Cuban-American travel and to lift the cap on remittances for family members. Cuban-American legislators protested, but in relatively muted fashion: the move was broadly popular with their constituents. As many as 50 Cuba-bound flights per week now leave American airports (mainly Miami's), packed with people, cash, and all manner of equipment to help relatives on the island survive and start small businesses. In fact, Cuban-Americans consistently favor more travel for all Americans and are clearly voting with their feet every time they board flights to Havana. A small majority even supports eliminating the embargo. Of course, those Cuban-Americans most frequently boarding the flights and most uniformly inclined to support wider policy change are less likely to be voting citizens, as they predominantly come from more recent generations of immigrants with lower rates of citizenship. But, Obama won the state of Florida in the 2008 election with only 35% of the Cuban vote as a whole, having dominated just the 18–35-year-old cohort. Non-Cuban Latino voters in the state proved much more crucial to Obama's victory there; nor is the conservative (or liberal) Cuban-American vote driven by the Cuba policy debate alone. Still, the political mythology in Washington persists: Cuban-Americans (including Havana-bound frequent fliers) will punish Obama at the polls should the White House go further toward overhauling a clearly failed policy toward the island. Obama won 49% of the Cuban vote in 2012, a stunning indication of new attitudes among these voters.

Although some Americans of non-Cuban origin can now travel under "people to people" programs (requiring strict institutional licenses issued by the Treasury Department's Office of Foreign Assets Control), by 2012 the administration had ceded to congressional demands that licenses comply with Helms-Burton criteria explicitly designed to use American visitors to foster anti-regime dissent. Thus, a major and probably unconstitutional paradox now holds. Cuban-Americans, whose representatives oppose change in U.S.-Cuba policy and are the convenient excuse for White House stasis, now have unlimited access to visit family, travel as tourists (they are Cuba's second highest source of tourism revenue), and invest (via remittances) in Cuba's emerging small business sector and real estate market. Yet almost all other Americans must beg (or pay lawyers to cajole) an under-staffed and politicized government bureaucracy for a sliver of that very privilege. A cynic might come away concluding that beneath the threats and tantrums prompted by any hint of White House common sense, Cuban-American members of Congress have carved out a stunningly exclusive earmark for their constituents: ethnicity-based access to a new market just a stone's throw from U.S. shores, without competition from the American public, and in likely violation of the 14th amendment.

Not all of the action has transpired in the narrow world of congressional-executive, or even electoral, politics. Obama's more open but still equivocal visa policy has authorized more Cuban scholars to attend conferences and teach in American universities (while still denying the petitions of others). Likewise, unprecedented numbers of Cuban artists, dancers, and musicians have toured throughout the United States. With help from both governments, in 2009 the Colombian megastar Juanes filled Havana's Revolution Square with 1,000,000 Cubans for a concert with 15 other bands from around the world. More recently, a children's theater group, La Colmenita, toured the United States with a play that promoted Cuba's top political request from the United States: the release from American prisons of the Cuban Five. Raul Castro's daughter, gay rights activist Mariela Castro Espín, did the same, while also publicly endorsing Obama's support for gay marriage and, not without controversy, explaining her father's policy priorities in major institutions such as the New York Public Library and the Council on Foreign Relations. Cuban-American financiers long opposed to change started visiting the island and talking to senior officials, quite plausibly assessing the possibility for investments in the not-so-distant future.

By the end of his (first) term, President Obama's Latin America policy had crashed on the shoals of domestic politics. The region's leaders delivered a stinging rebuke over the failure of his Cuba policy when he traveled to Cartagena, Colombia, for the 2012 Summit of the Americas, pledging there would be no more summits without Cuba present. Yet neither candidate dwelled on Cuba during the 2012 general election; as in 2008, the non-Cuban Hispanic role in allocating Florida's 27 electoral votes will likely prove more decisive in the outcome of the presidential race than the much-coveted, much-feared paper tiger of the *voto cubano*. The state of Florida itself, however, bought into some of the hype when it passed laws of questionable constitutionality aimed at mega corporations such as Brazil's Odebrecht, barring state government contracts with companies that do business with Cuba. Miami-Dade's media markets, meanwhile, are a bundle of contradictions. Hate speech toward advocates of policy change still flourishes on the airwaves, yet, increasingly, so do visiting artists and musicians from the island who themselves criticize U.S. policy. Some rancorous legacies of the past die hard, however. In April 2012, arsonists in Miami allegedly burned down the headquarters of one of the area's longest standing charter companies that flies Cuban-Americans to the island.

Two factors having nothing to with Cuban-American politics or campaign finance conspired against boldness from the Obama White House. Most obviously, neither Cuba nor Latin America rank as a high foreign policy priority. The second might be called the annoyance factor. Washington policy makers do not have the patience for navigating the frustrating diplomacy and toxic politics associated with Cuba. They express annoyance with the Cuban government for its skepticism of Washington's motives and political will. Americans policy makers can talk themselves into a view of Havana as obstreperous at best, or worst, likewise lacking interest in improving relations. In the second term, only President Obama himself will be able to cut through this thicket. With a series of unilateral steps requiring neither approval by the U.S. Congress or negotiations with the government of Cuba, the president can use his executive authority to substantially overhaul American policy toward Cuba and cement for his own legacy in the Americas the reputation as a courageous and visionary president, a stance he campaigned on in 2012.

Who is Alan Gross and why did he become a factor in U.S.-Cuba relations?

The George W. Bush administration increased spending for regime change programs in Cuba (also known by the more benign term "democracy promotion") from about $5 million in 2001 to $45 million by FY09. Upon taking office, the Obama administration allowed the programs to continue. Since the 9/11 attacks, moreover, the United States has outsourced to private firms a wide range of activities on an often blurry continuum between national security and development assistance.

Alan Gross is an American sub-contractor retained by one such private firm, Development Alternatives International (DAI), which received multimillion-dollar contracts authorized under the Helms-Burton law to conduct "technological outreach" in Cuba—mainly by disseminating services related to mobile devices and Internet access. After Gross made five trips to the island, Cuban police arrested him in December 2009 for importing and distributing sophisticated communications equipment in violation of Cuban law. According to his own trip reports, Gross designed a $600,000 program to help Cuba's small Jewish community (predominantly though not exclusively in Havana) install equipment intended eventually to give anti-regime activists (supported by additional USAID programs) access to Internet service. He confirmed this account to CNN host Wolf Blitzer subsequent to his arrest, relaying that his primary purpose was to test technology for future DAI programs using the Jewish community's network for his experiments. According to the Associated Press, on his trip in December 2009, Gross brought a surveillance-thwarting, wide-spectrum subscriber identity module (SIM) card to the island intended to be used in connection with satellite phones capable of providing a localized wireless Internet network (known as

BGAN). This card would thus not only allow Cuban users access to uncensored Internet through non-state networks without risk of surveillance but also presumably give USAID contractors and their sub-contractors a way to communicate with activists on the island undetected by Cuban police and intelligence services.

Cuba's Jewish community has substantial and long-standing ties with Israel and the American Jewish community. Importantly, Cuba's Jewish institutions have never been a source of anti-regime activities, and they are among the few NGOs on the island with Internet access. In fact, Gross *chose* the Jewish community to test-drive the SIM/BGAN technology precisely because of its established national network, independent status, and relatively wide access to information and foreign contacts and support.

In August 2011, a Cuban judge sentenced Gross to 15 years in prison for attempting to "undermine the integrity and independence of Cuba." Cuban authorities accused Gross of carrying out a covert operation on behalf of the United States government in violation of Cuban law. U.S. officials, in turn, contended that Gross was only working to provide assistance to the Jewish community and was not involved in activities to threaten the government. In his trial, however, Gross stated that he was a "trusting fool" who was "duped"—though he never clarified by whom. By framing Gross as an experienced development worker striving to boost the prospect of his fellow Jews, the Obama administration quite cynically drew the American Jewish community into the dispute. Likewise, Gross's family and his lawyer actively sought the advocacy power of the American Jewish community to campaign for Gross's release. Weekly protests in front of Havana's "Interests Section," a mile from the White House, soon commenced, as did regular briefings at synagogues around the country. But for the first three years of his incarceration, the family showed little interest in publicly pressuring the White House itself to pursue Gross's release.

Talks between the two governments to gain Gross's release never got off the ground, foiled by accumulated mutual distrust and a lack of political will—especially in Washington. Ironically, Secretary Clinton declared there would be no negotiation regarding Gross's fate on the same day the U.S. government released $5 million to the government of Egypt in return for the release of "democracy promotion" workers there. Until 2012 when the Gross family filed a lawsuit against the U.S. government, his family and advisors, steered clear of publicly acknowledging that Gross had played a role in a broader program of U.S. policies aimed at destabilizing the regime, acknowledging only that Gross had no intention of doing harm.

Two years after his arrest, journalists substantiated the Cuban government's claims that Gross's activities were part of a larger covert program. In a long published dossier, the Associated Press (AP) reported that the SIM card Gross installed was in fact a sophisticated communications chip available only to the U.S. Defense Department, CIA, and the U.S. State Department under special government license. The chip is designed to prevent satellite transmissions from being tracked within 250 miles. Gross claimed subsequently that he was merely testing "off-the-shelf" technology. But neither USAID nor the State Department refuted the AP's reporting, which has since been further substantiated by Gross's contracts with DAI.

In order to get members of the American Jewish community to transport computers, smart phones, and other equipment to Cuba, Gross introduced himself as a humanitarian development worker, not as a U.S. government contractor. A number of American Jews thus participated unknowingly in Gross's program by agreeing to bring equipment to Havana in their carry-on luggage while visiting the island on religious missions. Gross's trip reports—procured from his laptop at the time of his arrest by Cuban authorities and obtained separately by the AP— make clear that he understood the highly sensitive nature of his work as well as the risks to which he was exposing unwitting collaborators. Gross's reports describe the work as "very risky," offer guidance on "how to communicate securely in repressive environments," and warn that "detection of satellite signals will be catastrophic."

Up until Gross's detention, many observers felt that, despite a slow start falling far short of his rhetoric about a "new beginning" in relations with Cuba, President Obama might seek a gradual shift in attitudes and policy toward the island. Early in his administration, for instance, Obama had removed restrictions on Cuban-American travel and remittances. Gross's imprisonment, however, brought diplomacy to a standstill. In January 2011, the administration did proceed with a long-considered but limited expansion of government-regulated educational and cultural travel. Numerous Obama administration officials, however—particularly from the State Department—made public statements suggesting that further liberalizing steps would be contemplated only if Cuban authorities first released Gross. Such statements risked sending the implicit message to hard-liners in Congress that the only way to hold the line against further change and keep the embargo and other Cuba policies in place might well be prolonging Gross's imprisonment, or at least the programs that sent him there, programs the Cuban government clearly sought to compel the administration to change. Over the course of Obama's first term, protecting the fundamental strategy behind the Helms-Burton programs became one of the top political objectives of hard-liners in Congress. The Obama administration, in turn, allowed itself to be pressured into shelving any broader new agenda toward Cuba. In 2010, for instance, the Senate Foreign Relations and the House Foreign Affairs committees led an initiative intended to detoxify the programs that sent Gross to Cuba in the first place. Initially agreed to by the State Department, the proposed measures were presented to the Cuban government in recognition that securing Gross's release would require changing the context that had set him on the path to arrest. This effort, however, died when the House of Representatives changed hands in the November 2010 mid-term elections. Unwilling to risk a fight with hard-liners, the Obama administration began attacking the legitimacy of Cuban laws and demanding Gross's immediate, unilateral release. The Cuban government concluded that the Obama administration lacked the political will to undertake a new set of policies and gradually raised its position to include a full-blown prisoner swap: Alan Gross for the Cuban Five.

Why is Cuba still on the State Department's list of countries supporting terrorism?

Cuba has been on the U.S. list of state sponsors of terrorism since 1982. The U.S. government's rationale for keeping Cuba on this list has changed only slightly in recent years. Continuing the Bush administration's logic, the Obama White House at first justified Cuba's presence on the list in part with Havana's sustained critique of "the U.S. approach to combating international terrorism." But by this standard, dozens of countries, including close allies of the United States, would likewise be eligible for censure.

The Obama administration later removed the Bush-era criteria and settled upon three long-standing explanations for Cuba's continued inclusion on the list: first, that individuals affiliated with extremist groups like the FARC in Colombia and ETA in Spain "continue to reside in Cuba"; second, that fugitives wanted in the United States are now living in Cuba, where they have received government benefits; and third, that Cuba has "strategic deficiencies" related to money laundering.

In 1998, American intelligence agencies concluded that Cuba no longer posed a threat to U.S. national security. This conclusion still stands. Indeed, intelligence experts have been hard-pressed to find evidence that Cuba currently provides weapons or training to any active international terrorist groups. Moreover, the State Department has recently acknowledged Cuban collaboration with global counterterrorism efforts in several written reports, specifically citing Cuba's cooperation with Spanish efforts to investigate ETA members suspected of living on the island. Also, Cuba assists the United States in running security checks at several Cuban airports at times. Cuba, like Mexico, has long hosted talks in Havana between successive Colombian governments and representatives of the Colombian insurgent group, the FARC. In 2012, Cuba's diplomatic mediation helped pave the way for the first serious set of peace talks between the FARC and the government of Colombia since the 1990s.

The continued designation of Cuba as a state sponsor of terrorism reinforces the perception that U.S. policy is outdated and politicized—particularly at a time when actors in states such as Yemen (operations base for a powerful terrorist affiliate group, Al-Qaeda in the Arabian Peninsula) and Pakistan (where Osama Bin Laden lived before his death in 2011) pose considerably greater national security threats to the United States. Ultimately, Cuba's continued presence on the list responds not to foreign policy or national security considerations but to the perception that removing it would involve too high a domestic political cost. In order for trade and investment between the United States and Cuba to take off, Cuba must be removed from the list. The executive branch has the authority to do so without an act of Congress, but any White House ready to take this step will have to notify Congress in advance. That means having the political will to face down the handful of legislators, Cuban-Americans in large measure, who remain avidly committed to the status quo.

What happened to Luis Posada Carriles?

Despite his well-documented ties to the bombing of a Cubana Airlines flight in 1976, as well as a string of Havana hotel bombings in 1997, today Luis Posada Carriles lives as a free man in Miami. In 2007, a federal district court in El Paso, Texas, indicted Posada on multiple counts of fraud, making false statements, and using false identification documents in connection with his 2005 reentry into the United States after several years in hiding. A few months later, Judge Kathleen Cardone dismissed all counts against him, and Posada was released. A U.S. appellate court overturned this decision in 2008, ordering the case returned to trial. In 2009, under President Obama, the U.S. Department of Justice filed several new charges against Posada, including charges for making false statements about his involvement in the 1997 Havana bombings. This represented the first time Posada's role in violent acts against Cuban targets had been referenced specifically in connection with the charges levied against him. It thus appeared to represent a notable and symbolically resonant shift in the U.S. government position, given that Posada got his start in the early 1960s as a Central Intelligence Agency recruit. However, in 2011, Posada was found not guilty on all counts: perjury, obstruction of justice, and immigration fraud. The Cuban government denounced the acquittal and charged the United States with continuing to protect a known terrorist.

With a leadership transition underway in Venezuela, what are the enduring features of Cuba's relationship with Hugo Chavez?

Washington loves a good charismatic caudillo to anoint as its foil in Latin America. Over the last decade, Fidel Castro deftly, albeit unofficially, turned over that job to Venezuela's Hugo Chavez. Though the Cuban revolution's ties to Venezuela stretch back over half a century, Fidel didn't invent Chavez—the former army paratrooper emerged from his own country's history. The Cuba-Venezuela relationship, however, extends beyond the Castro-Chavez friendship and is not one that will be cast aside once either man is gone.

Chavez came of age during the Cold War, when, to avoid a repeat of the 1959 Castro revolution, the United States deployed throughout Latin America its considerable arsenal to keep the left weak through covert operations, counterinsurgency, coups, or meddling with elections. During this period, between the 1950s and the late 1980s, unelected generals ran most of Latin America, with American blessing, training, and support. At the time, Venezuela (and Colombia) stood out to a self-satisfied Foggy Bottom and to some political scientists as reassuring exceptions to South America's right-wing military regimes: twin poster children for democracy, albeit elite-brokered, shallow, and one that coexisted with extreme inequality and poverty—not to mention disfranchisement of poor majorities. Although solidly ensconced in the barracks, a nationalist strain in Venezuela's military seeded Chavez's skepticism about American power, which in turn became in his view inseparable from Washington's entrenched backing of Venezuela's elite.

Although Hugo Chavez was only five years old when Fidel Castro took power in 1959, their fates were already intertwined. Before launching an insurgency against Washington's Cuban surrogate Fulgencio Batista, as a young Havana lawyer Castro also had developed a belief in the inextricable link between American power and Cuba's and Latin America's thwarted economic and political development. As armed revolution unfolded in Cuba, in Venezuela in the late 1950s a coalition of church, society, student, labor, and business groups peacefully pressured the military to ease itself out of power. But Cuban revolutionaries needed international help. In 1958, the political wing of Fidel's 26th of July Movement persuaded a transitional Venezuelan president, navy commander Wolfgang Larrazabal, to ship weapons to Cuba's Sierra Maestra, giving a boost to Fidel's final push to topple Fulgencio Batista. Just three weeks after taking power, in January 1959 a triumphant Fidel flew to Caracas to say thank you. In contrast to the stoning of Richard Nixon's motorcade received during a 1958 visit, crowds cheered as Fidel preached the new gospel of Latin American unity, people-to-people solidarity, and revolution, themes Chavez would try to advance decades later.

But with oil rents greasing the wheels, Venezuelan elites looked aghast at the Cuban revolution and took up the banner of social democracy and Christian democracy, organizing themselves into a two-party system that lasted until the end of the 1980s, when their heavily subsidized petro-state became financially and politically unsustainable. And a short-lived guerrilla insurgency supported by Cuba was crushed in the 1960s, and non-violent leftist efforts to diversify Venezuelan politics never truly got off the ground. As a young army officer and with the spirit of General Simon Bolivar animating his political thought, Chavez incubated his anti-elite, anti-imperial vision of continental, popular unity in this context.

The Venezuela-Cuba relationship developed in three distinct periods. The first, likely one element that persuaded Chavez of Fidel's value as a resource for reshaping Venezuela's military and security institutions, dates back to the flight of Batista loyalists to Venezuela after Castro's revolution in 1959. These exiles worked for the CIA and with Venezuelan counterparts as a rearguard during the Bay of Pigs and Operation Mongoose. That deeper and still untold history is essential to understanding the significance of the second period.

Fast forward to Fidel's illness in 2006, when the first photos we saw of him were with Chavez at his hospital bedside: by then, the Cuba-Venezuela relationship had become linked by billions in subsidies, transfers, direct investment in energy and infrastructure, thousands of advisors, and a joint drive to build new regional institutions without the United States to shove member countries around.

As for the next phase, Chavez' successors—whomever they may be—won't quickly undo the layers of bilateral and regional togetherness. Venezuela's poor, whom the opposition now understands it must attract, derive direct benefits from the misiones, which would not be possible without Cuba. ALBA and Petrocaribe will not immediately unravel without Chavez. In his absence, we might expect a modified status quo for the near to medium term.

Contrary to the clichés, Cuba, the biggest beneficiary of Chavez's largesse, never put all of its strategic eggs in one basket. After learning the bitter lessons of excessive dependence on Spain, the United States, and later, the Soviet Union, Fidel and Raul Castro likewise recognized that Hugo Chavez was to be a transitional figure in Venezuelan history, even if the party machine they helped him construct continues to dominate politics in Venezuela. And the new regional institutions forged from the Havana-Caracas relationship helped Cuba engineer its way back to the center of Latin American diplomacy.

SUGGESTIONS FOR FURTHER READING

Andersen, John Lee. *Che Guevara: A Revolutionary Life*. Grove Press, 1997.

Arenas, Reinaldo. *Before Night Falls: A Memoir*. Penguin, 1994.

Bardach, Ann Louise. *Cuba Confidential: Love and Vengeance in Miami and Havana*. Vintage, 2003.

Behar, Ruth. *An Island Called Home: Returning to Jewish Cuba*. Rutgers University Press, 2009.

Blight, James G. and Peter Kornbluh, eds. *Politics of Illusion: The Bay of Pigs Invasion Reexamined*. Lynne Rienner, 1998.

Blight, James G. and Janet M. Lang. *The Armageddon Letters: Kennedy, Khrushchev, Castro in the Cuban Missile Crisis*. Rowman & Littlefield, 2012.

Brenner, Phil, Marguerite Rose Jiménez, John M. Kirk, William M. LeoGrande, eds. *A Contemporary Cuba Reader: Reinventing the Revolution*. Rowman & Littlefield, 2008.

Brotherton, P. Sean. *Revolutionary Medicine: Health and the Body in Post-Soviet Cuba (Experimental Futures)*. Duke University Press, 2012.

Castro, Fidel. *La contraofensiva estratégica: De la Sierra Maestra a Santiago de Cuba*. Oficina de Publicaciones del Consejo de Estado, 2011.

Castro, Fidel, w/ Katiuska Blanco. *Guerrillero del Tiempo*. Editora Abril, 2012.

Cháves, Lydia, ed. *Capitalism, God, and a Good Cigar: Cuba Enters the Twenty-First Century*. Duke University Press, 2005.

Cluster, Dick and Rafael Hernández. *The History of Havana*. Palgrave MacMillan, 2006.

Combs, Jack. *The Cubans*. University of Virginia Press, 2010.

Connors, Michael and Brent Winebrenner. *The Splendor of Cuba: 450 Years of Architecture and Interiors*. Rizzoli, 2011.

De la Campa, Román. *Cuba on My Mind: Journeys to a Severed Nation*. Verso, 2002.

De la Fuente, Alejandro. *A Nation for All: Race, Inequality, and Politics in Twentieth Century Cuba*. University of North Carolina Press, 2001.

De los Angeles Torres, Maria. *The Lost Apple: Operation Pedro Pan, Cuban Children in the U.S., and the Promise of a Better Future.* Beacon Press, 2004.

Domínguez, Jorge. *Cuba Hoy: Analizando su Pasado, Imaginando su Futuro.* Editorial Colibrí, 2006.

Domínguez, Jorge. *To Make the World Safe for Revolution: Cuba's Foreign Policy.* Harvard University Press, 1989.

Eire, Carlos. *Waiting for Snow in Havana: Confessions of a Cuban Boy.* Free Press, 2003.

Fernandes, Sujatha. *Cuba Represent! Cuban Arts, State Power, and the Making of New Revolutionary Cultures.* Duke University Press, 2006.

Franqui, Carlos. *Family Portrait with Fidel.* Vintage, 1985.

Garcia, Maria Cristina. *Havana USA: Cuban Exiles and Cuban Americans in South Florida, 1959–1994.* University of California Press, 2006.

Gjelten, Tom. *Bacardi and the Long Fight for Cuba: The Biography of a Cause.* Viking, 2008.

Gleijeses, Piero. *Conflicting Missions: Havana, Washington, and Africa, 1959–1976.* University of North Carolina Press, 2002.

Gott, Richard. *Cuba: A New History.* Yale University Press, 2007.

Grenier, Guillermo and Lisandro Pérez. *The Legacy of Exile: Cubans in the United States.* Allyn & Bacon, 2002.

Guerra, Lillian. *Visions of Power in Cuba: Revolution, Redemption and Resistance, 1959–1971.* University of North Carolina Press, 2012.

Guillermoprieto, Alma. *Dancing with Cuba: A Memoir of the Revolution.* Vintage, 2005.

Hansen, Jonathan. *Guantánamo: An American History.* Hill and Wang, 2011.

Harris, Alex. *The Idea of Cuba.* University of New Mexico Press, 2007.

Ibarra, Jorge. *Prologue to Revolution: Cuba, 1989-1958.* Lynne Rienner, 1998.

Lipman, Jana. *Guantánamo: A Working-Class History between Empire and Revolution.* University of California Press, 2008.

Martí, José. *Selected Writings.* Penguin Classics, 2002.

Matos, Huber. *Como Llegó la Noche.* TusQuets, 2004.

Mills, C. Wright. *Listen Yankee: The Revolution in Cuba.* Ballantine, 1960.

Moore, Robin. *Music and Revolution: Cultural Change in Socialist Cuba.* University of California Press, 2006.

Oltuski, Enrique. *Vida Clandestina: My Life in the Cuban Revolution.* Jossey-Bass, 2002.

Ortíz, Fernando. *Cuban Counterpoint: Tobacco and Sugar.* Alfred A. Knopf, 1947 (paperback by Duke University Press, 2003).

Padura, Leonardo. *La novela de mi vida.* Tusquets, 2002.

Patterson, Thomas G. *Contesting Castro: The United States and the Triumph of the Cuban Revolution.* Oxford University Press, 1994.

Pérez, Louis A. *Cuba in the American Imagination: Metaphor and the Imperial Ethos.* University of North Carolina Press, 2011.

Rathbone, John. *The Sugar King of Havana: The Rise and Fall of Julio Lobo, Cuba's Last Tycoon.* Penguin, 2011.

Sartre, Jean-Paul. *Sartre on Cuba*. Ballatine, 1961.

Schoultz, Lars. *That Infernal Little Cuban Republic: The United States and the Cuban Revolution*. University of North Carolina Press, 2011.

Scott, Rebecca. *Degrees of Freedom: Louisiana and Cuba after Slavery*. Belknap Press of Harvard University Press, 2008.

Sweig, Julia E. *Inside the Cuban Revolution: Fidel Castro and the Urban Underground*. Harvard University Press, 2002.

Symmes, Patrick. *The Boys from Dolores*. Pantheon, 2007.

Tattlin, Isadora. *Cuba Diaries: An American Housewife in Havana*. Broadway, 2003.

Thomas, Hugh. *Cuba: The Pursuit of Freedom*. Eyre and Spottiswoode, 1971.

INDEX